BAD
LEADERSHIP

LEADERSHIP <small>FOR THE</small>
COMMON GOOD

HARVARD BUSINESS SCHOOL PRESS

CENTER FOR PUBLIC LEADERSHIP
JOHN F. KENNEDY SCHOOL OF GOVERNMENT
HARVARD UNIVERSITY

The Leadership for the Common Good series represents a
partnership between Harvard Business School Press and
the Center for Public Leadership at Harvard University's
John F. Kennedy School of Government. Books in the series aim
to provoke conversations about the role of leaders in business,
government, and society, to enrich leadership theory and
enhance leadership practice, and to set the agenda for
defining effective leadership in the future.

OTHER BOOKS IN THE SERIES

Changing Minds
by Howard Gardner

Predictable Surprises
by Max H. Bazerman and
Michael D. Watkins

BAD
LEADERSHIP

WHAT IT IS,

HOW IT HAPPENS,

WHY IT MATTERS

BARBARA KELLERMAN

HARVARD BUSINESS SCHOOL PRESS
Boston, Massachusetts

Printed in the United States of America
08 07 06 05 04   5 4 3 2 1

Library of Congress Cataloging-in-Publication Data
Kellerman, Barbara.
   Bad leadership : what it is, how it happens, why it matters / Barbara
Kellerman.
      p. cm.
   ISBN 1-59139-166-0
  1. Leadership. 2. Decision making. 3. Personality and occupation. I. Title.
   HD57.7.K47 2004
   658.4'092—dc22

                                                    2004014041

The paper used in this publication meets the minimum requirements of the
American National Standard for Information Sciences—Permanence of Paper
for Printed Library Materials, ANSI Z39.48-1992.

For Jessica and Jake

We have fed the heart on fantasies,
The heart's grown brutal from the fare.

—William Butler Yeats

CONTENTS

ACKNOWLEDGMENTS

I am grateful to Jonathan Greenwald for giving me his hand, always.

And to Warren Bennis for lending a hand with unfailing intelligence and humor.

And to James MacGregor Burns for extending his hand when I most needed it, at the start.

I want to thank my close colleagues at the Center for Public Leadership—David Gergen, Ronnie Heifetz, and Scott Webster—for being, well, my close colleagues.

Finally I note for the record that this book benefited at every turn from the smart support of John Canady and Abigail Williamson; that my exchanges with Sarah Chace, Harris Collingwood, Michael Horn, Todd Pittinsky, and Suzanne Rotondo further fed this work; that my editor Jeff Kehoe and my associate Samir Randolph were important to the final product; and that my colleague Richard Hackman, was generous and "reliable."

WEBS OF
SIGNIFICANCE

T HIS BOOK IS ABOUT the dark side of the human
condition. It paints leadership in shades of gray—
and in black.

In spite of all the work on leadership that assumes it by definition to be good, I describe how we exercise power, authority, and influence in ways that do harm. This harm is not necessarily deliberate. It can be the result of carelessness or neglect. But this does not make it less injurious, and in some cases calamitous.

Often a leader is assumed to be all-powerful. But we must remember that leaders acting alone are not responsible for bad leadership. Thus, the web symbolizes the many different strands that always constitute the leadership process.

What are the webs of significance—the webs of leadership? Threaded through the whole is the leader. The leader may or may not hold a formal position of authority; position is not the point. Rather, it is the leader as protagonist that matters. As I define it, a *leader* chooses a particular course of action and then in some way gets others to go along; or, more subtly, the leader encourages the led to "choose" the course that the group will follow.

That followers matter is a presumption now widely shared. Still, even sophisticated students of leadership tend to focus on leaders and shortchange followers.

Our fascination with the man (usually it is a man) on the white horse remains constant. Like most other animals, we have tended to look to strong males to provide what's most important: safety and security. Robert Sapolsky, baboon expert extraordinaire, describes a troop leader and alpha male named Solomon. "Solomon was in his silver years and resting on his laurels, persisting out of sheer psychological intimidation. He was damn good at it. He hadn't had a major fight in a year. He would just glance at someone, rouse himself from his regal setting and saunter over, at the most swat him, and that would settle things. Everyone was terrified of him."[1]

The human animal resembles the baboon. We, too, have typically deferred to males whose strength and capacity to lead ostensibly have been proven. Still, there is no leadership without followership. Leaders *cannot* lead unless followers follow, passively or actively.

Finally, leadership does not take place in a vacuum. All leader-follower stories are set in the particular contexts within which they unfold. Robert Caro, author of a prodigious multivolume biography of Lyndon Johnson, titled the third volume *Master of the Senate*. As the title implies, this is a tale about a legislator, but it is also, inevitably, about the legislature within which he did his work. Caro makes plain that it is impossible to understand Johnson's power over his fellow senators without understanding the Senate itself. Johnson, Caro writes, was "master of an institution that had never before had a master, and that . . . has not had one since." So, he continues, "This book is a study of —the story of—America's Senate itself."[2]

Webs of leadership are tangled, the strands—the leader, the followers, and the context—hard to separate one from the other. Unlike great tapestries, in which countless threads are precisely woven into magical panoramas, webs of leadership are not so neatly delineated.

James O'Toole has used a nineteenth-century painting by the Belgian artist James Ensor to make a similar point. *Christ's Entry into Brussels* is a vast canvas of particular people—including one leader and many followers—in a particular place. But the crowded and chaotic street scene leaves us uncertain. So O'Toole asks, "Where is Christ in all this confusion? Shouldn't he be in the forefront, *leading* the parade? Shouldn't he be the visual focus of the painting?"[3]

Ensor's work is a radical departure from the art that preceded it. For nearly two millennia Christ—the leader/Redeemer—*was* the center of attention. But on this particular canvas, he is in the background, "almost lost in a throng of revelers that threatens to engulf him."[4] O'Toole's point is that Ensor was the first to illustrate the modern condition: one in which secular democracy has rendered traditional forms of leadership nearly obsolete.

The painting depicts the complex nature of a leadership process in which more than one player is center stage and in which backdrop matters. Yes, Christ is in the frame; and so there is, as we can plainly see, a leader. But the uncertain relationship between Christ and everyone else, and the obvious importance of the setting, the street scene in Brussels, depicts a dynamic that is complex and fluid rather than simple and preordained.

To see leadership in shades of gray, and in black, is to see it in a way that's another sort of departure from the past. What does "bad leadership" mean? Does it mean leadership that is immoral, unethical? Or does it mean leadership that is incompetent, ineffective? And what about the word *leader* itself? Isn't there a widely held view, at least in the United States, that it is good to be a leader because to be a leader is, ipso facto, to be good?

Questions like these have no easy answers. This should not intimidate us, but it does. Bad leadership is a phenomenon so ubiquitous it's a wonder that our shelves are not heavy with books on the subject. But they are not. Maybe there's a connection: Maybe we avoid the subject because bad leadership is located in what Harlan Cleveland refers to as the "untidy" world of human relations.[5] Bad leadership may be even untidier than good leadership.

Can you easily explain followers who willingly, sometimes even eagerly, do the bidding of leaders who are evil?

As we shall see in the pages that follow, even in the untidy universe of bad leadership, patterns emerge. Seven types of bad leadership are identified, which begin to impose an order on the whole.

Finally there is the ultimate question: What is to be done to maximize good leadership and minimize bad leadership? To address this issue, each of the seven stories on each of the seven types concludes with some thoughts about what leaders, and followers, could have done differently—what they could have done to prevent bad leadership in the first place or stop it after it started.

As the final chapter further suggests, this book is intended also to be prescriptive. I take it as a given that we promote good leadership not by ignoring bad leadership, nor by presuming that it is immutable, but rather by attacking it as we would a disease that is always pernicious and sometimes deadly.

PART ONE

THE BAD SIDE

But I'd shut my eyes in the sentry box,
So I didn't see nothin' wrong.

—Rudyard Kipling

CHAPTER ONE

CLAIMING
THE BAD SIDE

W HEN HE WAS INSTALLED as president of Harvard University in October 2001, Lawrence Summers delivered a speech in which he declared that "in this new century, nothing will matter more than the education of future leaders and the development of new ideas."[1] In this single sentence the new head of Harvard made at least two important assumptions: that people can be educated in ways that relate to being leaders, and in ways that relate to being *good* leaders.

This kind of positive thinking explains why leadership education has become a big business. The "leadership industry"—so tagged because in recent years it has grown so big so fast—is dedicated to the proposition that leadership is a subject that should be studied and a skill that should be taught. To meet the burgeoning demand for leadership education and training, a cadre of experts has emerged. These leadership scholars, teachers, consultants, trainers, and coaches work on the optimistic assumption that to develop leaders is to develop a valuable human resource.

The academic work that supports the leadership industry generally shares this positive bias. The titles of many of the best and most popular leadership books of the past twenty years send messages that make the point. Targeted primarily at those in the corporate sector, they include Thomas J. Peters and Robert H. Waterman's *In Search of Excellence: Lessons from America's Best-Run Companies*;[2] Rosabeth Moss Kanter's *The Change Masters: Innovation & Entrepreneurship in the American Corporation*;[3] Warren Bennis and Burt Nanus's *Leaders: The Strategies for Taking Charge*;[4] John Kotter's *A Force for Change: How Leadership Differs from Management*;[5] Noel Tichy's *The Leadership Engine: How Winning Companies Build Leaders at Every Level*;[6] and Jay Conger and Beth Benjamin's *Building Leaders: How Successful Companies Develop the Next Generation*.[7] Each of these books assumes that people can learn to be leaders and that to be a leader is to be a person of competence and character.

Good cheer of this kind is in even greater evidence among those who write for the general public. Authors such as Steven Covey, Kenneth Blanchard, and Spencer Johnson continue to sell tens of millions of books that suggest that you too can learn how to be a (good) leader, and in no time flat.[8]

By now such optimism has come to pervade not only American schools of business but also American schools of government. On the reasonable assumption that if leadership education makes sense for graduate students entering the private sector, it also makes sense for those entering the public and nonprofit sectors, schools of government now offer courses on how to manage and how to lead. Moreover, even though bad political leadership is as ubiquitous as bad business leadership, the prevailing view of leadership is rather relentlessly positive. As John Gardner wrote in the first of a series of highly influential leadership essays, "In our culture popular understanding of the term [leadership] distinguishes it from coercion—and places higher on the scale of leadership those forms involving lesser degrees of coercion."[9]

In this book I argue that there's something odd about the idea that somehow leadership can be distinguished from coercion, as if leadership and power were unrelated. In the real world, in everyday life, we come into constant contact not only with good leaders and good followers doing good things but also with bad leaders and bad followers doing bad things. In fact, anyone not dwelling in a cave is regularly exposed, if only through the media, to people who exercise power, use authority, and exert influence in ways that are not good. Still, even after all the evidence is in—after the recent corporate scandals, after the recent revelations of wrongdoing by leaders of the Roman Catholic Church, and before, during, and after political leadership all over the world that is so abhorrent it makes us ill—the idea that some leaders and some followers are bad, and that they might have something in common with good leaders and followers, has not fully penetrated the conversation or the curriculum.

The positive slant is recent. Historically, political theorists have been far more interested in the question of how to control the proclivities of bad leaders than in the question of how to promote the virtues of good ones. Influenced by religious traditions that focused on good and evil, and often personally scarred by war and disorder, the best political thinkers have had rather a jaundiced view of human nature.

Machiavelli provides perhaps the best example. He did not wrestle with the idea of bad—as in coercive—leadership. He simply presumed it. He took it for granted that people do harm as well as good, and so his advice to princes, to leaders, was to be ruthless. Consider this morsel about how leaders should, if need be, keep followers in line: "Cruelties can be called well used (if it is permissible to speak well of evil) that are done at a stroke, out of the necessity to secure oneself, and then are not persisted in but are turned to as much utility for the subjects as one can. Those cruelties are badly used which, though few in the beginning, rather grow with time."[10]

As the Gardner quotation makes plain, today leaders who use coercion are generally judged to be bad. But to Machiavelli, the only kind of bad leader is the weak leader. Machiavelli was a pragmatist above all, familiar with the ways of the world and with a keen eye for the human condition. And so, to him, the judicious use of cruelty was an important arrow in the leader's quiver.

Although it seems counterintuitive, America's founders thought like Machiavelli, at least insofar as they also believed that people required restraint. They were products of the European Enlightenment, but as they saw it, their main task was to form a government that was for and by the people but that would simultaneously set limits on the body politic and on those who would lead it.

To be sure, the emphasis was different. Whereas Machiavelli was concerned primarily with the question of how to contain followers, the framers of the U.S. Constitution were concerned primarily with the question of how to contain leaders. Alexander Hamilton, for example, was, in comparison with his peers, a proponent of a strong executive. But even he considered it ideologically important as well as politically expedient to focus not on the possibilities of presidential power but on its limits.

In *The Federalist Papers*, Hamilton acknowledged America's "aversion to monarchy"—to leaders who inherit great power. He dedicated an entire essay to distinguishing between the proposed president, on the one hand, and the distant, detested British monarchy, on the other, an essay that made one main point: The U.S. Constitution would absolutely preclude the possibility that bad leadership could become entrenched. The very idea of checks and balances grew out of the framers' presumption that unless there was a balance of power, power was certain to be abused. Put another way, the American political system is the product of revolutionaries familiar with, and therefore wary of, bad leadership.

But as sociologist Talcott Parsons observed, on matters that relate to the importance of power and authority in human affairs, American social thought has tended toward utopianism.[11] For whatever reasons, most students of politics shy away from the subject of bad leadership and especially from really bad leaders, such as Stalin and Pol Pot. In other words, no matter how great and obvious its impact on the course of human affairs, "tyranny as such is simply not an issue or a recognized term of analysis."[12]

The question is, why do we tend toward utopianism on matters relating to the importance of power and authority in human affairs?[13] Why do we avoid the subject of tyranny in our leadership curricula, thereby presuming that tyrannical leadership is less relevant to the course of human affairs than democratic leadership? Why does the leadership industry generally assume that a bad leader such as Saddam Hussein has nearly nothing in common with a good leader such as Tony Blair, or that the Nazis were one species and the Americans another? Is Bernard Ebbers really so very different from Louis Gerstner Jr.? How did *leadership* come to be synonymous with *good* leadership?[14] Why are we afraid to acknowledge, much less admit to, the dark side?

These are the questions to which I now turn.

The Light Side

We want to read books about good leaders such as John Adams, Jack Welch, and Nelson Mandela. We don't want to read books about bad leaders such as Warren Harding, David Koresh, and Robert Mugabe.

This preference is natural. We go through life accentuating the positive and eliminating the negative in order to be as healthy and happy as possible. As Daniel Goleman put it, "[O]ur emotional and physical well-being is based in part on artful denial and illusion." In other words, for us to cultivate an "unfounded sense of optimism" serves a purpose. It is in our self-interest.[15]

In the leadership industry, this disposition has now moved from the level of the individual to the level of the collective. Those of us engaged in leadership work seem almost to collude to avoid the elephant in the room—bad leadership.[16] We resist even considering the possibility that the dynamic between Franklin Delano Roosevelt and his most ardent followers had anything in common with the dynamic between Adolph Hitler and his most ardent followers; or that John Biggs, the admired former CEO of TIAA/CREF, has skills and capacities similar in some ways to those of Richard Scrushy, the disgraced former CEO of HealthSouth.

As we have seen, the human predisposition to denial and optimism does not stop everyone from assuming the role of the hard-nosed pragmatist. Machiavelli and Hamilton understood that the human animal cannot be relied on to be good, and they prescribed accordingly. So what happened in the recent past to explain why the leadership industry and the general public have become positively disposed?

Reason 1: The Use of Language

In 1978 James MacGregor Burns, a Pulitzer Prize–winning historian and political scientist of impeccable repute, published *Leadership*, a book now widely regarded as seminal. The time was right. Even in higher education, there was growing support for the idea that "great men" mattered; and in the wake of Vietnam and Watergate and the assassinations of John Kennedy, Robert Kennedy, and Martin Luther King, Jr., Americans were increasingly persuaded that there was a "crisis of leadership."

Because the book itself was impressive, because for decades there had been nearly no good work on leadership per se, and because *Leadership* was published just as questions about governance in America became urgent, Burns's work had considerable impact. In fact, his two types of leadership—transactional and transformational—became part of the leadership lingo among those interested in both political and corporate leadership.

Thus the way in which Burns chose to define the words *leader* and *leadership* mattered. "Leadership over human beings is exercised when persons with certain motives and purposes mobilize . . . resources so as to arouse, engage, and satisfy the motives of followers," he wrote. "This is done in order to realize goals mutually held by leaders and followers." Burns was unwilling to call those who "obliterate" followers "leaders." Instead he labeled them "power wielders." "Power wielders," Burns argued, "may treat people as things. Leaders may not."[17]

The fact that Burns's book came out just when the leadership industry was beginning to grow also explains his strong impact on how people understood the word *leadership*. Even now it is Burns's particular definition of leadership—a definition that excludes leaders who, even though they may exercise power, authority, or influence, fail to "arouse, engage, and satisfy the motives of followers"—that dominates the field. Warren Bennis, one of the gurus of corporate leadership, has taken a semantic stance similar to Burns's. In the new (2003) introduction to his classic *On Becoming a Leader*, Bennis restates the position he took when the book was first published (1989): that leaders engage others by creating shared meaning, speaking in a distinctive voice, demonstrating the capacity to adapt, and having integrity. In other words, like Burns, Bennis generally assumes that to become a leader is to become a good leader.[18]

Reason 2: Business Trumps Everything Else

During the last quarter of the twentieth century the leadership industry developed primarily in response to the demands of American business. The reason was simple: By the mid-1970s, American business was in trouble. As Rosabeth Moss Kanter put it in *The Change Masters*, published in 1983, "Not long ago, American companies seemed to control the world in which they operated." Now, she went on, they were in a much scarier place, one in which factors such as the control of oil by OPEC, foreign competition (especially from Japan), inflation, and regulation "disturb[ed] the smooth workings of corporate machines and threaten[ed] to overwhelm us."[19]

In response to the growing concern, American business (and American business schools) began pouring millions of dollars into developing a cadre of people who might fix what was wrong. The content of the behavioral sciences changed, and a new area of study developed with remarkable rapidity: leadership as a business management skill. Scholars, teachers, and consultants were now being paid very well indeed to teach people to lead companies that ran smoothly—and turned a profit.

Thus, during the past few decades corporate America and the

schools that study and serve it started slowly to equate the learning of leadership with the learning of good leadership. It can be argued that this new definition of the word *leadership* accounts more than anything else for the explosive growth of the leadership industry. In particular, in keeping with the spirit of American capitalism, programs and curricula that claim to grow (good) leaders fill seats—and coffers.

Reason 3: The American National Character

The leadership industry is an American product—an American seed planted in American soil and harvested almost entirely by American experts. It is small wonder that the industry mirrors the American experience, in particular its self-help optimism.

Repeatedly, America's great leaders have given voice to this sense of the possible. In his Farewell Address, George Washington foretold an America that would "give to mankind the magnanimous and too novel example of a people always guided by an exalted justice and benevolence."[20] In his second inaugural address, Abraham Lincoln spoke of binding "the nation's wounds,"[21] even though North and South had not yet finished fighting their excruciating Civil War. On the steps of the Lincoln Memorial, Martin Luther King, Jr., described his dream, in which his children would "one day live in a nation where they will be judged not by the color of their skin but by the content of their character."[22] And both John Kennedy and Ronald Reagan borrowed from John Winthrop the picture of America as a city on a hill. As Reagan put it while running for president the first time, "We can meet our destiny—and that destiny is to build a land here that will be, for all mankind, a shining city on a hill."[23]

Our newfound belief in the individual and collective benefits of leadership learning originates from this wellspring. We presume that to be a leader is to do good and to be good. We presume that all of us can, and that some of us will, build "a shining city on a hill."

The Dark Side

But the leadership industry has a problem that years ago I named Hitler's ghost.[24] Here is my concern. If we pretend that there is no elephant and that bad leadership is unrelated to good leadership, if we pretend to know the one without knowing the other, we will in the end distort the enterprise. We cannot distance ourselves from even the most extreme example—Hitler—by bestowing on him another name, such as "power wielder." Not only was his impact on twentieth-century history arguably greater than anyone else's, but also he was brilliantly skilled at inspiring, mobilizing, and directing followers. His use of coercion notwithstanding, if this is not leadership, what is?

Similarly, it makes no sense to think of corporate lawbreakers as one breed, and corporate gods as another. Why would we preclude people at the top of the Enron hierarchy—chairman Kenneth Lay, CEO Jeffrey Skilling, and CFO Andrew Fastow—from being labeled leaders just because they did not "realize goals mutually held by leaders and followers"? The fact is that Lay, Skilling, and Fastow were agents of change. What they did affected the lives and pocketbooks of tens of thousands of Americans, many of whom were not Enron employees. Let's be clear here. These men were not just a few rotten apples. Rather, they created, indeed encouraged, an organizational culture that allowed many apples to spoil and, in turn, ruin others.

Thus the fundamental proposition of this book: To deny bad leadership equivalence in the conversation and curriculum is misguided, tantamount to a medical school that would claim to teach health while ignoring disease. Some might argue that the differences are merely semantic—that although Burns and Bennis equate the word *leadership* with good leadership, the rest of us are free to define leadership as we see fit. But words matter. Inevitably, the fact that the overwhelming majority of leadership experts use *leadership* to imply *good* leadership affects how we think about a subject that is far more complex, and frightening, than this dewy-eyed view would suggest.

Limiting leadership to good leadership presents three major problems.

- *It is confusing.* Try telling the average undergraduate, or a non-American, or the proverbial man on the street, that the most reviled of recent American presidents, Richard Nixon, was something other than a leader. Most folks use the word *leader* as it has always been used: to refer to any individual who uses power, authority, and influence to get others to go along. The *New York Times* does not refer to former Liberian president Charles Taylor as a "power wielder," even though he stands accused of murder, rape, abduction, and other crimes against humanity. Nor is L. Dennis Kozlowski, the astonishingly successful former CEO of Tyco, considered by most people to be any the less a corporate leader because it was finally revealed that he was greedy to the point of being corrupt.

- *It is misleading.* As Bernard Bass has observed, "[T]here are almost as many different definitions of leadership as there are persons who have attempted to define the concept."[25] For example, leadership can be considered the exercise of influence, or a power relation, or an instrument of goal achievement, or a differentiated role. The point is that each of these definitions is value-free. It makes no sense therefore to distinguish between leaders and power wielders. In fact, to compare them is not to compare apples and oranges, but apples and apples.

- *It does a disservice.* All of us want good leadership—to live in a world of good leaders and good followers. We want good leadership at home, at work, and in the various communities of which we are members. One way to increase the probability of good leadership is to encourage as many people as possible to study it, teach it, and practice it. But another way is to encourage as many people as possible to explore bad leadership. How will we ever stop what we refuse to see and study?

Americans are familiar, of course, with bad leadership. We are not strangers to ineffective leaders and followers, nor to unethical leaders and followers. But it is also true that at the highest national level, the United States has never had a leader who was bad in the extreme. Unlike people in most of the rest of the world, Americans have never suffered under authoritarian rule, and so the dark side of public leadership has remained at a remove. Our bad leaders tend to disappoint because they are inept or corrupt, and not because they are despots. Even the worst of our national leaders, presidents such as James Buchanan, Warren Harding, or even Nixon, who resigned before he could be impeached, tend to be judged stupid, maladroit, sleazy, or ignoble rather than tyrannical.

But the American experience is not everything. Leaders and followers can be bad in ways that are of a different magnitude. In a foreword to *The Black Book of Communism: Crimes, Terror, Repression*, Martin Malia identifies several regimes by the brutal tyrants who led them: "Stalin's Gulag, Mao Zedong's Great Leap Forward and his Cultural Revolution, and Pol Pot's Khmer Rouge." Malia reminds us, in the event we need reminding, that Communism was a "tragedy of planetary dimensions"; its victims are estimated to number between 85 and 100 million. Moreover, he makes clear that it is impossible to understand what happened without understanding those who were immediately responsible.[26]

Those who are immediately responsible for bad leadership include bad followers just as much as bad leaders. Like leaders, followers run the gamut. At the extreme, there are those who commit "crimes of obedience." Herbert Kelman and Lee Hamilton demonstrated that such crimes take place not only in contexts of conflict—for example, when members of the military engage in sanctioned massacres—but also in political and bureaucratic settings. They point out that the burglars were the "foot soldiers of political espionage" in the original Watergate crime, and that the wrongdoing in Nixon's White House continued in a series of "cover-up actions" that reached all the way down the chain of command to the clerical staff.[27]

So bad leadership is not solely the fault of a few bad leaders. We are all, every one of us, in this together.

Archbishop Desmond Tutu has said that his experience of South Africa taught him "two contradictory things." On the one hand, we "have an extraordinary capacity for good." But on the other hand, we have "a remarkable capacity for evil—we have refined ways of being mean and nasty to one another [through] genocides, holocausts, slavery, racism, wars, oppression and injustice."[28]

Because leadership makes a difference, sometimes even a big difference, those of us who desire to make the world a better place must do what Tutu did. We must come to grips with leadership as two contradictory things: good and bad.

CHAPTER TWO

REASONS FOR
BEING BAD

POLITICAL PHILOSOPHERS have generally agreed on one important thing: People in a state of nature are not, in the usual sense of the word, "good." This is not to insist that people are bad but rather that the human animal cannot be relied on to behave well.

Because virtually all men, women, and children live in groups, and because some men, women, and children are bad some of the time, the overriding question is how bad behavior can and should be constrained. Freud wrote that primitive peoples lived in groups "ruled over despotically by a powerful male" and that only later, along with the beginnings of religion and social organization, was the "paternal horde transformed into a community of brothers."[1] It is this transition—from natural humans living in a "paternal horde" to more civilized humans living in a "community of brothers"—that has been grist for the mill of political philosophers from Aristotle and Confucius to Montesquieu and Mill. The most pressing political concerns have been and continue to be about governance: how people in groups are best ordered and organized.

In the classic *Leviathan*, English philosopher Thomas Hobbes (1588–1679) asserted that people in their natural state are rapacious and aggressive. Therefore, to ensure what's most important—self-preservation—individual rights must be subsumed under the rights of a state charged with keeping order. Hobbes argued that without strict political arrangements and rule by a leader with an iron fist, we would inevitably descend into chaos and war.[2]

Jean-Jacques Rousseau's (1712–1778) view of human nature was much different from Hobbes's. But by the time he wrote *The Social Contract*, a small book that had a big impact on eighteenth-century Western thought, Rousseau similarly argued that it was in our self-interest to surrender at least some individual rights. Unlike Hobbes, Rousseau did not consider people territorial and aggressive.[3] Still, he concluded that we are most likely to lead a good life by living in organized groups in which the whole, a community of some kind, is authorized to govern the individual parts.[4]

As we have seen, Machiavelli's (1469–1527) *The Prince* spoke to the virtue of order, however secured. Thus the ruler's first responsibility was to do whatever was required to impose it. Like Hobbes, Machiavelli asserted that we can choose to be free or to be ruled, but if we opt for the former over the latter we do so at our peril.[5] The trade-off for followers is obvious: less freedom in exchange for more security.

Machiavelli wrote about restraints because his primary interest was in securing the power of the leader. John Locke (1632–1704) wrote about restraints because his primary interest was in securing the rights of the led. Curiously, the premise that underlies the work of these two very different political thinkers—and indeed of virtually every great treatise on government—is more or less the same: To contain the dark side of human nature, some sort of structure, generally enforced by law, must be imposed. In other words, although it seems counterintuitive, the philosophers of the European and American Enlightenment were every bit as concerned with how to control the people as they were with how to liberate them. Whereas Locke's more tempered view of human

nature permitted him to consider the primary function of government to be the protection of property and not, as with Hobbes, the protection of life, the result is not very different from that of his great predecessor. Like Hobbes, Locke preached the need for constraints imposed by government and the rule of law.[6]

America's founders generally followed Locke's line of thought, which can be described as simultaneously enlightened and pragmatic. As *The Federalist Papers* testify, when the time came to codify a political system, Alexander Hamilton, James Madison, and John Jay argued for checks and balances. Why? It was because they did not trust all the people all the time. Simultaneously hopeful and hard-nosed, *The Federalist Papers* remind us of "both the light and dark sides of human nature—of man's capacity for reason and justice that makes free government possible, of his capacity for passion and injustice that makes it necessary."[7]

For those of us with a particular interest in leadership, the seminal readings in political theory are a treasure trove. Together they provide the single best explanation of why leaders lead and followers follow: self-interest. In nearly every case, leaders and followers engage to protect against the anxiety of disorder and the fear of death.

Of course our willingness, even our eagerness, to live with limits means that they must first be established and then enforced. Someone must do this collective work. That is, someone, or several someones, must lead this effort, and this is why, except for diehard anarchists, not one of the great political philosophers has a worldview that dispenses with leaders altogether.

Let me make clear that even though I have focused so far on political arrangements, the need for leadership applies to every area of human endeavor. All of us belong to groups and organizations of various kinds, ranging from the family to the work place. Virtually every one of these groups and organizations maintains some kind of order, and some kind of order means some kind of leadership.

In *Lord of the Flies*, William Golding tells of a band of boys brought together accidentally, having no resources other than the

ones they alone can muster. Soon the motley crew becomes an organized group, with a clear leader. Almost imperceptibly but with growing self-confidence, Ralph takes on the role. " 'I'm calling an assembly,' he said. One by one, the [others] halted, and stood watching him." Ralph, emboldened by the attention and sensing that he's filling a vacuum, continues. " 'With the conch. I'm calling a meeting even if we have to go on into the dark. Down on the platform. When I blow it. Now.' "[8]

Ralph's grab for power—and the other boys' willingness, at least initially, to go along—tells us what we already know. Most of the time someone is willing, even eager, to lead, however obscure and uncertain the rewards. And most of the time others are willing, even eager, to follow, however obscure and uncertain their reasons for doing so. Of course, the type of leadership that emerges will depend not only on the group members but also on the nature of the task at hand.

A question arises: Given that the need for leadership is demonstrable and universally shared, and given that the roles of leader and followers are readily filled, why does so much go so wrong so often?

Why Do Leaders Behave Badly?

In this book I do not explore the psychosocial genesis of individual behavior. But even to approach the question of how to minimize bad leadership, we must have some understanding of what motivates it.

Leaders are like everyone else. They—we—behave badly for different reasons, and they—we—behave badly in different ways.

Sometimes the context fosters bad behavior. A city in which corruption has long been tolerated is more likely to be defrauded by its elected officials than is one that has a long and strong tradition of good government.

Sometimes followers entice leaders to go astray. People in positions of authority are not immune to the influence of others,

especially close advisers who, although perhaps misguided, are nevertheless determined and single-tracked.

But, in the main, leaders behave badly because of who they are and what they want.

Traits

Leadership scholars used to think that the leader's traits were more important than any other variable to the way leadership was exercised. But now they're more skeptical. Traits once considered of paramount importance, such as intelligence, are viewed as having fuzzy and imprecise denotations. (Cognitive intelligence? Emotional intelligence? Practical intelligence?) And traits considered essential in some situations are now seen as virtually irrelevant in others. In any case, the explanatory power of traits is now viewed as less than it once was. It is now widely agreed that to overemphasize the leader's traits is to underemphasize other important variables, such as the situation, the nature of the task at hand, and of course the followers.[9]

But even though the trait theory of leadership is out of fashion, at least in academe, it's silly to pretend that traits don't matter. Traits once considered of consequence still are.[10] And average people who exercise leadership still exceed the average members of their groups in traits such as intelligence (however defined), sociability, persistence, alertness, verbal facility, level of energy, and adaptability.

In short, the trait approach to leadership is a relatively simple way of understanding why people behave the way they do. Moreover, whether a leader has or lacks a particular trait is likely to tell us a fair amount about how and why good, or bad, leadership was exercised.

Consider the explanatory power of an ordinary trait such as greed. Greedy leaders crave more—more success, more money, more power, or more whatever, such as sex. This is not to say that all leaders who aspire to have more are bad. In some measure, rewards such as money and power are simply the benefits expected from hard work. Rather, when leaders' appetites for more are excessive, it is likely to intrude on their capacity to exercise leadership for the common good.

American business has been riddled in recent years by scandals brought on primarily by rich corporate leaders who apparently wanted nothing so much as to get even richer. One of the poster boys for wrongdoing in the mutual fund industry was Richard Strong. Charged with sins ranging from late trading to improper market timing, Strong was finally forced to resign as chairman, chief executive, and chief investment officer of Strong Capital Management, a firm he had founded. Similarly, Raymond Cunningham, chief executive of Invesco, one of the world's biggest money managers, was hit by civil fraud charges filed by both the Securities and Exchange Commission and New York State Attorney General Eliot Spitzer. Cunningham reportedly was engaged in a massive mutual fund scheme from which he and his cronies profited handsomely while ordinary investors suffered millions of dollars in losses.

But greed is not measured in dollars alone. Because the modern American presidency offers heady, extravagant benefits, it comes as no surprise to learn that those who sit in the Oval Office are also inclined to want more, sometimes more than they can, or should, have. Lyndon Johnson wanted both guns and butter—American dominance abroad and the Great Society at home. Richard Nixon tried further to tighten his already tight grip on the American political system. And Bill Clinton's presidency will long be stained by his uncontained appetites. When leaders are unwilling or unable to control their desire for more, bad leadership will be the result.

Greed is likely to be most pernicious when it entails a hunger for power. Sometimes this results in little more than the leader's unwillingness to share power by, for example, delegating tasks and consulting with others.[11] But in its more extreme form, a craving for power can be dangerous. It is no stretch to say that the root cause of totalitarianism is a leader whose need for control is all-consuming.

Character

Psychologists and psychiatrists base their analyses of character on clinical observations. Historians and political scientists, on the other hand, assess character by studying the behavior of public officials over long periods.[12] In any case, character is considered the core of the personality system, the foundation on which personality structures develop and operate. Unlike traits, which are viewed as amenable to change, character is a more permanent condition, fundamental and fixed. Character is embedded in who we are; it *is* who we are.[13]

As the word is commonly used, we also presume that to know a person's character is to know his or her moral compass. When we say of leaders such as Nelson Mandela and Jimmy Carter that they are men of good character, we are saying they are good men, decent and honorable deep down as well as to all appearances.

The connection between character and leadership is easiest to make at the extreme. Political scientist Betty Glad studied three very bad leaders: Hitler, Stalin, and Saddam Hussein. She concluded all three were "malignant narcissists" who, in effect, could not help being aggressive and sadistic in their relations with others.[14] Put another way, malignant narcissism is not considered to be a mere trait. To label these three men malignant narcissists is to stamp their characters and to tell us what we need to know about why they behave as they do.

Why Do We Follow Leaders Who Behave Badly?

Unless followers are pressured or coerced into going along with bad leaders, they resist them—right? Wrong. We know full well that bad leaders of various kinds abound and that their followers usually follow, even when they know that their leaders are misguided or malevolent. Why? The answer to this question matters, because we can't expect to reduce the number of bad leaders unless we reduce the number of bad followers.

Individual Needs

Even bad leaders often satisfy our most basic human needs, in particular safety, simplicity, and certainty.

The quest for safety, for self-preservation (think Hobbes), is arguably the strongest of our basic needs.[15] Before anything else, we seek food, shelter, and protection from harm. As infants and small children, we are completely dependent on adults, usually our parents, to meet these primary needs. Consequently, one of the first things we learn during childhood is to follow—to do what our parents tell us to do. Getting along by going along is one of life's earliest lessons. Freud explicitly connected parenting and leading: "We know that the great majority of people have a strong need for authority which they can admire, to which they can submit, and which dominates and sometimes even ill-treats them. We have learned from the psychology of the individual whence comes this need of masses. It is the longing for the father that lives in each of us from his childhood days."[16]

Of course, our need for safety plays itself out at many levels other than the original, familial one, and this is why we follow the leader in everyday life. To be a well-behaved child is generally not to question the teacher, even when the teacher is somehow bad. When we are adults on the job it's the same: By and large we toe the line. We do what we're told and play by the rules, even when the rules are unfair, and those who set them badly equipped or disposed. We follow because the cost of not following is, more often than not, high.[17]

We also follow because of our need for simplicity and stability. Leaders, even bad ones, can provide a sense of order and certainty in a disordered and uncertain world. Moreover, to resist leaders is to invite confusion and upset. To resist leaders is demanding in a way that going along is not.

It has been suggested that the construct of the leader itself is a manifestation of our preference for simple as opposed to complex explanations. To have a leader is to have an observable someone, potentially replaceable, who is responsible for what happens.[18] In any case it's hard to argue with the proposition that leaders help us to make sense of the world in which we operate. Bill Gates explains and now even symbolizes the success of Microsoft, just as Cardinal Bernard Law came to explain and finally even to symbolize the cover-ups that stained the Roman Catholic Church.

Among the most compelling explanations for our willingness to obey authority is the need to keep things simple. Many reasons have been given to explain why, in Stanley Milgram's notorious experiment, ordinary people designated as "teachers" were willing to inflict painful shocks on those designated as "learners."[19] It was dismaying in any case, indeed horrifying, to discover how readily the likes of you and me hurt others if ordered to do so by someone with power or authority. Milgram himself explained it by saying that his "teachers" shifted their moral concern from the "learners" to the authority figure, in this case the experimenter who gave the instructions.[20] But it has also been argued that the teachers (followers) obeyed orders to inflict pain because of their overriding need to keep things simple in a stressful situation. Evolution favors creatures that make quick decisions based on their prior experience. So yet another reason to follow leaders, even bad leaders, is simply because it's often easiest to assume that they know what they're doing.[21]

Finally, sometimes followers follow bad leaders because of their our need for certainty. Although we are always vulnerable to existential angst, it can reasonably be argued that in the wake of September 11, 2001, for Americans at least this vulnerability became more acute. In our eagerness to quell our anxiety, we are more willing than we would be otherwise to go along with leaders who give the appearance of being strong and certain.[22]

Group Needs

Followers follow bad leaders not only because of their individual need for safety, simplicity, and certainty but also because of the needs of the group. Groups go along with bad leaders because even bad leaders often provide important benefits. In particular, leaders maintain order, provide cohesion and identity, and do the collective work.

As we have seen, political theorists agree that we require leaders to keep the peace. Empirical evidence supports this proposition. Hierarchy, it turns out, is the natural order of things. Patterns of dominance and deference among primates are particularly relevant. Although some thinkers quarrel with the notion that there is any link between the human animal and, say, the baboons referred to in the introduction to this book, it's hard to imagine that there exists no connection at all. As *Lord of the Flies* suggests, whenever a group forms, a leader will emerge. Our nonhuman ancestors—primates—exhibit the same behavior; that is, they exhibit social ranking. Therefore our own social, political, and economic hierarchies are in keeping with, rather than opposed to, our primate heritage.[23]

These connections also pertain to the role played by all leaders, including bad ones, in providing the group with cohesion and identity. Human groups have evolved from small-scale societies to the complex nation-states that characterize the modern world. This evolution has had implications for leadership systems. In general, the more complex the society is, the greater the number of groups, organizations, and leaders.[24] Leaders hold groups and organizations together as they develop and change. Leaders enable groups and organizations to distinguish themselves one from the other. And leaders at the top symbolize the whole.

The final point usually is underestimated: Leaders meet the needs of groups and organizations because they take on the collective work. In fact, as societies increase in size, they become even more dependent on leaders to order, organize, and carry out their collective activities. "Thirty people can sit around a campfire and arrive at a consensual decision; thirty million people cannot."[25]

No one has written about this phenomenon as persuasively as Robert Michels, an early twentieth-century German social scientist. After observing firsthand the gap between the socialist ideal of egalitarian governance and what actually transpired, Michels concluded that *all* groups and organizations, even those that deeply value collective decision making, develop oligarchic tendencies. Michels's "iron law of oligarchy" says simply that, utopian ideologies notwithstanding, there will always be leaders. There will always be those tasked with getting the group's work done.[26]

For reasons that are now quite clear, followers have good and sound reasons for following, even when their leaders are bad. To meet their needs, as individuals and as members of groups, followers usually conclude that it's in their interest to go with the flow. Another, perhaps more persuasive way of putting it is this: *Not* following is not in their interest. Not following can entail risk—to family, to position, and even to life. In particular, actively to protest against the powers that be takes time, energy, and, more often than not, courage.

Why Do Followers Behave Badly?

It's one thing for followers to follow bad leaders merely by going along. It's quite another for them to lend bad leaders strong personal support. What I am arguing is this: Followers who knowingly, deliberately commit themselves to bad leaders are themselves bad.

Followers' dedication to bad leaders is often strongest when their leaders are very bad, as opposed to only somewhat bad. Again, it's a matter of self-interest. Followers usually have no particular incentive to lend strong support to a leader who is merely ineffective. Going along is good enough. On the other hand, intimates of frankly unethical leaders often stand to benefit financially or politically from the relationship.

The corruption that took place in companies such as WorldCom and HealthSouth by no means involved only the CEOs. Both Bernard Ebbers and Richard Scrushy were surrounded by small groups of followers who knew what the score was, participated actively in the wrongdoing, and stood to profit substantially from the company's fraudulent practices. These members of the two men's respective inner circles were separate and distinct from the larger group of followers, who were out of the loop and who, whatever suspicions they might have had, were not directly involved in the corruption.

The most extensive study of bad followers has been the case of Nazi Germany. At the risk of oversimplifying but in the interest of distinguishing among the kinds of followers, I will divide Germans during the Nazi period into three groups: bystanders, evildoers, and acolytes. (Only a handful of Germans actively opposed Hitler, and they often paid with their lives.)

Bystanders went along with Hitler and the Nazi regime, but they were not fervent Nazis. Bystanders' motivations ranged from self-interest (on matters relating to stability and security) to being part of a national group (Germany was, after all, their *Heimat*, their homeland) that was cohesive and provided a sense of identity.

Evildoers were members of units such as the SS-Einsatzgruppen. One of this unit's first goals during the Second World War was to massacre as many Soviet Jews as possible. The 1941 slaughter at Babi Yar, a ravine in Kiev, was testimony to its efficiency: In only two days members of this unit shot to death 33,771 Jews. Why did members of the German SS become, in the words of Richard Rhodes, "masters of death"?[27] The reasons varied. Some were genuine sadists. Others had been persuaded that they were killing "vermin." Still others turned brutal because they themselves were being brutalized by violence or the threat of violence. Finally, however weak in retrospect this line of argument, German soldiers were like soldiers everywhere. They were told what to do and they did it.

Acolytes were true believers: followers who were deeply committed to Hitler personally and to his political program. Although the acolytes who constituted Hitler's inner circle stood handsomely to profit from their association with the Führer, in fact most were mesmerized by his charisma and ideas long before realizing rewards such as money and power. As early as 1923 Hermann Göring referred to Hitler as the "beloved leader of the German-freedom movement."[28] And only a few years later, in 1926, Joseph Goebbels gushed, "He [Hitler] is a genius. The natural, creative instrument of a divine fate . . . I feel completely bound to him. The last doubt in me has disappeared."[29]

Most people behave rationally most of the time. In Hitler's Germany, bystanders behaved badly either because they had no issue with the Nazi agenda or because, if they did, they calculated that the cost of resisting was greater than the cost of doing nothing. Evildoers behaved badly because it's how they were told to behave. And acolytes behaved badly because behaving badly is what they wanted to do. Acolytes were so dedicated to the Führer that his wish was, literally, their command.

Until now, I have spoken of bad leaders, bad followers, and bad leadership as if the different ways of being bad were more or less alike. But we know that being bad takes different forms. Because our interest in these matters is practical as well as theoretical, these differences may be of consequence. For example, holding a callous corporate leader accountable is one thing; holding a corrupt elected official accountable is a different thing entirely. Similarly, we know that deposing an incompetent mayor is rather a different undertaking from deposing an evil dictator. It is therefore important to make meaning of being bad, a task I turn to next.

CHAPTER THREE

MAKING MEANING OF BEING BAD

I N A TALK I once gave to the New Haven Jewish community, I referred to Hitler as a bad leader. The words were hardly out of my mouth when a member of the audience rose to differ. "Hitler may have been 'bad' as in 'ethically bad,'" he said. "But he was a good leader in that he was very effective."

The man was right. Given the ideology of National Socialism and the particulars of the Nazi agenda from 1933 to 1941 (when Germany made the mistake of invading the Soviet Union), Hitler's political and military strategies were nearly impeccable. Moreover, even between 1941 and 1945—the period leading up to Germany's defeat—at least one of Hitler's most cherished objectives, the annihilation of European Jewry, was realized with astonishing efficiency. Does this make Hitler a "good" leader?

If the lines of demarcation between effective and ethical blur for a leader as obviously evil as Adolph Hitler, it is no wonder that judging other leaders, less extreme, is harder. Was Ronald Reagan a good president? In many ways he was effective, much more effective than his Hollywood career might have predicted. But to liberal Democrats, who even in retrospect detest his domestic agenda in particular, to label Reagan a "good" president seems absurd.

The lack of clarity about what exactly defines a good leader, and how to distinguish a good leader from a bad one, is mirrored in the follower. Consider this question: Should followers follow the leader, or the dictates of their consciences? On the one hand, a strong argument can be made that to maintain order and get work done, followers should go along with their leaders except in dire circumstances. On the other hand, followers are not sheep, nor should they necessarily be part of any herd.

When Argentines took to the streets in early 2002 to protest the parties and politicians who had been discredited by the country's economic collapse, one might say that by noisily insinuating themselves into the political process they were being disruptive. Or one might take the opposite view: that by speaking out for what they believed, they were doing what good followers should do.

In an infamous case, Sherron Watkins, at the time vice president of corporate development at Enron, sent Kenneth Lay, Enron's CEO, a six-page memo in 2001 detailing her fears that the company would implode in a wave of accounting scandals. At first glance Watkins appears to be a good, even a very good, follower. But a closer look suggests that the picture is more complex. After the scandal broke and Watkins testified before Congress, some saw a traitor, a woman who was flagrantly disloyal to former colleagues at every level and indeed to Enron itself.

If we ask whether the end justifies the means, we further complicate the conversation. A letter sent anonymously to the president of a major university complained about the coach of the women's basketball team. The coach, a woman, was described as abusive to the point of creating an "extremely unhealthy and unproductive team environment." Specifically, her "primary leadership tools" were "criticism, public humiliation, demands of compliance, screaming and yelling, pitting players against one another, and other 'old-school' boot camp techniques."[1] Here's the question: Should the coach be judged on the basis of her performance, or that of her team?

The same issue arose with regard to Bobby Knight, once the legendary basketball coach at Indiana University (since 2000 he has been at Texas Tech University). Although as individuals his players were at the mercy of his frequent verbal and infrequent physical abuse, his team as a whole did brilliantly. How should Knight be judged? He got the end part right: His team was a winner. But his means were questionable: He browbeat undergraduates. So, finally, our assessment of a coach or leader, such as Knight, is bound to be subjective, personal, and value-driven. You might not like the idea of anyone ever striking a twenty-year-old. But given Knight's remarkable record as a winning coach, I might not find it so objectionable.

Clearly, means versus ends issues are like good versus bad issues: impossible to sort out with precision. No wonder the leadership industry simplifies things. No wonder it defines leaders simply as "people who do the right thing."[2]

But as we know, sometimes leaders do the *wrong* thing. Even the best and brightest aren't precluded from being seduced by power. Some of the twentieth century's most eminent intellectuals fell for really bad leaders in a really big way. The great German philosopher Martin Heidegger joined the Nazi Party because he longed to "return to some imaginary pre-modern idyll." Other Europeans of high repute, such as the leading French writer and philosopher Jean-Paul Sartre, became enamored of Stalin because there was nothing they hated so much as bourgeois capitalism.[3] Nor were Americans exempt from such foolish flirtations, especially, again, with Stalin. Out of willful ignorance and misguided optimism, writers such as Lillian Hellman and John Steinbeck spent years making excuses for the Soviet despot, apparently believing that all would be right in the end.

I do not underestimate the challenge of explaining followers like these, nor do I minimize the task of explaining bad leadership more generally. But if we have any hope of moving from bad leadership to better leadership, we must strike a balance between looking at the light and seeing in the dark.

Ineffective Leadership Versus Unethical Leadership

Bad leadership falls into two categories: bad as in ineffective and bad as in unethical. This distinction is not a theoretical construct. Rather, it is based on the empirical evidence. Look around and you will see that all bad leadership is bad in one, or sometimes both, of these ways.

The distinction between ineffective and unethical brings us back to the question of means and ends. Let's assume that Bill and Hillary Clinton's ambitious health care proposal was a well-intentioned initiative that, initially at least, had the support of most of their followers. But the means used—the ways in which the president and the first lady tried to get the American body politic from point A to point B—were inadequate to the point of being hapless. By the time the proposal was dead, even many of its early supporters had abandoned it. We can say, then, that at least in the area of health care policy, President Clinton was not a good leader. His good intentions notwithstanding, he was ineffective. Even his supporters would have to admit that his strategies and tactics were not up to the task, and so the job never got done.

By the same token, sometimes leaders and followers deploy effective means to unethical ends. It has become clear that for many years Boston's Cardinal Bernard Law (along with others in the Roman Catholic hierarchy) considered it his main mission to protect the good standing of the church. The problem was that this mission took precedence over the more immediate and humane one: to shield parishioners from predatory priests. Finally, the wrongdoing that kept the clergy's misconduct hidden from public view—the transfers, the payments, and the cover-ups—undermined the very church that the Cardinal wanted so badly to secure.[4]

Ineffective Leadership

Ineffective leadership fails to produce the desired change. For reasons that include missing traits, weak skills, strategies badly conceived, and tactics badly employed, ineffective leadership falls short of its intention.

One way to think about an ineffective leader is to reverse the ideal: If the ideal leader has traits such as intelligence, persistence, flexibility, and an even disposition, the leader who lacks many of these will likely run into trouble. The same holds for leadership skills. If the ideal leader is able to communicate, mobilize, collaborate, and make good decisions, leaders who are unwilling or unable to employ such skills are less likely to perform well than their better-disposed and better-endowed counterparts.

The rule for followers is analogous: Ineffective followers lack, or do not demonstrate, the traits and skills necessary for good followership. Robert Kelley found that the best followers were "strong, independent partners with leaders. They think for themselves, self-direct their work, and hold up their end of the bargain. They continuously work at making themselves integral to the enterprise, honing their skills and focusing their contributions, and collaborating with their colleagues."[5] By these measures, ineffective followers are weak and dependent, and they refuse in any significant way to commit or contribute to the group.

A final point: Leaders are generally judged ineffective because of the means they employ (or fail to employ) rather than the ends they pursue. Most leaders set goals that seem reasonable to at least a substantial minority of their constituents. But not many leaders and followers have the capacity to reach these goals. To be sure, the deck is often stacked against them. Context matters a great deal, and the challenges they face are, objectively, difficult. But in many cases leaders and their immediate followers simply lack the traits and skills required to surmount the long odds.

By all accounts Gray Davis, California's erstwhile governor, was in a situation fraught with political peril. The state was faced with formidable challenges, in areas ranging from deficits to demographics, and the citizens were restless. Even though no one complained that Davis was unethical, the impression gradually became widespread that he and his team were ineffective—so ineffective that in a special recall election he was unceremoniously dumped.

Unethical Leadership

Unethical leadership fails to distinguish between right and wrong. Because common codes of decency and good conduct are in some way violated, the leadership process is defiled.

In chapter 1, I take issue with James MacGregor Burns's definition of the word *leadership*, in which leadership is, necessarily, an ethical act. Let me now return to the exact way that Burns uses the word, particularly in the phrase "transforming leadership." For Burns, leadership is implicitly ethical in that it "is done to realize goals mutually held by leaders and followers." In his view, transforming leadership goes a step further; it's even better. "Such leadership occurs when one or more persons engage with others in such a way that leaders and followers raise one another to higher levels of motivation and morality."[6]

In Joanne Ciulla's collection of essays, *Ethics: The Heart of Leadership*, Burns takes yet another cut. Here he distinguishes among three types of leadership values: ethical values, moral values, and end values. Although he does not so group them, Burns is writing, on the one hand, about the leader's private self (the leader is honest, kind, and so on) and, on the other hand, about the leader's public self (the leader furthers the common interest).[7]

Burns goes on to suggest the following.

- Ethical leaders put their followers' needs before their own. Unethical leaders do not.

- Ethical leaders exemplify private virtues such as courage and temperance. Unethical leaders do not.

- Ethical leaders exercise leadership in the interest of the common good. Unethical leaders do not.

Most contemporary leadership scholars agree that the first principle is critical. Robert Greenleaf's "servant leader" leads because of a desire to serve others.[8] Joseph Rost sees leadership as "noncoercive influence" that leaves followers free to decide for themselves whether to go along.[9] And Edwin Hollander is content to bestow on leaders benefits, such as money and prestige, if in turn the leaders are accountable to followers.[10]

The second principle might seem new, and especially pertinent in a time of relentless media intrusion into the private lives of leaders such as Bill Clinton and Jack Welch. Although in recent years the question of whether a leader's private behavior impinges on public performance has been a hot topic, political philosophers have been interested in the issue for centuries. In general, the tolerance for moral fallibility, even if evident only behind closed doors, has been low. Confucius declared, "He who rules by virtue is like the polestar, which remains unmoving in its mansion while all the other stars revolve respectfully around it." In response to a question from Lord Ji Kang ("What should I do in order to make the people respectful, loyal, and zealous?"), Confucius urged him to be what today we call a role model: "Approach them with dignity and they will be respectful. Be yourself a good son and a kind father, and they will be loyal. Raise the good and train the incompetent, and they will be zealous."[11]

To act in accordance with the third principle is to exercise power, authority, and influence in the interest of the public welfare. To be sure, the contemporary literature on democratic theory argues that each of us, every citizen, bears the individual burden of assessing "the moral authority of political mandates."[12] But a good case can be made for the proposition that political leaders have a special responsibility to support the government and uphold the law only if they can do so in good conscience. If they cannot—if they are expected, for example, to uphold what they consider an unjust law—they are morally obliged to try to change course. One need hardly add that corporate, nonprofit, and military leaders should be held similarly accountable.

Ciulla argues that "leaders who do not look after the interests of their followers are not only unethical but ineffective."[13] At the same time, she takes the position that the standards to which we hold leaders should be the same as those we hold for everyone else—no lower and no higher. How then might this translate? If we accept Aristotle's dictum that virtues such as honesty and justice are acquired by practicing them, then leaders should do as Aristotle instructed: They should practice virtue because they want and intend to be virtuous.[14]

Nor are followers exempt. Like leaders, they are accountable for what they do.

- Ethical followers take the leader into account. Unethical followers do not.

- Ethical followers exemplify private virtues such as courage and temperance. Unethical followers do not.

- Ethical followers engage the leader and also other followers on behalf of the common good. Unethical followers do not.

Kelley found that followers were more troubled by ethical issues than were leaders. It's common for followers to be faced with an ethical dilemma: a situation in which they feel obliged by authorities to behave in ways that make them uncomfortable. Kelley writes that exemplary followers address the problem by demonstrating a "courageous conscience." Such followers have "the ability to judge right from wrong and the fortitude to take alternative steps toward what they believe is right."[15] Followers who lack a courageous conscience, particularly those who do not act even when something is obviously and egregiously wrong, are unethical.

Kelley is not, of course, suggesting that followers take on leaders freely and easily. In fact, his work supports the first principle, which clearly implies that leaders cannot be effective without cooperative followers. But followers are more obligated to the community as a whole than they are to any single individual, including the leader.

Kelley's research was conducted in the corporate sector. In contrast, John Rawls's seminal volume *A Theory of Justice* is about public life. Here too followers—citizens—are obliged to resist if resistance, rather than acquiescence, is in the common interest. Rawls describes civil disobedience as a "public, nonviolent, conscientious yet political act contrary to law usually done with the aim of bringing about a change in the law or policies of the government."[16]

Note that if a protest such as this one is successful, followers become leaders. Consider first the followership and then the leadership of Martin Luther King, Jr.—a subtle transition he described in a letter. "As the weeks and months unfolded," King wrote from his Birmingham, Alabama, jail cell in 1963, "we [Negroes] realized that we were the victims of a broken promise. The signs remained. Like so many experiences of the past we were confronted with blasted hopes, and the dark shadow of a deep disappointment settled upon us. So we had no alternative except that of preparing for direct [nonviolent] action, whereby we would present our very bodies as a means of laying our case before the conscience of the local and national community."[17]

The mixture of the ineffective and the unethical in bad leadership can never be known or measured precisely. This is a truth of the human condition. The important tasks then are to develop a greater awareness of the dynamics of bad leadership, and a better understanding of the different ways that leaders' actions can be both ineffective and unethical. Thus, I propose a typology of bad leadership that will highlight and distinguish the various ways in which we lead badly.

Types of Bad Leadership

After looking at hundreds of contemporary cases involving bad leaders and bad followers in the private, public, and nonprofit sectors, and in domains both domestic and international, I found that bad leadership falls into seven groups, which I have typed as follows:

- Incompetent
- Rigid
- Intemperate
- Callous
- Corrupt
- Insular
- Evil

To posit a typology is to invite argument. No less an expert than Max Weber, the German sociologist whose three types of authority—rational-legal, traditional, and charismatic—continue to influence leadership scholars some eighty years after his death, was wary of his critics. "The fact that none of these three ideal types . . . is usually to be found in historical cases in 'pure' form, is naturally not a valid objection to attempting their conceptual formulation in the sharpest possible form," Weber wrote. "Analysis in terms of sociological types has, after all . . . certain advantages which should not be minimized."[18]

Let me echo Weber's defense and provide a few cautionary notes about this typology in particular:

- These types are no "purer" than any other types, including Weber's.

- The range is wide. Some leaders and followers are very bad; others are less bad. Moreover, in some cases the consequences of bad leadership are major, in others minor.

- Opinions change. When Harry Truman left office in 1953, his approval rating was a dismal 32 percent. But in 2000, historians rated him among the greatest of American presidents, just behind Lincoln, Franklin Roosevelt, Washington, and Theodore Roosevelt.[19]

- Views differ. About Thomas Krens, controversial director of New York's Guggenheim Museum, two contrasting questions were asked. Was Krens "an egomaniac who squandered the museum's resources on a quest to expand his empire"? Or was he instead a "brilliant, misunderstood radical who inherited an institution with a relatively small endowment and stagnant program and wanted to try something more daring than mounting the umpteenth Picasso show"?[20]

- As it is used here, the word *type* does not mean personality type, nor do I intend to suggest that to be rigid, for example, is a personal trait in evidence at every turn. Rather, *rigid* refers to a set of behaviors in which leaders and followers mutually engage and that results in bad leadership.

Nevertheless, dividing the universe of bad leadership into seven types gives us, as Weber says, certain advantages. First, the ability to distinguish among the ways of being bad orders an untidy world, where the idea of bad leadership is as confusing as it is ubiquitous. Second, the seven types serve a practical purpose. They make it easier to detect inflection points—points at which an intervention might have stopped bad leadership or at least cut it short. Finally, the types make meaning of being bad. They enable us to know better and more clearly what bad leadership consists of.

Before I describe the seven types, two additional notes. First, the first three types of bad leadership tend to be bad as in ineffective, and the last four types tend to be bad as in unethical. I set up a continuum in which the first type of bad leadership, incompetence, is far less onerous than the last type of bad leadership, evil. But of course the lines blur: Sometimes leaders and followers are ineffective and unethical. For this reason I simply describe the seven types of bad leadership in sequence. Second, although one of my themes is that bad followers are as integral to bad leadership as are bad leaders, in the following section the brief examples allude only to the leader.

Incompetent

Bernadine Healy served effectively as dean of the Ohio State University Medical School and as the first woman director of the National Institutes of Health. But during her brief tenure (1999–2001) as head of the American Red Cross, Healy lost her touch. She was a driven professional, determined rapidly to change the deeply ingrained Red Cross culture, with which she was unfamiliar. In short order, members of the staff, as well as the fifty-member Red Cross board, decided that Healy was too assertive, too critical, and too pitiless. Once she compounded her errors by presiding over a debacle involving donations accumulated in the wake of the attack on the World Trade Center, she was dismissed. In short, whatever Healy's previous successes, and for whatever reasons, as leader of the Red Cross she was incompetent.[21]

> **Incompetent Leadership**—*the leader and at least some followers lack the will or skill (or both) to sustain effective action. With regard to at least one important leadership challenge, they do not create positive change.*

Incompetent leaders are not necessarily incompetent in every aspect. Moreover, there are many ways of being incompetent. Some leaders lack practical, academic, or emotional intelligence.[22] Others are careless, dense, distracted, slothful, or sloppy, or they are easily undone by uncertainty and stress, unable effectively to communicate, educate, or delegate, and so on. Note also that the impact of incompetent leadership is highly variable. Sometimes, as in the case of pilot error, it leads to disaster. At other times it amounts to mere bungling.[23]

The case of incompetent leadership on which this book centers is that of Juan Antonio Samaranch, president of the International Olympic Committee from 1981 to 2000. His accomplishments were considerable, but toward the end of his tenure something went badly wrong. During his final years in office, Samaranch and his close followers ignored and thus implicitly sanctioned wide-spread corruption in the Olympic movement, thereby disgracing the very games they were supposed to honor as well as sustain.

Rigid

As soon as he took office, Thabo Mbeki, who succeeded Nelson Mandela as president of South Africa in 1999, took issue with the West and its approach to AIDS. Mbeki maintained that HIV did not cause AIDS, that leading AIDS drugs were useless and even toxic, and that poverty and violence were at the root of his country's rapidly growing problem with the lethal disease.

As a result of his hostility to the West and his notoriously unyielding quest for an African remedy, Mbeki continued to withhold from HIV-positive pregnant women the antiretroviral drugs that would have cut in half the transmission of the disease to their babies.[24]

> **Rigid Leadership**—*the leader and at least some followers are stiff and unyielding. Although they may be competent, they are unable or unwilling to adapt to new ideas, new information, or changing times.*

Mbeki can be described by Barbara Tuchman's phrase "wooden-headed"—a leader who consistently refuses to be "deflected by the facts."[25] Rigid leaders can be successful up to a point. But if they refuse to change with the changing wind, the result will be bad leadership.

The case of rigid leadership examined in chapter 5 is that of financial analyst Mary Meeker. During the 1990s, while the prices of technology stocks skyrocketed, Meeker rode high. But when the market changed, she did not. Unable or unwilling to acknowledge that the party was over, Meeker and her like-minded collaborators told her legions of listeners to hold on to their stocks even as the market tanked.

Intemperate

Russian President Boris Yeltsin, an alcoholic, was often intoxicated in private and in public, much to the embarrassment of his government and the Russian people. In 1999, to take only one example, Yeltsin was too drunk to get off a plane to greet the visiting prime minister of Ireland, who was left cooling his heels on the tarmac.[26] Alcoholism is a disease. But Yeltsin's failure to treat his problem affected his capacity to serve as Russia's head of state.

> ***Intemperate Leadership***—*the leader lacks self-control and is aided and abetted by followers who are unwilling or unable effectively to intervene.*

In their book *Leadership on the Line*, Ronald Heifetz and Marty Linsky cautioned leaders to control their impulses: "We all have hungers that are expressions of our normal human needs. But sometimes those hungers disrupt our capacity to act wisely or purposefully."[27] Because we live in a time when all top leaders are grist for the media mill, the risk of such disruption is far greater than it was in the past.

The case of intemperate leadership on which this book focuses is that of Marion Barry Jr. Although Barry was elected mayor of Washington, D.C., no fewer than four times, almost throughout his time in office he lived a life of excess. In the end, his own inability to control his various hungers, particularly for crack cocaine, and his followers' inability to get him the proper help, dearly cost him as well as the city he had been elected to govern.

Callous

Most Americans who have any interest in such matters know the story of Martha Stewart. She has become rich and famous by figuring out that homemaking—cooking, gardening, sewing, entertaining, cleaning, indeed every conceivable domestic chore—could reflect artistry as well as drudgery.

But even before her indictment on charges stemming from insider trading, Stewart had acquired a bad reputation. Although she is a brilliantly accomplished and hard-working business-woman, nearly from the start of her career she has been rumored to be unpleasant and unkind, particularly to employees. How many of these personal attacks are the consequence of Stewart's being a woman in a man's world is difficult to say. Most observers would agree that the rules for women at the top of the corporate hierarchy are different from the rules for men. Most would likely also agree that if Stewart is not exactly a monster or a sociopath, she can be mean. Described variously as a harridan, an uncaring mother, and nasty to those in her employ, Stewart has made bad manners part of her legend: "Neighbors and acquaintances said she was aloof, inconsiderate, and selfish. Employees said she was 'hot-tempered and unreasonable and left them little time to cultivate a garden of their own.' It was as if she created a vision that none around her could live in."[28]

Callous Leadership—*the leader and at least some followers are uncaring or unkind. Ignored or discounted are the needs, wants, and wishes of most members of the group or organization, especially subordinates.*

Al Dunlap, the former CEO of Sunbeam Corporation, is the case of callous leadership described in chapter 7. Brought in in 1996 to turn around the fortunes of the appliance maker, Dunlap, through his abrasiveness, instead depleted morale and impaired the company's ability to function. As Sunbeam continued its downward spiral, Dunlap, with the support of his closest followers, cut himself off from the company and willfully ignored its ignominious descent. By the end of his tenure in 1998, Sunbeam had filed for bankruptcy.

Corrupt

In 1983, Michigan mall developer A. Alfred Taubman bought Sotheby's, the legendary auction house known, along with Christie's, for having cornered the market on the sale of fine art, jewelry, and furniture. Because the auction business had become increasingly competitive, by the mid-1990s Taubman and his Christie's counterpart, Sir Anthony Tennant, were illegally conspiring to raise commission rates.

A few years later the scheme was discovered, and in 2001 Taubman was found guilty of price-fixing, sentenced to a year and a day in prison, and ordered to pay a $7.5 million fine. In addition, Sotheby's and Christie's were ordered to settle class action suits with more than one hundred thousand customers for $512 million.[29]

Taubman did not act alone. For her part in the price-fixing scheme, Sotheby CEO Diana (Dede) Brooks was sentenced to six months of home detention, three years of probation, and one thousand hours of community service. Brooks, a Yale-educated former Citibank executive whose tenure at Sotheby's had been viewed as highly successful, was spared a more severe sentence only because she cooperated with government investigators to provide evidence against Taubman.

> *Corrupt Leadership—the leader and at least some*
> *followers lie, cheat, or steal. To a degree that exceeds the*
> *norm, they put self-interest ahead of the public interest.*

Corrupt leaders are usually motivated by power or greed—by the desire, in any case, to acquire more of a scarce resource. For example, to make more money, corrupt leaders take bribes, sell favors, evade taxes, exaggerate corporate earnings, engage in insider trading, cook the books, defraud governments and businesses, and in other ways cut corners, bend rules, and break the law.

Chapter 8 tells the story of William Aramony, once the highly respected head of United Way of America. Aramony's tale is not unfamiliar: It is about the head of a large organization caught lying, cheating, and stealing. But it is at odds with how we think about charitable organizations and those who lead and manage them.

Insular

When the streets of Monrovia began to run with blood, Liberians begged President George W. Bush to intervene, to stop the conflict by sending troops. At first he dithered, siding for a time with those who said, in effect, "Our hands are too full to rescue a distant people determined to murder one another."[30]

Those who chose to differ, Secretary of State Colin Powell among them, argued for intervention on the grounds of national interest and because they considered it the right thing to do. "Liberia is not just another African country," one interventionist argued. "It is an American creation, founded by former slaves 150 years ago, reflecting our image and legacy."[31]

In terms of American foreign policy this might be considered yet another debate between isolationists and interventionists. But as far as the quality of leadership is concerned, the debate over whether or not to intervene in Liberia reflected the tension between those who believe that leaders are responsible only to their own constituencies and those who consider that they have a broader mandate—one that includes trying to stop large numbers of men, women, and children from being hacked to death, even in a distant land.

> *Insular Leadership—the leader and at least some*
> *followers minimize or disregard the health and*
> *welfare of "the other"—that is, those outside*
> *the group or organization for which*
> *they are directly responsible.*

Bill Clinton is the exemplar of insular leadership, as profiled in chapter 9. Although the president knew of the genocide in Rwanda, he paid it little attention. Having been burned by his experience in Somalia in particular, Clinton, along with the rest of his foreign policy team, made the decision to steer clear of a calamity that was taking place far from home.

Evil

In 1991, Foday Sankoh, an itinerant photographer and army corporal with a primary school education, gathered a group of guerillas and started a civil war in Sierra Leone. Sankoh was known for his extraordinary charisma. But his followers, many of them poor boys from the countryside, were notorious above all for their brutality. They killed, raped, and spread terror across the small West African nation by chopping off the hands, arms, and legs of innocent civilians—men, women, and children alike. Sankoh was unperturbed. In fact, when some of his close associates spoke out against the flagrant abuses and violations of human rights, they were summarily executed.[32] In 2000, Sankoh was captured by British troops operating under the auspices of the United Nations; later he was turned over to the Special Court for Sierra Leone. The seventeen-count indictment charged him with crimes against humanity, including murder, rape, and extermination. Foday Sankoh died in custody in July 2003.

> **Evil Leadership**—*the leader and at least some*
> *followers commit atrocities. They use pain as*
> *an instrument of power. The harm done to men,*
> *women, and children is severe rather than*
> *slight. The harm can be physical,*
> *psychological, or both.*

Evil leaders are not necessarily sadistic. But some experts argue that our notion of evil should include the intent not only to terrorize but also to prolong suffering. They believe that all evildoers derive some sort of satisfaction from hurting others.[33]

The case of evil leadership described in chapter 10 is that of Radovan Karadzic. As Bosnian Serb president during the early and mid-1990s, Karadzic, along with his followers, was responsible for the rape, murder, and pillaging of thousands of Bosnian Muslims and Croats, and for the infamous massacre in Srebrenica.

The Heart of Darkness

Making meaning of being bad is difficult. Consider this confusion: The *American Heritage Dictionary of the English Language* properly refers to Hitler as an "absolute dictator." But, perhaps because he was a wartime ally, the same dictionary describes Stalin only as a "Soviet politician who was general secretary of the Communist Party and premier of the U.S.S.R." This, even though we now know that Stalin was directly responsible for the deaths of some twenty million people.[34]

Moreover, like all typologies, the one in this book raises questions just as it provides answers. It's fair to ask, for example, whether leaders should be considered incompetent if the demands on their time preclude attention to all matters of importance. Similarly, one might reasonably wonder whether leaders are intemperate if they are not monogamous but still not promiscuous. The questions pertain to followers as well. Are you corrupt if you cheat, ever so slightly, on your taxes, knowing that many others are doing the same thing? Am I evil if my leader compels me to commit evil acts?

To avoid as far as possible the inevitable pitfalls of the inevitable complexities, I use only cases in which the evidence of bad leadership is overwhelming. In other words, because I recognize that even generally competent leaders are sometimes incompetent and that even generally kind leaders are sometimes callous, the examples of bad leadership used in this book are at the extreme—virtually indisputable.

The paradoxes of leadership—leaders who are, for example, corrupt and effective at the same time—further complicate the difficulty of making meaning of being bad. As I describe in more detail later, in 2000 Vincent A. (Buddy) Cianci Jr., the mayor of Providence, Rhode Island, was sentenced to five years and four months in jail after being convicted of soliciting bribes for city contracts. But before being thrown into prison, Cianci had "transformed Providence from a grimy industrial backwater into the liveliest, most appealing city in New England."[35]

New York mayor Rudolph Giuliani presents a different kind of paradox. In the wake of 9/11, Giuliani was hailed as a hero, a leader worthy of comparison to Churchill. But before his appointment with history, Giuliani's approval ratings had been low. The mayor's rigid refusal to reach out to members of New York City's minority communities, particularly to people of color, meant that in at least one important way, he was inadequate, a bad leader.

Finally, problems of objectivity and subjectivity inevitably muddy the water. In all but the most egregious cases, opinions will differ about who deserves to be called a bad leader and why. As far as possible I head off this argument by choosing to focus on cases of bad leadership on which there is broad consensus.

The heavy lifting notwithstanding, we know three important things:

1. Sometimes leaders, and followers, make a difference.

2. Sometimes this difference is significant.

3. Sometimes the outcome is bad.[36]

We turn now to the seven types of bad leadership: incompetent, rigid, intemperate, callous, corrupt, insular, and evil. The chapters that follow are about the dark side—about how we get caught in webs we ourselves spin. It is my hope and intention that by discussing and distinguishing among the primary forms of bad leadership, we might ourselves avoid becoming entangled, both as bad leaders and as bad followers.

PART TWO

LEADING
BADLY

*Man is an animal suspended in webs
of significance he himself has spun.*

—Clifford Geertz

CHAPTER FOUR

INCOMPETENT

JUAN ANTONIO SAMARANCH

> **Incompetent Leadership**—*The leader and at least some followers lack the will or skill (or both) to sustain effective action. With regard to at least one important leadership challenge, they do not create positive change.*

INCOMPETENT LEADERS are ubiquitous. Sometimes they are so obviously and extremely incompetent that we wonder how they were able to assume leadership roles in the first place. And sometimes they're just incompetent enough to interfere with their own best-laid plans to sustain stability or create change.

Leaders are incompetent for various reasons. Some lack experience, education, or expertise. Others lack drive, energy, or the ability to focus. Still others are not clever enough, flexible enough, stable enough, emotionally intelligent enough—or whatever enough.

In addition, leaders are incompetent in various ways, ranging from miscalculation to mismanagement, from silliness to stupidity, from carelessness to callousness. Incompetent leaders may be bad at meeting challenges such as mastering information, coping with complexity, minding the store, making decisions under conditions of uncertainty, managing change, managing conflict, managing crises, or managing themselves. Some leaders are unwilling or unable to employ necessary and appropriate leadership strategies such as envisioning, prioritizing, communicating, educating, inspiring, persuading, mobilizing, organizing, coalition building, listening, adapting, getting information, managing, delegating, coordinating, negotiating, implementing—well, you name it.

In other words, to the question of exactly in what ways leaders are incompetent, there is only one reply: Let me count the ways. And how exactly are followers incompetent? By ignoring or discounting warning signs, and by letting bad leadership linger.

Brief Examples

Abdurrahman Wahid

Every now and then there is a leader who is incompetent nearly across the board. An example is Abdurrahman Wahid. In October 1999, Wahid, a half-blind Muslim cleric, became president of Indonesia, the world's fourth most populous country. Wahid succeeded Achmed Sukarno and Mohamed Suharto, despots who, in the wake of Dutch rule, promised democracy and reform but instead delivered repression and corruption. Only after Suharto was ousted did the Indonesian people finally have free and open elections.

Because Wahid was Indonesia's first democratically elected head of state, hopes for him were high. Political instability and economic crises notwithstanding, he was expected to undertake major reforms that were badly needed and long overdue.

On the surface, the optimism was justified. Wahid had defeated his rivals by brilliant political maneuvering. He headed the forty-million-strong Muslim Nahdlatul Ulama, one of the largest religious organizations in the world. Wahid was a veteran political player whose progressive vision of Islam seemed in keeping with Indonesia's future as a global player of major consequence.[1] And in a country rife with ethnic conflict, he preached tolerance and promised to let democracy flourish.

Moreover, in contrast to Sukarno and Suharto, Wahid enjoyed a refreshingly modest lifestyle. He lived in a plain house in Jakarta, on a small street crowded with children and vendors. And after he became president, his manner and style remained simple. He appeared at all except the most formal functions in sandals, a batik shirt, and the traditional black hat known as a *peci*.[2]

But it was apparent almost immediately that the early faith in Wahid was misplaced. His perilous health, which included declining eyesight, diabetes, kidney failure, and a series of strokes, combined with bizarre behavior even as he moved into the presidential palace, soon brought confusion and disillusionment.

When he first became president, Wahid's unusual history and personality seemed to be assets. But soon the contrast between his inclination toward the traditional world of Javanese mysticism, on the one hand, and his vision of a modern, progressive Indonesia, on the other, made him increasingly difficult to read. His management style was capricious. His policy preferences were inconsistent. And he proved capable of appearing literally to laugh off Indonesia's most pressing problems.

In particular, Wahid was erratic and bewildering with regard to his political and economic agenda: He ran his cabinet like a bus terminal (twenty-two ministers came and went in a two-year period), clashed with members of parliament, and made rash statements to the press. He traveled frequently and refused to return home when ethnic conflicts erupted into violence. He ignored financial scandals that ultimately stained his own reputation for incorruptibility, he alienated members of the military, political, and business elites, and finally he failed to secure the crucial support of the international financial community. Potential investors in Indonesia's economy, including the International Monetary Fund, were legitimately concerned that Wahid knew little (and cared less) about economic management, that his economic ministers were at loggerheads with each other and with him, and that his political aims interfered with economic policymaking.[3]

Finally, Wahid shunned and ignored even his own advisers, appeared haughty and autocratic to those he should have cultivated as allies, and retreated into the world of supernatural omens and spirits.[4]

The end was swift. In July 2001 Wahid declared a state of emergency and suspended parliament. But few followed where he led, or rather tried to lead. Senior generals mutinied and resigned en masse, and parliament voted 591 to 0 to impeach Wahid and replace him with his vice president. Initially Wahid resisted his ouster. But finally he succumbed to the inevitable. Wahid moved out of the presidential palace twenty-two months after moving in.

Some of his most fervent followers took to the streets to protest, but the violence was short-lived. In the end, there was overwhelming agreement that whatever his strengths in other circumstances, as leader of the Indonesian nation Wahid was incompetent in nearly every respect.

The question is how so incompetent a leader came to be president in the first place. The answer: It was because Wahid's followers were as incompetent as he, even if through no fault of their own. In other words, there was incompetence on all sides. Ordinary Indonesians had no experience with civil society. They had no democratic traditions, no familiarity with free elections, and no way of knowing how to assess the various candidates. Even members of Indonesia's political elite made the mistake of assuming that once Wahid was in office, his eccentricities would somehow be assets or at least would not be liabilities. It is no surprise, then, that their first time out, Indonesia's voters chose a leader who, whatever his virtues, was woefully incompetent as head of state.

Jill Barad

Another case of incompetence so egregious it rapidly resulted in the corporate equivalent of a palace coup is that of Jill Barad, briefly CEO of Mattel, Inc., the largest and most successful toy firm in America.

Despite the strength of its brand, during the 1980s, following a diversification spree and the collapse of its video game business, Mattel came close to bankruptcy. The company avoided demise only by shedding its nontoy assets and focusing on four core businesses, including the legendary Barbie doll.

Jill Barad joined the company's little-known novelties division in 1981. Within a couple of years she was named one of two product managers on the Barbie team and was charged with reviving what had once been Mattel's mainstay; by the late 1980s she was credited with nearly single-handedly transforming Barbie from dated doll to prized collectible.[5] Clearly, Barad had played a key role in Mattel's transformation from a company in trouble to one whose operating profits were growing 26 percent a year. (Barbie accounted for fully 35 percent of the company's revenue.)

In 1989 Barad decided to capitalize on her success. She threatened to leave Mattel for a top job elsewhere (Reebok International) unless she was promoted. Her gamble paid off. CEO John Ammerman gave Barad what she wanted: the copresidency of Mattel's U.S. operations.

Three years later, Barad went to Ammerman again, this time demanding his assurance that she would succeed him. "There was some trepidation on both sides," Ammerman said later. "My retirement was still a long way away." Even so, on the spot he made her president and chief operating officer, doubled her compensation (to $2 million annually), and gave her a contract that included a guaranteed payout of five years' compensation in the event she was passed over for CEO.[6]

In 1995, Ammerman expanded Barad's responsibilities still further. And in January 1997 Jill Barad was appointed CEO of Mattel, Inc.

Her situation was as singular as Barad herself. Then as now, nearly none of America's largest companies had a woman CEO. And then as now, most women in senior management downplayed or even hid their femininity. Barad, though, stood out. In high heels and Chanel suits, she was glamorous and radiant—in the words of *Business Week*, "more Hollywood than corporate."[7]

Variously called fierce, flamboyant, and emotional, the new CEO soon announced plans to shed unprofitable assets, chucked her predecessor's preoccupation with quarterly earnings, and decided that Mattel should merge with The Learning Company, which controlled the market for educational software. Barad viewed the $3.6 billion deal as a huge opportunity for Mattel, a way for the world's largest toy maker to establish an online presence and thereby secure its future in an economy that was certain to be increasingly Web-based.

But Barad's time of flying high was short-lived. Only three years after becoming CEO, she was forced to resign.

The most obvious reason for her rapid collapse as CEO was the disastrous merger with The Learning Company. In the fourth quarter of 1999, the operation lost a staggering $183 million. And for the year overall, Mattel—which in 1998 had earned a profit of $206 million—had a loss of $82.3 million. As Barad put it when she announced her departure, "The board of directors and I view the performance of The Learning Co., and its effects on our results, as unacceptable. Therefore, the board and I have agreed that I resign effective today."[8]

Barad's short tenure inevitably raises questions about whether women CEOs are more vulnerable to criticism than their male counterparts. Probably. But it is also true that as CEO of Mattel, Barad was cast in a role that demanded leadership skills and capacities very different from those of the marketing expert she had been, and a role for which she was, it turned out, ill suited.

Mattel's acquisition of The Learning Company, over which she presided and in which she persisted, was considered one of the worst in recent corporate history. To digest the merger, the company had to cut three thousand jobs, or 10 percent of its work force. Moreover, Mattel's preoccupation with The Learning Company resulted in the decline of core businesses. Sales of Barbie declined 14 percent during the second year Barad served as CEO.

But Barad's incompetence amounted to much more than making a terrible business decision. As soon as she ran into trouble it became clear that, although she had been with Mattel for many years, she had failed to build a constituency of good friends and dependable allies. She had no political base. Again, gender may have been part of the problem. As one woman executive put it at the time, "These people calling [Barad] abrasive, have they met Ted Turner? Have they met Michael Eisner? Compared to most CEOs, she is not abrasive. But maybe compared to their wives she is."[9]

Even allowing for this bias, Barad's interpersonal skills, especially her capacity for collaboration, had long been called into question. Widely viewed as controlling and temperamental, especially with male subordinates, throughout her tenure at Mattel Barad had had run-ins with colleagues, who would then proceed to quit.[10] In other words, the fiasco with The Learning Company notwithstanding, emotional intelligence was not Barad's strong suit.

Of course, this story about leadership is like every other such story: Barad was not alone in her incompetence. At the least, John Ammerman, along with Mattel's board, acceded far too readily to Barad's repeated demands for promotion—even as Ammerman, in any case, had second thoughts (as he later admitted). Note the curious twist. In the late 1980s and during the 1990s, on the matter of Barad's successive promotions at Mattel, it was the board who followed and Barad who led. As famously testified by the case of Enron, among others, the passivity of Mattel's board was at the time by no means unusual.

Juan Antonio Samaranch: Blind Eye, Deaf Ear

The Prologue

The incompetence of Wahid and Barad became apparent early on, and as a result they held their jobs at the top only briefly. In contrast, Juan Antonio Samaranch served as president of the International Olympic Committee (IOC) for nearly two decades before his bad leadership became an open secret.

His case is more typical. In general, leaders who exhibit incompetence are not, like Wahid and Barad, so grossly and obviously bad so early in their tenure that they are quickly sacked. Rather, most leaders are closer to the example of Samaranch: competent in some ways and incompetent in others; competent at some times and incompetent at others.

As president of the IOC, Samaranch achieved considerable results. He led the Olympic movement from the precipice of fiscal disaster to new heights of popularity and prosperity, and he, more than anyone else, was responsible for transforming the IOC into a "transnational nongovernmental commercial giant" in world sport.[11] But during the years of his long tenure, Samaranch gradually became complacent and careless. Ultimately his sloppy management led to widespread indiscretion and corruption, even among members of the IOC. In the end, his failure to uncover and correct the growing wrongdoing resulted in an ugly scandal that discredited him personally and dishonored the games he was supposed to ennoble as well as secure.

The Context

In 1896 a French physical fitness buff, Baron Pierre de Coubertin, persuaded the city of Athens to host the first modern Olympiad. The rules of the games reflected de Coubertin's idealism, and they were strict. Only amateurs could compete, and no prizes of value would be awarded. "The goal of Olympism," de Coubertin declared, "is to place sport at the service of the harmonious development of man, with a view to encouraging the establishment of a peaceful society."[12]

For most of the twentieth century, the Olympics were held on a fairly regular basis, but predictably they fell somewhat short of this imagined ideal. In particular, for many years the games as an instrument of peace and goodwill fell victim to the vicissitudes of international politics.

For example, in 1916, the games were canceled because of the First World War, and again in 1940 and 1944 because of the Second World War. Still, the idealism that had characterized both the original and the more modern Olympic games was never entirely lost. For example, throughout even the most difficult period of the

Cold War, American and Soviet athletes were expected to be, and mostly were, friendly and sportsmanlike.[13]

After the Cold War was over, the importance of politics immediately decreased and the importance of money, big money, quickly increased. During the late 1980s and 1990s in particular, there was an enormous rise in the power of the modern Olympic movement to raise vast amounts of revenue from the sale of television rights worldwide, and from marketing the Olympic five-ring symbol to multinational corporate giants, who used it to hawk their wares.[14]

Although the goals of the modern Olympiad are ostensibly achieved through various national and international committees, in fact it has one supreme authority: the International Olympic Committee. The IOC describes itself as an international, non-governmental, nonprofit organization that serves as the "umbrella" of the Olympic movement. Moreover, the IOC owns all rights to the Olympic symbols, such as the flag, motto, and anthem, as well as to the games themselves.

Since the end of the Second World War, the IOC has had only four presidents.[15] Avery Brundage served from 1952 to 1972, retiring from his post at the age of eighty-four, with a stern warning about creeping commercialization.[16] He was succeeded by the Irish-born Lord Killanin, who made some important changes but turned out to be a transition figure. Killanin, in turn, was succeeded by a little-known Spaniard, Juan Antonio Samaranch.

When Samaranch became president of the IOC, the mood of the Olympic movement was grim. In 1972 eleven Israeli athletes had been murdered in Munich. And the fiscal disasters and political boycotts that had additionally plagued the games in Montreal (1976) and Moscow (1980) finally left the IOC demoralized and depleted. International sports had been a victim of the Cold War, and the IOC had less than a half million dollars in the bank. Many questioned the future of the Olympic games, and even those who did not expressed growing doubts "over just what the Olympics was all about."[17]

It was Samaranch who ushered in the Olympic movement as we now know it. As Robert Barney, Stephen Wenn, and Scott Martyn point out in *Selling the Five Rings*, their definitive study of Olympic commercialism, during the 1980s and 1990s the entire operation was transformed. The authors write, "The IOC became not only wealthier beyond its most optimistic expectations but extraordinarily more powerful in the context of global sport."[18] In fact, the IOC increasingly came to resemble a multinational corporation, with headquarters in Lausanne, Switzerland, and a "quasi-chief executive officer" in Samaranch.

When Samaranch took over from Killanin, the fee paid by NBC Television for the U.S. rights to broadcast the Moscow games was $87 million. Sixteen years later, the IOC signed three new contracts that promised by 2008 to fill the Olympic coffers with more than $5 billion.[19] It had become clear that Samaranch was never satisfied with anything less than the most he could get. Worried about the Olympic movement's nearly sole reliance on revenues generated by selling television rights, he pushed his IOC colleagues to get into the business of Olympic marketing. Soon he was aggressively seeking to protect the Olympic mystique, in the main to be able to exploit the Olympic symbols, which had become a valuable commodity.

The 1984 Olympics were a turning point. Los Angeles forbade the use of public funds to support the games, and for that reason Peter Ueberroth, the president of the local organizing committee, had to rely on the private sector for funding. Ueberroth, Samaranch, and other members of the IOC ultimately secured the participation of 140 countries and 163 companies, most of them large, multinational corporations. Moreover, they negotiated television contracts to enormous advantage and transformed the nature of corporate sponsorship. From being a financial liability that no city other than Los Angeles had been willing to accept, the games had become a highly lucrative business.

The next fifteen years were ones of unstoppable growth. The broadcast and marketing programs in Lillehammer (1994) generated more than $500 million, and the games in Atlanta (1996) reached a record-breaking audience of more than 3.2 billion people in 214 counties. But with all the changes, the original Olympic ideals remained on the books. The Olympic movement, over which the IOC had "supreme authority," was supposed to be committed to sports ethics and fair play and opposed to "all forms of commercial exploitation of sports and athletes."[20]

The Leader

Juan Antonio Samaranch was born in Barcelona in 1920, the son of a wealthy self-made textile baron. By the late 1940s Samaranch had matured into a passionate sportsman and dapper ladies' man whose position was enhanced by marriage to a society beauty with family money older than his own.

From an early age Samaranch was ambitious. He joined the youth fascists under Generalissimo Francisco Franco, later rising steadily through the ranks of Franco's autocratic regime. Samaranch eventually became the rough equivalent of a junior under-secretary of sport, a position that by 1966 gave him the standing suitable for membership in the IOC.[21]

Occasionally Samaranch's years of loyalty to Franco came back to haunt him. One of Samaranch's detractors claimed that under his jurisdiction, Spain had failed to create a nation of sportsmen, construct much-needed sports facilities, and earn the respect of its global competitors.[22] Samaranch defended himself, insisting that he was "not ashamed" of anything and that Franco, moreover, had done "good things" for the Spanish people: "He kept us out of World War II. He created a middle class. He chose a good successor, the king."[23]

In any case Samaranch's place in the world of Spanish sport enabled him to cultivate the patronage of Avery Brundage. He sent Brundage letters praising his intelligence and love for the Olympic ideal and promised to devote himself to Brundage's work. Samaranch even invited Brundage's wife to his beautiful home on the Spanish coast. Eventually Brundage arranged for Samaranch to join the IOC.

After Franco's death in 1975, Samaranch made the transition from autocracy to democracy without apparent effort. According to Ernest Lluch, a former Spanish health minister who knew Samaranch for years, he is a "great chameleon" who "adapts to everything."[24] To underscore the point, only two years after Franco died, Samaranch was appointed by the new Spanish government to be its first ambassador to Moscow.

Samaranch has said that he started thinking about the presidency of the IOC shortly after becoming a member in 1966. "Moscow was preparing the Olympics of 1980, and I knew that going there would be a good move."[25] Samaranch had planned his move carefully. He had turned down the ambassador's post in Vienna in favor of Moscow, primarily to play a major role in the Olympic games.

During this period he acquired, in addition to Brundage, a second patron, Horst Dassler. Dassler, the clever and hard-driving CEO of Adidas, recognized far earlier than most people the big money to be made by associating particular products with particular athletes. As far back as the Melbourne Olympics in 1956, Dassler was paying athletes to wear his shoes: "Winners Wear Adidas" was the company's slogan.[26]

Dassler had been doing business with the Eastern bloc since 1960, so when Samaranch ran for president of the IOC, Dassler proved an invaluable ally. With Dassler's backing, Samaranch could count on the Soviet Union and all its East European allies. This support, together with that of the Hispanic countries, his natural constituency, enabled Samaranch to win the IOC's top job on the first round with an absolute majority of forty-seven votes. In retrospect, the association with Dassler can be seen as an inflection point. It was the first time Samaranch tied himself closely to someone whose primary interest was in the money to be made from global sport.

When Samaranch took office, being president of the IOC was not a coveted position. "Everybody was writing the Olympic obituary," said one former IOC member. "We were politically and financially bankrupt."[27] The difficult circumstances provided Samaranch with a golden opportunity to use his new leadership role to make something out of nearly nothing.

The early years of Samaranch's tenure were by most measures successful. After the Soviet boycott of Los Angeles, he coaxed 160 nations (of the 167 then in the Olympic movement) to attend the 1988 games in South Korea. Moreover, in response to his personal diplomacy and the occasional handsome gift, the IOC gained many new members. By 2000, more than 80 percent of the members had joined under Samaranch.

He also made key administrative changes, virtually all of them designed to enhance the political strength and fiscal health of the IOC. They included the establishment of a full-time residential presidency in Lausanne, the implementation of a stronger executive board, the decision to grant individual international sports federations the right to determine which athletes were eligible for the Olympics (a move that opened the door to professional athletes), and the establishment of a new commission charged with capitalizing on the "most valuable unexploited symbol in the world"ı the Olympic rings [28]

During the early years of his presidency, Samaranch's strong performance both as an administrator and as an entrepreneur brought him many admirers outside the Olympic movement and permitted him to exercise complete control within it. He was hardworking, tenacious, and interpersonally skilled. Moreover, in important ways he understood what had to be done. If the Olympics were to thrive over the long term, they would have to be more inclusive, bring in more professional athletes, and attain a firmer financial footing. As Olympic historian John Lucas put it, "In the first years of his reign, [Samaranch] made more positive, uplifting changes than all the other IOC presidents put together." [29]

But as the years went on, as Samaranch presided over the nearly complete transformation of the IOC from sports movement into commercial giant, the original Olympic ideal faded. With associates such as Dassler, Samaranch protected the fiscal and political interests of the IOC at the expense of its high ideals. [30] The negative impact of the infusion of corporate capital on the Olympic movement and its parent figure, the IOC, became increasingly evident. [31] For all his early accomplishments, Samaranch was unwilling to check the growing costs of his relentless drive for more money and greater expansion. And so by the time he resigned as president, the reputation of the IOC had become badly tarnished, many of his IOC colleagues had been discredited, and the games themselves had become no more, if no less, than global sports extravaganzas.

Over time Samaranch had grown careless. His increasingly exclusive focus on financial expansion caused him to turn a blind eye and a deaf ear to problems ranging from enveloping commercialism to a proliferation of incidents involving performance-enhancing drugs to growing corruption. His ignorance of these problems gradually evolved from inattention to rank mismanagement and incompetence. His refusal to address the IOC's increasingly long list of troubles bespeaks a man whose insatiable ambition ultimately intruded on his capacity for good decision making and sound judgment.

He was leader and steward of a movement of high ideals, but Samaranch grew sloppy and sleazy. Among his many other mistakes, he willingly, even eagerly, engaged with bad people. Olympic awards were bestowed on malevolent dictators such as East Germany's Erich Honecker and Romania's Nicolae Ceausescu, even though the first was widely rumored to be running a state-sponsored doping system and the second was an especially vicious despot. Disreputable people were invited to become members of the IOC, including Major General Francis Nyangweso of Uganda, who had served under Idi Amin; South Korea's Kim Un-Yong, who was a senior member of the Korean Central Intelligence Agency under the dictatorship of Park Chung-Hee; and Jean-Claude Ganga of the Congo Republic, who, although known as an antiapartheid activist, was also reputed to be spectacularly greedy (he was called the "human vacuum cleaner") and was later accused of accepting more than $250,000 in bribes to bring the games to Salt Lake City.[32]

To maintain the IOC's original ideals, the expansion over which Samaranch presided should have been mediated by a transparent organizational culture and controls at every level. Instead, there was an almost complete lack of administrative oversight. And so, even though the IOC was responsible for hundreds of millions of dollars in annual revenues, and for choosing the site of the games—worth fortunes to the selected cities—this public and powerfully symbolic organization was allowed to become a "nongovernmental, nonprofit, private association of unsalaried men and women who voted in secret, chose new members by co-option, and published no overall accounts."[33] The power granted the IOC by the Olympic Charter—"the Olympic Games are the exclusive property of the IOC which owns all rights relating thereto"—turned out to be a gold mine. But Samaranch failed to stand guard.

Over time, he also acquired bad habits. Given the increased stakes, local Olympic committee officials, eager to bring the games to their respective cities, began courting Samaranch personally—and he, in turn, was content to be courted. The Nagano Olympic Committee hired a private three-car train for Samaranch in 1991, at a cost of $7,000, with a view to winning the 1998 winter games, which it did. While in Nagano, Samaranch stayed at the imperial suite of the Kokusai 21 Hotel for nearly a month at a cost of more than $75,000. Although Samaranch always denied any personal wrongdoing, in retrospect it's clear that on such occasions he was, at the least, insensitive to appearances.

His lack of oversight eventually led to a string of financial abuses. When Toronto bid for the 1996 summer games in the late 1980s, twenty-six members broke the rules by bringing more than one guest or staying longer than the allotted time. Although local officials warned the IOC that "blatant abuses" had taken place, abuses that finally inflated the cost of Toronto's bid for the Olympics to $14 million, the IOC failed effectively to respond. As a spokesman for Samaranch put it, "We wanted to react. But you can't just pick 26 IOC members and shoot them."[34]

Samaranch's failure to exercise sufficient oversight was the reason things went from bad to worse. When Berlin bid for the 2000 summer games, twenty IOC members descended on the city for stays of five days or more, and they accepted gifts worth about

$85,000. By the time the story in Salt Lake City began to unfold, the situation had gotten out of hand. By then gifts and outright payments to members of the IOC, and the use of agents offering to sell blocs of votes, were considered business as usual.[35]

The biggest scandal in the history of the Olympic games broke in November 1998, when a Utah TV station obtained a letter in which a member of the Salt Lake City Olympic Committee informed the daughter of an African member of the IOC that an enclosed check for $10,114.99 would have to be its last payment for tuition. The obvious question was why Utah organizers were paying college costs for the daughter of an influential Olympic executive.

But by then this particular payment was only one of many. To secure the games for Salt Lake City, local organizers had played by what now were the rules of the game: They had engaged in bidding practices that were blatantly corrupt.[36]

As a result of the scandal six IOC members were expelled, four resigned, and ten were warned. For his part, the increasingly imperial Samaranch scoffed at suggestions that he had in any way tolerated, not to speak of fostered, the culture of sleaze that now characterized the IOC. He had long held the reins, and he personally had selected more than 80 percent of the IOC membership, but that did not stop him from claiming that he had had no knowledge of any wrongdoing. Moreover, evidence to the contrary notwithstanding, he insisted that he personally was a man of simple tastes. "I am a normal person. I may be of nobility, but I am not a rich man," Samaranch said. "I travel widely, but I stay in small suites. I have no yachts or planes, and I don't like fancy lunches or dinners."[37]

After Salt Lake City, the chameleon-like Samaranch changed yet again, this time into a strong advocate for change at the IOC. But it was too little and too late to salvage his reputation. For all he had accomplished, the gap was now too wide between what the Olympics were supposed to be and what they had become. As one commentator put it, "For all the talk about bringing people of the world together . . . the Olympics are really no different from the Super Bowl or any other ostentatious sporting display."[38]

Samaranch had extended an open invitation to big business. But his failure to exercise the proper oversight in this regard was, finally, key to the incompetence that left a permanent stain on his presidency. That the longtime head of the IOC had grown so careless and complacent as to ignore or dismiss the selling-out of the Olympic games was confirmation that, as the supreme leader of the "supreme authority," Samaranch was incompetent. On the surface it might seem that he was corrupt more than anything else, but that's incorrect. He liked living well, and he liked the money and status his position afforded, but Samaranch's story is not one of personal enrichment; rather, it is one of personal aggrandizement. Because he was left for twenty years to preside over the IOC unchecked and unchallenged, he failed to pay attention to what mattered other than money; failed to establish an organization that provided the necessary checks and balances; and failed to correct his own bad habits.

The Followers

Like most leaders, Juan Antonio Samaranch had various groups of followers. The most important was the International Olympic Committee, whose members, along with Samaranch, were accountable for whatever transpired in the Olympic movement.

For all intents and purposes, members of the IOC were in thrall to their leader throughout his two decades in office. To be sure, there were occasional dissidents who tried to swim upstream. Marc Hodler, a Swiss, tried for years to curtail the competition among cities vying for the Olympic games. In 1987, for example, he sent a letter, formally endorsed by Samaranch, to members of the IOC, the national Olympic committees, and the candidate cities stating that "gifts of value are not permitted" and reminding IOC members that they were not allowed to stay for more than three days in any city bidding for the games. But Samaranch never followed up; nor did he give the letter any teeth by stating that transgressions would be punished. And so, of course, it was ignored.[39]

In any case, Hodler was the exception to the rule. Because virtually all members of the IOC benefited in some way from their association with the Olympic movement, and because the history and culture of the IOC did not exactly encourage their resistance to authority—Brundage had also been something of an autocrat—members were generally loath to take on the president.

Moreover, the IOC did not constitute a coherent whole. It had grown rather rapidly to more than one hundred members and was peopled by many different types from many different cultures and countries. Consequently, IOC members had as little opportunity as they did incentive to organize a protest against the central office in Lausanne. Even at the end, when Samaranch had become a public embarrassment, there was no movement from within to take him on. As the *Washington Post* put it, "There appears to be no groundswell of antipathy within the IOC urging Samaranch to fall on his sword—largely because of the strong loyalties he commands from members he appointed. Even his most ambitious rivals for power . . . have reaffirmed their faith in seeing him carry the Olympic banner into the new millennium."[40] To prove the point, in March 1999, only a few months after the scandal in Salt Lake City hit the front pages, IOC members gave Samaranch an overwhelming vote of confidence.

Samaranch's failure to exercise oversight was obviously mirrored by IOC members. As a collective, they too failed to pay attention to what mattered other than money; they too failed even to try to establish an organization that would provide the necessary checks and balances; and they too failed to correct their own bad habits. As Samaranch's successor, Jacques Rogge, put it, "We are collectively responsible for not having been tough enough to address the problem. I'm saying we are responsible, not him [Samaranch] personally."[41]

But IOC members are by no means the only followers who deserve blame for permitting sleaze to permeate the Olympic movement. Members of the national Olympic committees and city officials, only too eager to pay for the privilege of bidding for the games, came to accept and some of them to participate in the growing corruption. In 2003, Salt Lake City's David Johnson and Thomas Welch were finally acquitted by a federal judge, who found fault with the government's case. Nevertheless, these two men, who presided over the effort to bring the games to Utah, were among those who, whatever their intent, appeared to be engaged in shady practices. Welch, known as the "pre eminent giver of gifts and cash," proclaimed his innocence on the grounds that this was how the IOC's game was played: "The whole atmosphere was, hey, you're paying homage to these people [Samaranch and the rest of the IOC]. We don't like that, but . . . that's the rush if you want to join the fraternity."[42]

Samaranch's close associates also failed him. Horst Dassler, known for his drive and business acumen, not only did not restrain Samaranch from his corporate excesses but actually encouraged them. Similarly, Richard Pound—Montreal tax lawyer, chancellor of McGill University, founder and head of the World Anti-Doping Authority, key member of the IOC, and for years one of Samaranch's closest colleagues—was a "loyal lieutenant" to Samaranch, apparently refusing even in private to criticize him.[43]

Finally, sports fans around the world were also among Samaranch's followers, albeit at a remove. The truth is that no one seemed to care very much that, as Olympics scholar James Hoberman put it, Samaranch "hijacked" an operation whose greatest resource was "the ability to project the possibility of the unification of humankind."[44] In any case, no one lifted a finger to stop him.

All we really seem to care about now is the show—games in the summer and winter available for our viewing pleasure in our living rooms. Despite the occasional gripes about the selling of the Olympics, it is we who have allowed the games to reach a point where the original Olympic ideal seems merely quaint.

A final note: Samaranch did not generally operate in secret. Information about who he was and what he was up to was available for years. Although the mainstream press did not in any clear and consistent way expose his shortcomings, or at least not until the sleaze became blatantly obvious in Salt Lake City, it did not ignore the story. For example, just before the games in Lillehammer

(1994), *VG*, Norway's largest-selling newspaper, reported, "Juan Antonio Samaranch arrives in Norway today. He will be met by an opinion poll that is a complete disaster for him and the IOC." The paper went on to report that the IOC was considered a "careerist organization" whose members felt most comfortable with "red carpets and champagne."[45] And in a special supplement on the Olympics that came out even earlier, *Time* reported that although the IOC was now a well-endowed empire, it was stained by scandal. Samaranch, the piece went on, "seems to prefer the comfortable status quo to the house-cleaning necessary to restore the movement's soundness and integrity."[46] But because the reading public reacted to these occasional pieces with little more than a collective yawn, these reports never had legs.

In sum, although Samaranch's weaknesses were obvious even ten years into his twenty-year tenure as president of the International Olympic Committee, no one, inside or outside the Olympic movement, was offended enough, persistent enough, or courageous enough to take him on.

The Web

As Indonesia's head of state, Abdurrahman Wahid was grossly incompetent—so incompetent that in less than two years he was gone. Jill Barad's case is perhaps less clear, because she was a woman in a man's world, but she did make a famously costly business decision and she did fail to create a network of friends and allies that would have enabled her to survive her early humiliation.

The story of Juan Antonio Samaranch and his followers is much more complex. Perhaps the best way to think of it is as a trajectory in which Samaranch's performance as a leader and manager deteriorated over time. In the beginning, in part because the context was conducive and the Olympic movement badly in need of repair, Samaranch was in many ways effective. He became president of the IOC just when its urgent need for cash could be met by a new technology, television—and it was he who seized the moment and transformed the Olympics into a billion-dollar enterprise.

But, over time, things turned sour. Brundage had established a precedent in which the president of the IOC led by command and control, and the Olympic movement more generally was effectively devoid of checks and balances. Therefore, when Samaranch came into office he had no reason to expect that his performance would be closely monitored, and it was not. Nearly invulnerable to challenge by members of the IOC, by anyone else associated with the Olympic games, or by anyone from the outside, Samaranch was free to operate more or less as he saw fit. And so, after he had served about a decade as IOC president, his skills as leader and manager started to deteriorate. His failure in any meaningful way to respond to the growing sleaze and corruption brought scandal to an Olympic movement in which big business and big money had come to be more important than almost anything else.

Samaranch's incompetence was mirrored by the incompetence of his followers. Most went along passively; others actually encouraged his bad habits. Jean-Claude Ganga, and even David Johnson and Thomas Welch were examples of officials who, for reasons of self-interest, took advantage of the lax culture Samaranch had tacitly endorsed. Moreover, it's clear in retrospect that Samaranch lacked even one close associate who was willing to play devil's advocate; there was not a single colleague who with any regularity or reliability challenged him personally or in any other way took him on. In short, if in the end Samaranch fell down on the job, his followers fell down alongside him.

Samaranch's mismanagement was the external manifestation of his internal need to control. This was, after all, a man familiar with autocratic rule. A former member of the youth fascists and then a functionary under Franco, Samaranch did not find, in his earliest experiences with people and power, any examples of democratic virtues such as shared decision making, organizational transparency, and personal accountability. He was at ease with his own fiefdom and with the idea that leaders can exercise authority with impunity. Manifestly he felt no obligation to respond to the charges of arrogance and mismanagement that were leveled against him years before he left office.

Although he enjoyed living among the rich and famous, Samaranch was never charged with lining his own pockets. Rather, his hunger was for the next deal. He was obsessed with the idea of the Olympic games as mega-events entirely different from their smaller and much more modest predecessors. So he never stopped long enough to take stock. And he never said "enough." Enough growth. Enough money. Enough commercialization. Under Samaranch the Olympic ideal was subsumed almost entirely to the dollar.

Samaranch is no fool. He presumably concluded that the fiscal benefits that accrued to the IOC during his presidency outweighed the costs of the expansion. Moreover, because no one seemed to care very much that the integrity of the Olympic movement was being compromised, Samaranch had good reason to believe that his presidency would not be clouded by major scandal.

In 2001 former Olympic sailor Jacques Rogge, a Belgian physician with a reputation for integrity, was elected president in the IOC's first contested election in twenty-one years. Although the selection of Rogge as Samaranch's successor was intended to signal a major change in how the IOC did business, the culture of corruption was by then deeply entrenched.

A couple of years after new IOC rules had been put in place, after the debacle in Salt Lake City, the ban against committee members visiting bid cities was still being ignored; the promise of full financial disclosure remained unrealized; and the secret balloting on key issues continued, raising the kinds of questions that only greater transparency could address.[47] The fact that three members of the U.S. Olympic Committee's ethics commission resigned in protest in early 2003, only eighteen months before the 2004 summer games in Athens, further confirmed that concerns about the integrity of the Olympic movement continue.[48] In other words, Samaranch's mismanagement and his inattention to core values left a legacy that endures.

The refusal to hold Samaranch accountable continued even after he left office. Far from being sanctioned for what went wrong on his watch, he was rewarded by that vote of confidence and by perks that kept coming after his tenure ended. His son, Juan Antonio Samaranch Jr., was elected to IOC membership. The IOC agreed to maintain offices for Samaranch in his hometown of Barcelona as well as in Lausanne. And the International Olympic Committee gave him the right to continue to attend, and participate in, committee meetings.

Unlike Wahid and Barad, who were quickly forced out, Samaranch escaped nearly unscathed. This brings us to the question of what could have been done to preclude his incompetence in the first place or to stop it after it started.

The Benefit of Hindsight

Juan Antonio Samaranch's incompetence was strategic rather than tactical. It was not that he and his followers failed to get anything done. Rather, it was that they became obsessed with one goal to the virtual exclusion of any others.

Samaranch was an elegant and rather understated authoritarian, but an authoritarian nonetheless. His long tenure in office suggests a man who thought of himself as appointed for life; and the nature of his administration spoke fiefdom rather than democracy. It is precisely because Samaranch exerted such a high degree of control over everything and everyone that he was, in the end, incompetent. The games were, after all, a global enterprise, with national committees the world over. Therefore, his refusal to delegate meaningful responsibility to others resulted in a kind of weak federal system in which the individual parts were in a position to inflict damage on the whole. The fiasco in Salt Lake City was only the most visible manifestation of a leader and manager who was so inattentive, so out of touch, that he was caught by surprise and embarrassed by his own troops.

Nor was there any corrective. Most members of the IOC were personally beholden to Samaranch and therefore loyal to him in particular, rather than to the games more generally. Thus, as an instrument of oversight they were nearly useless. Not once did they seriously challenge their leader, his priorities, or his methods of (mis)management.

Above all, neither they nor anyone else protected Samaranch against his own worst enemy—himself. Especially in the waning years of his presidency, there was no one around to caution against the temptations that came with the territory, or against the creeping rot. And so the mission of the Olympic movement became more memory than anything else. In the pursuit of big money, the commitment to oppose "all forms of commercial exploitation of sports and athletes" was consigned to the dustbin of history.

CHAPTER FIVE

RIGID

MARY MEEKER

Rigid Leadership—The leader and at least some followers are stiff and unyielding. Although they may be competent, they are unable or unwilling to adapt to new ideas, new information, or changing times.

I T HAS OFTEN BEEN SAID of late twentieth and early twenty-first century leadership that nothing matters so much as having the capacity to adapt to change. For this there are two reasons. First, change occurs faster, more often, and sometimes more suddenly and dramatically than before. For Americans at least, the world after September 11, 2001, has never been the same as it was before. And second, the amount of information available is nearly overwhelming. Moreover, what is fact on one day often becomes fiction on another. When scientists declared that instead of helping women stave off heart disease, hormone replacement therapy might actually contribute to it, the conventional wisdom went out the window. Small wonder that leaders and followers who hold fast to the familiar are likely to lag behind.

Brief Examples

Robert Haas

Levi Strauss & Co. had a long, proud history of benevolent leadership and management. But in 1997 the company, which had staked its name and reputation on protecting its employees, was obliged to send thousands of them packing. CEO Robert Haas sought, on the one hand, to justify his decision and, on the other, to reaffirm his commitment to every member of the Levi Strauss family: "I believe that if you create an environment that your people identify with, that is responsive to their sense of values, justice, fairness, ethics, compassion, and appreciation, they will help you be successful."[1]

Haas was compelled to violate some of his company's most fundamental values—justice, fairness, compassion, and appreciation—because he had failed to foresee the effects of an economy that was growing globally, and particularly the effects of these changes on Levi Strauss. As a result, Haas stayed too long with policies and practices that could no longer be sustained. When Levi Strauss announced plans to shut down twenty-nine factories and eliminate sixteen thousand jobs, *Fortune* described the sad scenario as a "failed utopian management experience." Moreover, Haas was blamed personally for his failure to adapt to the new and changing markets. Levi Strauss, *Fortune* concluded, had come "apart at the seams."[2]

Sumner Redstone

Viacom is one of the few mega-media companies to have survived the era of mega-mergers in good shape. But Sumner Redstone, its octogenarian CEO, had long been in denial concerning his own eventual demise. His rigid refusal even to address the issue of who would succeed him left Viacom vulnerable.

The widely reported tensions between Redstone and the company's president, Mel Karmazin, further contributed to the sense of unease. In January 2003 relations between the two men were said to have grown poisonous, and although peace broke out a couple of months later, Redstone's need to dominate everything and everyone, and his reluctance to quit center stage, made the situation unnecessarily tense and even precarious.

Put bluntly, the chairman and controlling shareholder of Viacom long refused to consider himself mortal, and so he continued to resist planning for an orderly transition in the event he became disabled or dead. "Viacom is me. I am Viacom," Redstone said. "That marriage is eternal, forever."[3]

Vladimir Putin

In 2000 the Russian submarine *Kursk* sank to the bottom of the Barents Sea, with 118 men on board. President Vladimir Putin's response was curious. Unwilling to cancel his Black Sea vacation to visit the site and commiserate with the families of the victims, he remained at a remove for more than a week.

More critically, he refused to immediately request the kinds of assistance—especially from the United States—that might have saved lives. In fact, Putin turned down help that was promptly offered. After a week, Norwegian divers were finally permitted to come in and do in one day what the Russians had been unable to do in seven. They pried open the sunken submarine's emergency escape hatch, but by then to no avail.

"Why did Mr. Putin and his generals resist asking for foreign help until it was too late?" asked *New York Times* foreign affairs columnist Thomas Friedman. "Because they feared it would sully the honor of Mother Russia's army and puncture Russia's pretense to still being a super power."[4]

Mary Meeker: Queen of the Net

The Prologue

Mary Meeker was one of the legendary leaders of the frenzied boom in online stocks that characterized the equities markets during the mid- to late 1990s. A friend of Amazon.com's Jeff Bezos, AOL's Steve Case, and eBay's Meg Whitman, Meeker was not a leader in the conventional sense. That is, she had no direct power or formal authority over her followers. Rather, she was an opinion leader. From her prominent perch as a financial analyst at the Wall Street firm of Morgan Stanley Dean Witter & Co., Meeker wielded great influence. When she spoke, people listened. More to the point, when she told them to do something, they did it. Tens of thousands bought stocks solely on the basis of Meeker's personal recommendations.

As long as the Internet bubble remained intact, everything was fine. Alan Greenspan's faint caution about "irrational exuberance" notwithstanding, Meeker gave her followers what they wanted: hot tips on hot stocks. But when the market turned bearish, she remained bullish. Long after she should have warned that owning stocks, especially the technology stocks in which she specialized, had become risky, Meeker refused to give the signal to sell. Moreover, her inability or unwillingness to adapt to new information and changing markets was not confined to a single incident or brief period. Rather, it came to define the nature of her leadership, just as it came to cost those who hung on her every word.

The Context

In January 1995, the Dow Jones Industrial Average stood at 3,800. In March 1999 it hit 10,000, and by May it had climbed another 1,000 points. The rise in the tech-heavy NASDAQ exchange was even more dramatic. In March 2000 the NASDAQ hit 5,000—an increase of 571 percent in six years.

What happened? What accounted for this upsurge, which only a few years later was widely viewed as merely a speculative bubble?

In the summer of 1994, *Time* ran the first of several cover stories on the Internet, describing it as "the nearest thing to a working prototype of the information superhighway."[5] In other words, by the mid-1990s the media establishment had concluded that the Internet was of signal importance and that it was here to stay. Moreover, fledgling businesses were starting to capitalize on what was soon being described as a "revolution" in information technology.

Although several companies could claim the title, if you had to pick one to represent the so-called New Economy, America Online (AOL) would be as good a candidate as any. In July 1993, AOL had two hundred fifty thousand subscribers. One year later it had a million. By early 1996, five million people were accessing the Internet through AOL.

Predictably, AOL's rapid growth was reflected in the price of the company's stock, which climbed steadily. Between 1992 and 1996, AOL's market value rose from $70 million to $6.5 billion. Moreover, strong backing by Wall Street insiders enabled CEO Steven Case to finance his plans for aggressive expansion. Mary Meeker, who by the mid-nineties was one of Morgan Stanley's star stock analysts, was one of Case's strongest and most visible supporters. As John Cassidy reported in his book *Dot.con*, which smartly and succinctly tells the story of the New Economy, Meeker had made a buy recommendation on AOL stock beginning in 1993.[6]

The rise of stocks in companies such as America Online, Netscape, and Yahoo! was part of a broader phenomenon. In the first four months of 1996 alone, Americans deposited about $100 billion in stock mutual funds. As recently as 1990, that figure had been a mere $12 billion for the entire year.[7] With all that money pouring into the equities market, prices climbed sharply. Between the beginning of 1995 and the end of May 1996, the Dow went up 45 percent, and the NASDAQ 65 percent.

For all the optimism, however, not everyone was an optimist. For example, well-known equities analysts Barton Biggs and Byron Wien—both older than most of their bullish colleagues and both also, like Meeker, based at Morgan Stanley—warned that because the markets had risen nearly without pause, they were vulnerable. Meeker, though, was undeterred. Her buy signals for stocks such as Netscape and America Online remained in place.[8]

The debates about whether or not the Internet was the harbinger of a genuinely "New Economy" continued. Still, the markets maintained their upward trajectory. Cautious money managers were left behind, and those who were willing to assume more risk were generously rewarded. Moreover, individual investors were no longer dependent on their brokers to make trades. Anyone armed with an online trading account could play the part of professional investor twenty-four hours a day, seven days a week. A click of the mouse displayed your portfolio. Another few clicks, and you could buy and sell stocks like a seasoned professional.[9] By mid-1996, about eight hundred thousand Americans had online trading accounts, and the number was increasing daily.

Throughout 1997, the markets continued to climb. Stocks rose another 7 percent during the first six months, and fans of the New Economy grew, both in confidence and numbers. Now, along with the investment professionals, their ranks included academics, journalists, and high government officials.

Even Alan Greenspan, the heretofore cautious chairman of the Federal Reserve, morphed into a bull—into a poster child, if you will, for the same irrational exuberance he had decried a year earlier. In July 1997 Greenspan went before members of Congress to deliver his semiannual report on monetary policy. He told the Senate Banking Committee that the economy's recent performance had been "exceptional," so exceptional that it could amount to a "once or twice in a century phenomenon that will carry productivity trends nationally and globally to a new higher track."[10]

The media first fueled, and then mirrored, the growing ebullience. In particular, CNBC, the cable network whose focus was business, itself contributed to the stock market boom. As Cassidy put it, "CNBC's reporters were enthusiastic, perky, and well informed. Together, they produced smart, entertaining television, which was all the more impressive for being largely unscripted. What they didn't produce was objective news."[11] The overwhelming majority of CNBC's on-air guests were bullish rather than bearish or agnostic. Although market pessimists were not banned, their unpopularity with viewers made it easier for CNBC to accentuate the positive and neglect the negative.

Spurred on by the gains of the recent past and by a new series of interest rate cuts, by 1999 the markets were in a state best described as euphoric. Most people knew that Internet stocks in particular were overvalued, but they couldn't resist joining the crowd, which, in many cases, included family, friends, and neighbors.[12]

On Friday, December 29, 1999, Muhammad Ali rang the opening bell of the New York Stock Exchange. By the end of the day, the Dow was at an all-time high of 11,497. For the year, it was up more than 25 percent. The NASDAQ, in turn, stood at 4,069. During the previous two years it had climbed more than 85 percent—the best performance ever by a major American stock index.

But then the worm turned. By the middle of 2000, interest rates had started to climb, many stocks outside the tech sector had lost value, and the equities market had generally become more volatile. By October 2000, the Dow Jones Composite Internet Index was down 54 percent from its high of only seven months earlier. Whether or not the collapse of the NASDAQ was, as Cassidy labeled it, a "turning point in American history," only time will tell.[13] What can be said for certain is that it was a time of tranoition the end of one era in which all things seemed possible and the beginning of another considerably more somber.

But despite the changing economic climate and dramatic declines in the markets, Mary Meeker held her ground. It was the ground beneath her that gave way. And so, with her buy recommendations for stocks such as Amazon.com, Priceline.com, and Yahoo! remaining in place, she became a scapegoat. Meeker was on the cover of the May 14, 2001, issue of *Fortune*, along with a headline that read, "Can We Ever Trust Wall Street Again?"

Still, Meeker held fast. While almost all signs were pointing downward, Meeker predicted that sometime during the next two or three years, the "nuclear winter" would give way to a "spring bloom." Soon, she proclaimed, the market value of leading stocks would make the market value just passed "look like chump change."[14]

The Leader

Mary Meeker was born in a small farming town in northeastern Indiana. When her father started to make some money, he bought stocks and brought his daughter along for the ride. In high school she got serious: She entered a stock-picking contest and watched her gains double. Meeker went on to attend DePauw University, with a major in business and psychology; after graduation she joined Merrill Lynch and earned an M.B.A. from Cornell. In 1991 she joined Morgan Stanley, which hired her mainly because of her expertise in personal computers.

Meeker caught the wave. She took the job at Morgan Stanley just as the revolution in information technology was beginning to have an impact on equity markets. For years to come, this head start gave her an enormous advantage. She understood before most of her competitors did that online communication was cheaper and more efficient than paper, and that as the Internet grew its usefulness would increase exponentially.

Moreover, her in-depth knowledge of emerging companies such as AOL, Netscape, eBay, Amazon.com, Dell, Compaq, and Microsoft shaped her views of the online world as it began to emerge in the early nineties. "If you looked at Microsoft and believed Bill Gates when he said, 'A personal computer on every desktop. A personal computer in every home,' it was easy to extrapolate, and see that Microsoft was going to be a big company," Meeker told Cassidy in a 1999 interview. "Simple as it sounds, I believed in 1993 that everyone would use E-mail someday."[15]

Friends describe Meeker as a plain-speaking, unpretentious Midwesterner with an immense capacity for hard work.[16] By the mid-1990s she in any case stood out. She was able to supply what the investment community demanded, and so she was promoted to a position in which she was free to opine as she saw fit.

Meeker's expertise, and her strong early track record in an equities market both unfamiliar and uncertain, was the source of her clout. In 1993, in a move she later described as "a defining event in my career," she recommended AOL to investors.[17] At the time, the company's shares sold for about 95 cents. Some six years later they were trading at $160. During roughly the same period, Meeker recommended ten other tech stocks, each of which also increased tenfold or more. In short, for most of the 1990s she continued to burnish her reputation as a stock picker of extraordinary judgment and foresight.

Meeker was no lightweight—that is, she was not just lucky. She did her own research on individual stocks and on the economy, and she reported her findings in a series of books. In 1995 she predicted the growth of tech stocks in a coauthored book titled *Internet Report.* (The book sold fifteen thousand copies and was downloaded more than one million times from Morgan Stanley's Web site.) A year later she came out with a second volume, *Internet Advertising Report.* The next year she published *Internet Retailing Report,* which made the same basic argument: The Internet was an "efficient and powerful new channel" for commerce. By 1997 Meeker was widely viewed as a "truly big-picture thinker" and one of the "best writers on Wall Street."[18]

But it took another year for Meeker to reach her apotheosis. In 1998, in an article in *Barron's,* she was anointed "Net Queen." Breathed *Barron's* writer Andrew Bary, "Just about everybody in America knows that Internet mania has been sweeping Wall Street lately. . . . But only the cognoscenti realize that a lot of this excitement has been whipped up by Mary Meeker, a 38-year-old analyst at Morgan Stanley Dean Witter. In Wall Street parlance, Meeker is known as the 'axe' for the Internet sector, meaning she is the most influential analyst around. Indeed, for big institutional investors, an Internet stock hasn't arrived until it has Meeker's stamp of approval."[19]

Except for a few brief pauses, Meeker was a strong bull during the entire dot-com era and beyond. To all appearances she genuinely believed that the strength of the markets was an indicator of a New Economy and that the old rules no longer applied. "Nothing has happened like this before," she maintained. "It just hasn't."[20]

In support of one of her favorite picks, Amazon.com, which she had long predicted would outperform the market, Meeker expressed the view that the age of the Internet was as different as it was new. "As we have said again and again—the world has never experienced as rapid/violent a commercial evolution of a fundamental business change as that being caused by the acceptance/usage of the Internet as a communications and commerce tool."[21]

In fairness, Meeker was no Pollyanna. During the late 1990s she was neither completely oblivious to, nor completely silent about, the dangers lurking in tech stocks. In January 1999 she warned investors to be prepared for a wild ride: "I'd be shocked if we didn't see a lot of volatility."[22] And later that year she cautioned that the days of easy dot-com money were over: "I think there will be only a couple of handfuls of companies that really succeed."[23]

Still, Meeker undercut her own expressions of doubt. While foretelling a "wild ride" in 1999, she simultaneously made clear that she remained strongly optimistic about Internet stocks for the long term, and she kept "outperform" ratings on her various favorites. (The phrase "the long term" is often used in discussions about money and markets, but exactly what it means to the individual investor is left vague.) And while observing that probably only a "couple of handfuls of companies" would ultimately succeed, Meeker claimed that she could point to these companies: "super-companies" such as AOL, Amazon.com, and At Home (which in September 2001 filed for bankruptcy). Moreover, when her words of caution sent technology stocks way down—that's how much influence Meeker had over her followers—Morgan Stanley rushed in to save the day. "There's nothing new" in what Meeker had said, a company spokeswoman insisted on one such occasion.[24]

What's clear in retrospect is that 1999 was a crucial year in determining Meeker's fate. She did see the warning signs; she did recognize that the markets were at levels perhaps dangerously high. But she downplayed the significance of voices she did not want to hear, and as a result she was caught in a trajectory of her own making.

In the end, Mary Meeker was unable to adapt to new information, new ideas, or changing times. Having achieved what was arguably the dominant position in the investment community—she was, after all, "Net Queen"—she stuck to her views and her stock picks long after it made good sense to do so.

Why did she not change in the face of change? There are many possible reasons: an early record of accomplishment that gave her good reason to believe she was smarter than her colleagues and competitors; the genuine belief that the New Economy was real; a mind so single-tracked and positively oriented that it did not easily admit new information that disconfirmed previously held opinions; a reluctance to give up a game she had dominated; a growing list of rewards, such as money (in 1999 she reportedly earned fifteen million dollars), fame, influence, and the thrill of the deal; and, finally, her deep entrenchment in a Wall Street culture in which others did what she did.

This last point is difficult to overestimate. Like other financial analysts caught in a web of conflicting interests, not only was Meeker in the business of giving investors supposedly objective advice, but she also worked for Morgan Stanley as an investment banker. In other words, while on the one hand Meeker continued to work as an independent stock analyst, on the other hand she had become something else entirely: a stock promoter who was expected to, among other things, pitch Morgan-sponsored stock issues.

Meeker's dual role became more questionable during the late 1990s, when the Internet boom became the Internet frenzy. Indeed, she was not entirely comfortable with the fact that some recent initial public offerings (IPOs) did not meet the three criteria she had earlier said were key: a big potential market, sound management, and an original product. "With every IPO the envelope is being pushed a little further and a little further," she noted. "At some point you have to scream, Uncle."[25] Still, Meeker's criticism of Wall Street as Wild West went only so far. As Cassidy has pointed out, "If she had really wanted to take a stand, she could have downgraded some of the leading Internet stocks, such as eBay, which was trading at about 1,600 times its revenues. This Meeker wasn't willing to do."[26]

Meeker was not alone in assuming two roles that would seem to be in conflict. During this same period, Jack Grubman worked for Salomon Smith Barney, supposedly as an independent analyst specializing in telecommunications stocks. What was not known then but is known now is that Grubman also advised the very companies whose stocks he was trying to sell. Grubman helped Salomon Smith Barney earn almost $1 billion in fees during the late 1990s, but by 2002 investors and lenders who had put money into the firms he recommended had lost an estimated $2 trillion.[27]

By 2000 the bloom was off the Meeker rose. Ranked by *Institutional Investor* in 1999 as the number one Internet analyst, in October 2000 she was charged with "pushing fool's gold." An article in the *New York Post* titled "Queen of the Internet Dethroned" pointed out that the stocks Meeker followed and recommended had not in fact outperformed the market, her "outperform" ratings notwithstanding.[28] The piece went on to charge that Meeker was caught in the catch-22 referred to earlier: To bring in business, she was hobnobbing with the rich and famous rather than providing the objective investment advice ordinary investors were looking for. In any case Meeker's rigidity made her unable carefully to watch and listen—and to tack accordingly.

By 2001 it was also an expensive indulgence. The investment community was calculating sums lost as a consequence of her bad calls, and the media that had built her up was cutting her down. In April, *Business Week* concluded that as a stock picker Meeker had a "mixed" record. For example, Meeker had downgraded the search engine Ask Jeeves, but only after the company warned of disappointing earnings. And she was plain wrong on Priceline.com, conceding too late that she had misjudged the size of the market.[29]

But it was *Fortune* that finally struck the fatal blow to Mary Meeker's reputation. In that May 2001 issue that had her on the cover, the magazine charged that Meeker had become "the single most powerful symbol of how Wall Street can lead investors astray." Meeker had maintained strong "buy' or "outperform" ratings on all except two of the fifteen stocks she was covering, *Fortune* reminded its readers, even in a market in which "Internet stocks have crumbled and entire companies have vaporized."[30]

Although crediting Meeker with once being far ahead of the pack, *Fortune* now took her to task. The magazine charged that she had compromised her position as an independent analyst; protected stocks she had followed and favored, even after they had lost a great deal of their value; developed a flippant attitude toward conventional measures of what a stock was really worth (she was using novel calculations based on anticipated margins and growth rates five years down the road); promoted her own celebrity (Morgan Stanley had hired a full-time PR person just to field Meeker's daily calls, including those from clients such as Barbra Streisand and Reggie Jackson); and relied too heavily on the research of others (by the late nineties Meeker was signing her name to reports written by assistants).

Once described as a big-picture thinker, Mary Meeker had become so caught up in the world she helped to create that she was no longer able to see the big picture. In only a few years, Meeker had been transformed from visionary Internet leader to rigid Internet has-been. By 2001 she was described as "stubbornly sticking" with previous buy ratings, even after stocks such as Yahoo! were off 94 percent from previous highs.[31]

Predictably, Meeker was anything but contrite. "I'm tired of the witch-hunt punching-bag stuff," she said in 2001. "Did we do some deals we shouldn't have done? Yes. Did we recommend some stocks we shouldn't have? Yes." But, she added, "It's difficult to get hit and hit and hit when we did a better job than any other firm."[32]

The Followers

Americans are spoiled. In one generation the average American home grew from fifteen hundred square feet to about twenty-two hundred square feet, and nearly three-quarters of new American cars have cruise control and power door locks. We spend $40 billion a year on our lawns alone—an amount roughly equal to the entire federal tax revenue of India.[33] In fact, those among us who are members of college-graduate households are richer than 99.9 percent of all human beings who have ever lived. But still we want more.

Moreover, because (as discussed in chapter 2) Americans are optimists who trust the system, we are willing to place bets on getting rich quick. This explains at least in part why, during the 1990s, many of us speculated in markets that had already gone way up. As David Brooks has put it, "The lure of plenty, pervading the [American] landscape, encourages risk and adventure."[34] An article in the *Journal of International Business Studies* confirms that Americans are more comfortable with the idea of taking risks, including financial risks, than citizens of any of the other nine nations studied.[35]

This tells us something about the base on which the New Economy was built. It also helps to explain why by 2001 nearly half of all American households held stocks either directly or through mutual funds.

Mary Meeker could not have been a leader in the financial services industry without legions of followers willing to put their money where her mouth was. She was the expert who told us what to believe and how to behave, and we freely went along. Because many of us continued to buy after the market had by every historical measure climbed too far too fast, it can fairly be claimed that the Internet boom and subsequent bust were as much our fault as they were the fault of Wall Street professionals who misled us. In other words, even though Meeker stayed stuck, her bad leadership depended absolutely on those of us who were so eager to make a killing that we fell in line.

Throughout the go-go nineties, Meeker's followers remained in hot pursuit. In 1999, Morgan Stanley's telephone operators took more calls for Meeker than for anyone else at the firm. On a typical day she received numerous voice and e-mail messages and many requests for interviews and appearances. To cope with the clamor, Morgan Stanley provided Meeker with a staff of six.[36]

Meeker's bid to add to the ranks of investors in her thrall was strongly supported by, among others, the media. As Cassidy observed, the overall standard of reporting during the dot-com heyday was dismal. The print media had fawned over and finally crowned Meeker "queen," and the electronic media, especially CNBC, had become a fan club for corporate America. "All across the country—in bars, banks, health clubs, airports, and doctors' waiting rooms—televisions were permanently switched to CNBC. The network's reporters didn't hype stocks directly. Rather they helped to create a populist investing culture in which adulation of the stock market was the norm."[37]

Moreover, for years CNBC acted as if there was no such thing as a conflict of interest. Network anchors failed to question guest analysts about dual loyalties. Nor were fund managers asked about positions they held in the stocks they touted.[38] But, of course, it takes two: one to sell and one to buy, one to lead and one to follow. Although the CNBC audience had good reason to believe that the so-called experts were objective analysts, many investors chose not to question the experts, not to cast doubt on those in positions of authority. Like Meeker herself, they— we— preferred to believe good news rather than bad; and so they— we—continued to hold even after the suspiciously rapid and strong run-up in prices.

Meeker also received support from the larger community of investment professionals. Although there were some exceptions— some financial analysts who kept their feet on the ground while the Internet bubble swelled—most, like Meeker, were caught up in the frenzy of speculation that characterizes a stock market bubble shortly before it bursts. In other words, Meeker belonged to a like-minded group whose members bought into the idea of a New Economy. Genuine dissidents were few, and even the occasional dissenting voices were drowned out by cheerleaders for Wall Street. The overwhelming majority of those who peopled the financial services industry shared Meeker's disposition to positive thinking.

Meeker's third source of support, however tacit, came from government regulators who did not seek aggressively to protect the interests of ordinary investors. The mutual fund scandals that broke in 2003—mainly because of ground-breaking investigations by New York State Attorney General Eliot Spitzer—are no more and no less than further testimony to the degree to which the government colluded in the excesses, if only unwittingly. This is not to absolve Meeker of bad leadership. Rather it is to indicate that she was part of a go-go economy in which those who were supposed to exercise oversight, but did not, also played a part.

On the day the World Trade Center was attacked, the bear market was eighteen months old. The Dow had reached its high in January 2000, and the NASDAQ three months later. Between 1990 and 2000, $14 trillion in paper wealth was created. But by 2001, only one year later, $4.5 trillion had vaporized.[39]

It was around December 2000 that the conventional wisdom started to change. Voices of caution were heard more frequently, and they had a greater sense of urgency. The *New York Times* featured articles with headlines such as, "How Did So Many Get It So Wrong?" and "Buy, They Say, But What Do They Do?"[40] The *Montreal Gazette* warned its readers, "Don't Follow the Herd: Investors Shouldn't Rely on Stock Analysts' Advice."[41] And Mary Meeker was savaged for having advised followers to buy Priceline at $165 a share in 1999 and then falling "silent" as the stock collapsed less than a year later.[42]

By 2001, many of Meeker's erstwhile followers were disenchanted. The "days when investors reacted to a favorable mention from Meeker by bidding a company's stock up ten or twenty points" were over.[43] In fact, Meeker's rigid refusal to change course during the changing times finally incurred her followers' wrath to such a degree that some turned on her full force: They sued her. In August 2001 the onetime queen of the Internet was the target of a trio of class action lawsuits alleging that her analysis of three stocks—AOL Time Warner, Amazon.com, and eBay—was biased. The suit charged that Meeker had acted not as an objective analyst but rather as a subjective salesperson whose main interest was to keep her corporate clients happy. Meeker was accused of being "virtually indistinguishable from an investment banker."[44]

Although the eight class action lawsuits against Mary Meeker were ultimately dismissed, the fact that they were filed is revealing. During the mid- to late 1990s, investors, especially individual investors as opposed to institutional investors, had good reason to believe that Meeker was providing advice based on her own independent research and judgment. But by 2001, many of Meeker's followers were angry over their losses, and some even felt duped. Ignoring their own earlier eagerness to follow the lead of a woman who symbolized the New Economy, they lashed out. The queen was dethroned by her subjects, who only two years earlier had hung on her every word.

The Web

By the time the twentieth century came to a close, it was apparent that the New Economy had disappeared. It turned out that valuations still mattered; that profits still mattered; that Internet companies were as vulnerable to bankruptcy as widget companies; and that the Internet did not produce change as dramatic as had the telephone or automobile. In short, by the new millennium the bubble had burst.

Mary Meeker's rigidity was a personal proclivity. It was also the product of a larger culture of optimism and greed. During the second half of the 1990s it was common for investment advisers to take big risks with our money. In fact, by 2003, at least some of the guilty—mostly institutions and not individuals—had been caught by the authorities. The nation's biggest brokerage firms, including Morgan Stanley, agreed to pay almost $1 billion in fines to end investigations into whether they had issued misleading stock recommendations and favored corporate clients with easy access to IPOs.[45]

Of course, not everyone on Wall Street was crooked or foolhardy or wooden-headed. For example, during the late nineties, Sallie Krawcheck, who has since been tapped by Citigroup to lead a separate division for its stock research and brokerage businesses, was in a position similar to Meeker's. But unlike Meeker, Krawcheck was able to adapt. Benefiting from her post at Sanford C. Bernstein, a small firm that had a reputation for giving thoughtful, independent financial counsel even during the go-go days of the New Economy, Krawcheck pushed her colleagues to down-grade stocks that looked increasingly risky.[46]

As we have seen, Meeker is not a leader as the term is usually used. She was not elected or appointed to anything, nor was she formally or even informally in charge of any group or organiza-tion. But the nature of her interaction with those who for years followed her advice makes an important argument for expanding the conventional conception of the word *leader*.

Meeker's reputation and high status, within both Morgan Stan-ley and the investment community more generally, enabled her, literally, to move markets. As we have seen, a favorable mention from Meeker could bid a stock up ten or twenty points. This ability to engage and enlist investors, to get them to do what she wanted them to do, grew out of what social scientists refer to as "expert power." Many of us bought stocks Meeker recommended because we believed that she knew more than we did (and more than even most of her peers) about equities and markets. We believed it possible, if not probable, that if we followed where Meeker led, we would make money.[47]

This case raises another question: Why call Meeker rigid? Was she not simply corrupt? Let me be clear here. There is no evidence that Meeker stayed with her stocks because her primary motiva-tion was to make money. This is not to say that she had no inter-est in money; clearly she did. Rather, it is to make two other points. First, Meeker was, like many of her peers, caught in Wall Street's web. Ensnared by the frenzied context in which she oper-ated and by followers eager to get rich quickly, she was a creature of her circumstance. Second, Meeker's failure to adapt to new in-formation and the changing environment was also the result of her apparently genuine, unswerving belief in the New Economy — the idea that the Internet had ushered in a new era of money and markets in which many of the old ways of doing things, including calculations of the values of stocks, were obsolete. Meeker was a workaholic whose hours were described as "death-defying." The New Economy was the base on which she had built her life, and those tech stocks she discovered early on were her progeny. To give all this up was, clearly, more difficult a change than she was willing or able to make.

Note also that during the various, if belated, government inquiries into wrongdoing on Wall Street, Mary Meeker was never singled out by regulators nor charged with any wrongdoing. In fact, despite the various dot-com fiascoes and scandals, Meeker suffered no more than slight damage to her reputation. She continued to remain at Morgan Stanley, emerging in 2003 as coleader of its technology research group.

In the end, one thing is clear. When the wind shifted, Meeker did not. Whatever the long-term future of the tech stocks dear to her heart for a decade, it will not change the fact that in the short term many of her followers lost a lot of money by doing as she did: standing pat in changing times.

The Benefit of Hindsight

This is a case of bad leadership in which the leader and her followers were joined at the hip. Although there were many other forces at play in this story, it is primarily about the relationship between, on the one hand, a leader promising a pot of gold and, on the other hand, followers who wanted nothing so much as to believe.

Mary Meeker was crowned queen of the Net. The problem was that the more successful she became, the more frenzied she became, and, finally, the more entrenched she became. A single-tracked woman who after years in the business was defined by her profession, Meeker was ultimately trapped in, and by, her own small world: all-tech-stocks-all-the-time.

Meeker came to believe that she and other like-minded people were dominating the so-called New Economy and that what had worked in the recent past would work in the future. But she failed to compensate for her increasingly narrow views. She failed to surround herself with people whose opinions were different from her own; she failed to admit new information and ideas; and she failed to diversify by becoming fully familiar with the market as a whole.

Above all, she made the mistake of falling in love with her own progeny, the very tech issues she had long followed and favored. Seduced by success, money, and fame, Meeker held fast long after she should have let go.

Meeker's growing rigidity was mirrored by those members of the media who declared stock market experts to be stock market gurus, and of course by individual investors who deluded themselves into thinking that if only they followed Meeker, there was little to lose and much to gain.

Meeker was an opinion leader. She was able to get her followers to do what she wanted them to do not because she was in a position to order them around, but rather because she was able to exercise influence. This means that whatever the mistakes Meeker made, individual investors were hardly free of blame. It was up to them (us) to learn about money and markets. It was up to them (us) to perform due diligence. It was up to them (us) to assess their (our) readiness to risk money in a risky market. And it was up to them (us) to remember the old stock market saw: Too much greed and too little fear is a dangerous thing. The bottom line? Meeker's followers were free agents. Just as she was rigid, so were they.

CHAPTER SIX

INTEMPERATE

MARION BARRY JR.

Intemperate Leadership — *The leader lacks self-control and is aided and abetted by followers who are unwilling or unable effectively to intervene.*

NO TYPE OF BAD LEADERSHIP seems as unnecessary, as careless and wasteful, as intemperate leadership. Although intemperate behavior usually plays out in private and is therefore ostensibly without public consequences, leaders, especially if they are highly visible, must presume that even a single lapse puts them and their followers at risk.

For at least two reasons, the need for leaders to abstain, or at least to be highly discreet, is far more important now than it used to be. First, our celebrity culture supports and even encourages the invasion of privacy. This means that well-known leaders—for example, Hillary Clinton in politics and Martha Stewart in the corporate world—are as likely to be on the cover of the *National Enquirer* as on the cover of *Newsweek*. And second, the information revolution guarantees that anything of public interest instantly becomes public knowledge.

When leaders lose self-control and their followers find out about it, it's a distraction, sometimes even a major distraction. Our appetite for scandal—a given when the leader is a star—and the resulting din of constant gossip derail the real work that needs to be done. When intemperate behavior is more egregious and enduring, as in substance abuse, it is destructive. In such cases, it's not a matter of work being derailed but of work not being done at all.

Brief Examples

Gary Hart and Jesse Jackson

We might think of them as bookends: Senator Gary Hart was one of the first modern American politicians to be tainted by sexual scandal, and the Reverend Jesse Jackson was one of the most recent. Times had changed during the fourteen-year gap between the two events—Americans became more tolerant of different lifestyles—but not so much so that Jackson was able to emerge unscathed.

In 1987, Hart told reporters, who were suspicious about his personal behavior, that they should follow him around. "I don't care. If anybody wants to put a tail on me, go ahead."[1] These words turned out to be the noose in which Hart hanged his promising candidacy for president.

Reporters from the *Miami Herald* tailed Hart and staked out his Washington townhouse. Soon he was caught on the arm of part-time model and aspiring actress Donna Rice. The next day the *Herald* led with the following headline: "Hart Has Relationship with a Woman." Twenty-four hours later, the paper reported that Hart and Rice had just spent two days together on a yacht with the unfortunate name of *Monkey Business*.

To be sure, even then, nearly two decades ago, polls showed that many voters were reluctant to cast their votes based on a candidate's private life. But when the *National Enquirer* published a shot of Rice and the senator aboard the *Monkey Business*—she nestled in his lap with her arm around his neck—it was all over. Hart's run for the presidency was so badly derailed that within a week of the original disclosure he withdrew from the race.

In 2001 it was revealed that Rev. Jesse Jackson had fathered an out-of-wedlock child with Karin Stanford, the director of the Washington office of his Rainbow/PUSH Coalition. America was shocked but not surprised. Rumors about Jackson's philandering had been around for years.[2] And by then public acceptance of the fallibility of leaders was widespread. Still, for Jackson to have had a baby with a woman other than his wife was no small matter.

"As her mother does, I love this child very much and have assumed responsibility for her emotional and financial support since she was born," said Jackson in a prepared statement he released because, in effect, the tabloids compelled him to do so. "This is no time for evasions, denials, or alibis. I fully accept responsibility, and I am truly sorry for my actions."[3]

It is impossible to measure precisely the impact of this revelation on Jackson's political standing. For many years he was the undisputed leader of black America, but Jackson's authority did not derive from any of the traditional sources, such as being elected or appointed to political office. Rather, he drew on informal, deeply personal bonds forged over many years with his legions of followers, both black and white.

Thus, although Jackson's relationship with Stanford had also raised questions about Rainbow/PUSH Coalition's bookkeeping practices, most of his followers stood by him. As political scientist Ronald Walters put it, Jackson's "ability to motivate people comes from the capital he has built up over the years."[4]

Still, Jackson's transgressions further fueled the growing impression that his influence was starting to wane. He was not compelled to retreat from public life, nor did his deep well of support among African Americans run dry. But the sharks circled. "What's his future?" asked Wyatt Tee Walker, the pastor of Harlem's Canaan Baptist church. "That's a no-brainer. Jesse's through. On a scale of 1 to 10, his credibility is about a 2."[5]

Others used the occasion to trash Jackson's leadership overall. Conservative columnist Andrew Sullivan cited Jackson's "nimble pirouettes over a recently conceived illegitimate child" and then went on to launch a full-scale attack: "Jackson's greatest betrayal, of course, is to the cause of civil rights. He once played a small but energetic role in the civil rights movement. But his actions in the last 20 years have trivialized its moral salience and dented its prestige."[6]

Obviously, during the years that separated the Hart and Jackson scandals, attitudes changed, and they have continued to evolve. The American body politic is less naive and less censorious than it was twenty years ago about sexual indiscretions and, for that matter, about sexual preferences. But even now the American people are not entirely oblivious of, or indifferent to, the sexual conduct of those who would be president or preacher.

James Bakker and Henry Lyons

James Bakker and Henry Lyons were leader-preachers. Bakker was a minister of the Assemblies of God, a televangelist who took in millions of dollars each year donated by his legions of faithful followers. Lyons was president of the National Baptist Convention, the nation's largest African American denomination, with more than thirty thousand churches. In the end, both men were also hoisted by their own petards: intemperance in matters of money and sex.

James Bakker resigned his ministry in March 1987. He had been head of the PTL Club (the letters stood for Praise the Lord and People that Love), and, with his wife, Tammy Faye Bakker, host of a daily talk program that aired on hundreds of stations around the country. In addition, the Bakkers were ringmasters of a 2,300-acre religious theme park, Heritage USA, the Christian Disneyland. For their labors, the Bakkers were amply rewarded. In 1986, for example, they received salaries and bonuses of $1.6 million.

Bakker said he was leaving the ministry because of an extramarital affair he admitted had taken place seven years earlier. He disclosed his wrongdoing in a statement that said he was "wickedly manipulated by treacherous former friends" who "conspired to betray [him] into a sexual encounter."[7]

But the matter was not so simple; nor was Bakker's transgression only sexual. His affair with Jessica Hahn was a red herring. In addition to the personal problems of Tammy Faye, who had disclosed shortly before her husband's resignation that she was undergoing treatment for drug dependency, it turned out that James Bakker had bilked his followers out of some $58 million.

Bakker's hunger for sex was apparently robust; later it was revealed that to "calm himself," he regularly had masturbatory sex with other men, sometimes subordinates who were pressured into it.[8] Even greater, however, was his hunger for money. Tammy Faye, in any case, had a "shopping demon," and so the Bakkers spent to excess. They had three houses, each decorated at enormous expense; a fleet of cars, including four Mercedes-Benzes and two Roll-Royces; and racks of expensive clothes and shoes. Their ministry once spent $100,000 for a private jet to fly the Bakkers' clothes from North Carolina to California; and a hundred dollars' worth of cinnamon rolls were bought, not to be eaten but only because they smelled good.[9]

Bakker eventually paid for his crimes. A couple of years after he resigned, a North Carolina jury found him guilty on twenty-four counts of fraud and conspiracy. But if his conviction capped "a devastating period of tumult within religious broadcasting" (well-known preacher Jimmy Swaggart had also confessed to an encounter with a prostitute), the damage was short-lived.[10] Only three years after the two men were mired in scandal, Assemblies of God churches were attracting more members than ever before.

The Reverend Henry Lyons became president of the National Baptist Convention (NBC) in 1994. Not only is the NBC the largest African American denomination, but it also has a proud history. The NBC has had an impact on every dimension of African American Christianity, including its music, preaching, and political activism. Martin Luther King, Jr., preached his first sermon in a National Baptist church. Aretha Franklin sang her first solo in a National Baptist church. And politicians have long flocked to meetings of the National Baptist Convention when they want to reach the black community.[11]

When Lyons assumed the NBC presidency at the age of fifty-two, he had a track record as a successful administrator at historically black institutions, including churches and schools. He twice had headed Jesse Jackson's presidential campaign in Florida, and he was known to be an electrifying preacher. And so when Lyons took office, he was widely hailed as a leader of promise who would "revitalize the denomination."[12] In fact, Lyons did get off to a strong start. He set an ambitious agenda, pledged that NBC would expand economic opportunities for its constituents, and committed himself to overhauling the organization's finances.

But less than three years after taking office, he ran into trouble. While Lyons was on a trip to Africa, his wife, Deborah, was arrested and charged with setting fire to the expensive waterfront home that her husband owned with another woman, Bernice Edwards. Lyons rushed back, and within a few days he and his wife held a press conference in which both insisted that it had all been a terrible mistake. Lyons described Edwards as "a close friend of my family for several years and a business partner of mine," and he "categorically denied" he was having an affair with anyone or misusing any funds to finance a lifestyle that included, among other things, one Rolls-Royce, two Mercedes Benzes, and that $700,000 waterfront home in St. Petersburg. Deborah Lyons concurred. She insisted she had set the fire accidentally and did not know "how the sheriff got it so wrong."[13]

It was later revealed that even before becoming president of the NBC, Lyons had twice come close to facing criminal charges on grounds of fiscal wrongdoing, and that he likely had fathered two children out of wedlock. It also turned out that in 1994 his "business partner," Bernice Edwards, was convicted of conspiring to embezzle $60,000 in federal funds from a school in Milwaukee.

Even after all the questions about Lyons's personal habits and professional practices, he hung tough and his followers held fast. Days after the 1994 press conference, the two hundred-member board of the NBC voted unanimously to keep Lyons as president.

And in spite of critics who called the decision a cover-up, some weeks later the board further declared that it would drop a church investigation into the various charges against Lyons. According to a writer for *Christian Century*, Lyons's supporters believed that they had defended God's honor by forgiving and retaining the embattled president. "They repeatedly invoked Jesus' admonition to forgive our brothers as many as 70 times seven. Another scriptural passage they offered was, 'Let those who are without sin cast the first stone.' " [14]

What church authorities were not willing to do, Florida state authorities were willing to do. About six months after the scandal first broke, Lyons was indicted on one count of racketeering and two counts of grand theft. (Meanwhile, Deborah Lyons had pleaded guilty to first-degree arson.) In time it was revealed that as far as money and sex were concerned, the Reverend Henry Lyons had little self-control. It was estimated that he had swindled his constituents out of more than $4 million; and in addition to his multiple affairs, he had been married previously—not once, as he claimed when getting his license to wed Deborah, but three times.

In March 1999 a Florida court found Lyons guilty of theft and racketeering. Only then did he resign as president of the NBC; and only then, as part of a plea bargain in which forty-nine other charges were dropped, did he plead guilty to federal counts of tax evasion and fraud. Although he sobbed and pleaded for mercy, Lyons was sentenced to five and one-half years in prison and ordered to repay almost $2.5 million of the $4 million he had stolen.

"I do ask for mercy today," Lyons told the judge before his sentencing. "I am 57. I don't have a lot of time to right all the wrong I have done. . . . I need to do at least 100 good deeds for every bad deed." [15] But this case was not about "every bad deed" standing somehow apart from every other bad deed. Rather, it was about a pattern of behavior that was nothing if not intemperate.

William Bennett

After he left government service, William Bennett, Secretary of Education under President Ronald Reagan, did not earn his millions as most of his former colleagues did—by lobbying. Rather, he became America's "self-appointed moral guardian, pontificating on everything from the unsuitability of gangsta rap to Bill Clinton's sexual peccadilloes."[16] Even his political enemies credited Bennett with making morality and responsibility integral parts of the political debate. He was a writer, a speaker, and a political operative. He was, in Joshua Green's words, "a commanding general in the culture wars."[17]

Bennett could often be seen on television opining in the fullness of his certitude, and he made an even greater impression through his bestselling books. For example, his edited collection, *The Book of Virtues*, was originally published in 1993 and sold millions of copies. Note that among the several virtues Bennett touted was moderation—the virtue of being restrained, of being temperate in all things.

In *The Book of Virtues*, Bennett approvingly quotes John Locke: "He that has not a mastery over his inclinations . . . is in danger of never being good for anything." Later he gives us an ancient Greek homily, "Nothing overmuch." And then, in the unlikely event we have missed the point, he goes on to explain, "The maxim calls not for total abstinence, but rather reminds us to avoid excess. We should know that too much of anything . . . may prove to be our undoing." Finally, at the end of the chapter on the virtues of self-discipline, Bennett turns to Tolstoy, who cautioned us to "set definite boundaries on our own appetites."[18]

Because Bennett had declared himself a leading arbiter of the virtuous, when it was finally revealed that he himself was intemperate and unable to "set definite boundaries" on his appetites, it was bound to be big news. Bennett, it turned out, had a gambling habit. Not a small gambling habit but a big gambling habit, and one that during the preceding decade was said to have cost him more than $8 million.[19]

Liberal columnists slammed him. For example, Frank Rich, writing in the *New York Times*, criticized Bennett's "compulsive, prolonged visits to a town [Las Vegas] that exuberantly epitomizes everything he was against in American culture."[20] And of course late-night comics had a field day. Rich summarized their collective humor: "Mr. Virtue, in a farcical belly flop out of 'Tartuffe,' is caught sinning."[21] But it was up to Bennett's natural constituency, America's conservatives, to dismiss him from his post as commanding general in the culture wars. And so they did. This appeared in an editorial in the *National Review*: "Bill Bennett is through. We speak, of course, of his public life. He is objectively discredited. He will not be proffered any public post by any president into the foreseeable future. He will not publish another book on another virtue." This is the consequence, the editorial concluded, of the "damage he has done to himself."[22]

Marion Barry Jr.: His Own Worst Enemy

The Prologue

Washington, D.C., is neither fish nor fowl—not, in matters of governance, an ordinary city, nor an ordinary state, nor an ordinary anything else. Moreover, perhaps more than in other cities, the politics of race run through Washington like a river of uncertainty and unrest. On the one hand, Washington has only one industry, the federal government. But on the other hand, it has a large population of African Americans, most of whom have no connection to the federal government.

Into this unusual mix came an unusual man: Marion Barry Jr. Generally considered the first militant black leader to be elected mayor of a major American city, Barry was at first an enormously popular figure whose gifts as an organizer and politician held out hope for a community that had long been beleaguered. He won the mayoralty in 1978, again in 1982 and 1986, and once more in 1994.

But nearly from the start it was a messy business. Barry's tenure as mayor was marred by fiscal crises and a series of corruption scandals—and Barry himself descended gradually but inexorably into a dependency on drugs. In the end, his inability to kick the habit brought about his own personal ruin and further damaged the sick metropolis he had been elected to salvage.

The Context

Once a rather small and sleepy southern town, after the Second World War Washington, D.C., began to grow, reflecting the superpower of which it was now the capital. More than ever before, Washington's most beautiful and prominent buildings and monuments became symbols of America's power and prestige; and more than ever before, the city became Mecca to tourists from around the world, impressed by its importance and grace.

But until the 1970s, Washington depended entirely on the federal government, which led and managed it. Consequently, America's capital differed from other municipalities in that it had not developed the political traditions or governing classes required to run City Hall. In this sense Washington more closely resembled a struggling former colony than a mature and independent civic enterprise able to run its own affairs.[23]

To the casual observer, Washington was misleading. Among other things, the poor were hard to see. As Harry Jaffe and Tom Sherwood pointed out in their indispensable book about the city, Washington hides its poor in public housing complexes that don't look rotten until you look carefully: "But the most deceptive and disturbing aspect of the capital city may be that nice-looking neighborhoods can be deadly."[24]

So the Washington scene is rather like a stage set: The props suggest well-being, and the business of running the federal government gets conducted; but behind the scenes, stories unfold that paint a different picture. This other picture is about three divides: between those who are somehow connected to the federal government and those who are not; between those who are relatively rich and those who are poor; and between those who are white Americans and those who are black Americans.

In the 1950s politicians running Washington from Capitol Hill were still treating the city like their "plantation."[25] Patronage was paramount. The social service budget was low, and the meager tax revenues were spent on projects intended for the benefit of the white business community. In fact, the white business elite had more clout in Washington than did anyone else except for a few members of Congress. By the mid-1960s the situation remained essentially unchanged: Washington had no home rule, and blacks had no say. Congress continued to run the city as if it were part of the federal government.[26]

But if Washington wasn't changing, America was. The civil rights movement, the women's movement, and the antiwar movement gave meaning to the phrase "power to the people." In time, even Washingtonians joined the fray, adopting the politics of protest that came to dominate America's political life in the late 1960s and early 1970s. Emboldened by President Lyndon Johnson's support for home rule and by the Free D.C. movement, formally launched in 1966, the people of Washington were catching on and catching up.

Free D.C.'s most prominent spokesperson was Marion Barry Jr. And so when the organization announced its most important political alliance to date—with the NAACP—it was Barry who did the talking.

Jaffe and Sherwood describe him on that day, February 26, 1966, as an activist in his prime. Dressed for the occasion in a white shirt, thin tie, and dark sport coat, Barry, who had been in Washington for only eight months, was already at the helm of the "biggest mass movement local Washington had ever seen."[27] Emboldened to invoke the *s* word ("Who is it that keeps D.C. in political slavery?"), Barry pulled no punches. "We want to free D.C. from our enemies," he declared, "from the people who make it impossible for us to do anything about lousy schools, brutal cops, slumlords, welfare investigators who go on midnight raids, employers who discriminate in hiring, and a host of other ills that run rampant through our city. The people in this city are tired of Gestapo cops."[28]

The day of this announcement was supposed to be all about Free D.C. As it turned out, it was all about Marion Barry as well. February 21, 1966, can be seen as the start of Barry's rise, and of his fall.

The Leader

In 1940, when he was four, his mother, Mattie , moved Marion Barry and his two sisters to Memphis, leaving the tiny town in Mississippi where they had been born. After she remarried, the boy did his growing up in a household that consisted of his mother and stepfather, two sisters, two half-sisters, and two step-sisters. Barry's family never experienced abject poverty, but, as his mother once said, "It was just so many mouths," and so from the age of eleven Marion Barry worked.[29]

In fact, he worked hard, obviously determined to better himself. He graduated from LeMoyne College, also in Memphis, and then went on, perhaps in part to avoid being drafted, to do graduate work in chemistry at Fisk. In addition to being a student, Barry had another life—in the civil rights movement. His prominence was confirmed when Martin Luther King, Jr., first came to Nashville to organize; Barry, who had started a local chapter of the NAACP, was one of King's first recruits.

Beginning in about 1959, Barry was deeply committed to advancing the rights of blacks. He played a role in the legendary sit-in movement at Woolworth's lunch counter in Greensboro, North Carolina. He led a drive in Memphis to desegregate the public library. And he was the first chairman of the Student Nonviolent Coordinating Committee (SNCC), known at the time to insiders as "Snick."

But in important ways Barry stood apart from even his closest associates in the civil rights movement. For example, after only five months as chairman of SNCC, he resigned to attend the University of Kansas for one year. As Congressman John Lewis, a legendary activist, now recalls it, "Barry would show up at meetings, dash in and dash out. He had a way of being in but not in."[30] Barry's private behavior was somewhat similar. In 1962 he wed a reportedly beautiful woman he had met at Tennessee State University; but by 1964 the marriage was over. Divorce papers filed a few years later alleged that Barry had "disappeared" and left his wife "impoverished." He was already developing a reputation as a womanizer and, on occasion, a mean one. Lewis recalls him as abusive; in any case in 1964 a woman on the SNCC staff charged Marion Barry with sexually assaulting her.

The next year Barry changed his life. He headed north, to Washington, D.C., where he became head of SNCC's local office.

As a result of a ten-year-old order to integrate Washington's public facilities, including its schools, and the political unrest now widespread across America, Barry arrived in a restless city. Thus was his timing perfect. The city was ripe for a would-be hero, preferably a black man who could take on, but also get along with, the white establishment. In short order, and in good part through his leadership of Free D.C., Barry was known as a man to know. The newspapers gave broad coverage to the various protests and boycotts he had had a hand in organizing, and the name of Barry, the "civil rights chieftain," became a household word.[31]

Whatever Marion Barry's deficits, such as unpredictability and unreliability, in those early days he was considered one of the few people in Washington who could bridge the divides of class and race. His growing skills as a conciliator were tested when violence erupted in the wake of the assassination of Martin Luther King, Jr. Barry was not, of course, a magician. But he was seen by both whites and blacks as better able than almost anyone else to connect to different groups, including the looters, most of whom were young. And so when the city tried to heal its wounds, during the period that followed the race riots, Barry became even more prominent. Less than three years after he arrived in town, "Marion Barry started to take his place among the city's power brokers."[32] He was transforming himself, and being transformed by others, from a civil rights activist to a mainstream politician.

At the same time, by the mid-1970s, there was another, far less savory Marion Barry than the one now being embraced by the Washington establishment. This Marion Barry's Youth Pride—a program designed to provide jobs for young inner-city African Americans—was reportedly riddled by corruption and graft. This Marion Barry's philandering was so egregious that his second wife, Mary Treadwell, threatened him with a pistol unless he changed his ways. (He did not, and they separated soon there-after.) And although this Marion Barry had stopped drinking rum and ginger ale, he had started using cocaine.

A home-rule bill finally passed both houses of Congress in 1973; and in 1974, in the first municipal election held under the new form of government, Barry was elected to the Washington city council. He was reelected in 1976, and in 1978 he announced his candidacy for mayor. He narrowly won the Democratic primary and easily won the general election. For a time at least, it seemed he had done so on his own terms. Although he had somewhat moderated his political persona, he remained true to himself. On the day he became mayor Barry was what he had been all along: "dark-skinned, unassimilated, and unashamed."[33]

During his first term as mayor, the patterns of Barry's life became entrenched. By day he tried to improve city services and to cope with an array of daunting problems, including budget deficits and high crime rates. And by night he hit the clubs, where by all accounts his life even then was marked by excess, particularly with regard to women and drugs.

But even as he planned to run for mayor a second time, Barry refused to see a connection between Barry by day and Barry by night. According to him, the people of Washington were not especially interested in things like the city budget; they just wanted services. He further claimed that almost no one cared that "he might be cheating on his wife or doing drugs, unless he became a hypocrite and started to crack down on junkies at the same time."[34] In fact, Barry himself told the story of a woman who said she'd heard he was sleeping with every woman old enough to say yes. It was a private matter, he replied, adding that his top female appointees would testify he had done more for women than any other mayor.

Barry won again in 1982, but the promising biracial coalition of four years earlier had largely evaporated. From that point on, Barry's political support came overwhelmingly from the black community.

Jaffe and Sherwood recount the story of Washington during the 1980s in a chapter titled "Greed City." For a variety of reasons that had little to do with the mayor and his black constituents (for example, the large infusion of foreign capital), the city was poised for a major revival. Money flowed, and Ivanhoe Donaldson, Barry's closest friend and political adviser, was seduced by its allure. Donaldson had started embezzling city funds in 1981. By 1984 it was a habit, and in 1985 he pleaded guilty to having taken $190,000 from city coffers.

Meanwhile Treadwell, Barry's wife and also the operations director of Youth Pride, had been indicted on charges of stealing and misappropriating funds from federally funded housing projects. And Karen Johnson, one of the many women in Barry's life, claimed she had sold him cocaine on twenty to thirty occasions. (Johnson was eventually sentenced to four months in jail.)

Barry's 1986 campaign for mayor of Washington, D.C., his third, has been described as a "besotted, drug-laden lark."[35] No matter. Seventy percent of the votes cast went to the incumbent.

Barry's third term amounted to something of a struggle between him and his inner demons, and between him and the federal officials determined to arrest and convict him of drug use and corruption. The city, of course, was caught in between. Polls showed that two out of three people now believed that corruption was a major issue in Barry's administration, and 47 percent said the mayor's own ethics were either "not good" or "poor."

By the late 1980s Barry was losing control and barely functioning. His excesses had taken their toll, and now, in addition to everything else, he was regularly using crack cocaine, a highly addictive and much stronger substance than what he had started on years earlier. The mayor's legal adviser, Herbert O. Reid, described the situation in stark terms: "If it walks, he fucks it. If it doesn't he ingests it."[36]

January 1990 marked the beginning of the end of Marion Barry's political life. As part of a sting operation jointly conducted by the FBI and the Washington police, Barry was lured to a downtown hotel by a longtime woman friend, a "stunning former model" named Rasheeda Moore.[37] When Moore agreed to cooperate, the rest was easy. The mayor of Washington was videotaped buying and smoking crack cocaine, arrested on the spot, and arraigned the next day.

Barry was charged with simple possession of cocaine, a misdemeanor, and released on the condition that he would agree to be tested for drugs each week. For the first time ever, he did not deny using drugs; nor did he say a word about his campaign for a fourth term, which was supposed to be launched in a few days.

From that point on, Barry's political career was erratic. Before his drug trial began, he promised not to seek a fourth term as mayor. But, unable to stay away, he tried to win a seat on the D.C. city council. He was unsuccessful the first time around, in the immediate aftermath of the sting operation, but after six months in prison Barry won his council seat. Emboldened by his victory, in 1994 Barry ran again for mayor, and again he won.

Throughout this period, it was well known that the city of Washington was in bad shape. In fact, the District was doing so badly in so many ways that in 1995 the federal government stepped in to take control of the city's fiscal affairs. Two years later President Clinton went further, transferring key D.C. programs back to the federal bureaucracy.

This was the cloud under which Barry served out his fourth term as mayor. At the ignominious end of his tenure, he declared he would never again run for any office, but in 2002 he tried one final comeback. He canceled his bid for another seat on the city council only after police reported finding small amounts of crack cocaine and marijuana in his Jaguar. Although Marion Barry denied he was using drugs, he was finished.

The Followers

In her book *The Last of the Black Emperors*, Jonetta Rose Barras describes Marion Barry on a bright spring day in 1994. Although no longer in his heyday, "dressed in an African-inspired suit, accented by the Kente cloth and matching kufti that had become his standard uniform for the previous two years, Barry exuded the pomposity of a Third World dictator. . . . A blend of race, cultural pride, and history underlie the admiration and respect most [blacks] hold for Barry. A wily, controversial personality, with indisputable civil rights credentials, he is lauded for his skill at out-maneuvering the 'white establishment.' "[38]

Barry's followers cannot be understood apart from the racial divide that characterized the context within which he operated. Nor can they be understood apart from his split personality. On the one hand, he was a militant black activist; and on the other hand, he was a bridge-building mayor. On the one hand, he was an ambitious and hard-working career politician; and on the other hand, he was his own worst enemy.

Originally, Barry's followers came in two colors: black and white. When he first became mayor, in 1978, white Washingtonians were on board. The white business establishment considered the mayor an ally in the search for economic opportunities, primarily through redevelopment. The white political establishment considered the mayor a partner in governing the city over which they finally had some control. And ordinary white citizens considered the mayor a doer who might just be able to build an effective and enduring multiracial coalition. In fact, no less venerable a white institution than the *Washington Post* pinned its hopes on Marion Barry. An editorial that appeared before the 1978 election read in part, "We find it, in fact, very nearly grotesque that his work with disadvantaged street youths, at one particularly turbulent time in this city's history, and his service among the shock troops of a great national movement for human rights at a tumultuous time in our national history, would somehow be counted against him in a campaign for mayor of the District of Columbia in 1978."[39]

It seems clear that Barry's credentials as a first-generation civil rights activist had deep appeal not only to blacks but also to moderate and left-of-center whites. They considered his transformation from protest politics to mainstream politics to be in their own interest, and in keeping with their liberal views.

Within the black community, Barry's position was of course strong. In fact, given that he had played a prominent role in the civil rights movement, he was, to many if not most African Americans, a hero. This is not to say that Barry drew on his past performance only. In fact, during most of the 1980s, black Washingtonians gave Barry credit for having improved city services. But even when things turned sour, Barry's credentials as a black activist stood him in good stead.

But if in the early rounds Barry was able to draw on the support of both black and white voters, things changed when his performance as mayor deteriorated and his personal excesses became widely known. First, the mayor's political base changed. By the mid-1990s Washington's demographics were different from what they had been ten years earlier. Many black residents, most of them poor and lower-middle-class voters who had given Barry his biggest majorities, had left town, most of them for the suburbs. Thus African Americans now constituted only 60 percent, rather than 70 percent, of the city's population. Gentrification had swept through neighborhoods once dominated by black middle-class families, and public housing had been replaced by mixed-income developments.[40]

Second, by the late 1980s, attitudes had changed. Most whites and many middle-class blacks were increasingly dismayed by the mayor's performance, summarized by the *Economist* as "steering Washington into an abyss." Schools and public services had deteriorated, the tax base had shrunk while the city's payroll had mushroomed, drugs flowed, and the murder rate had soared.[41] By almost any standard of urban horror, Washington in the early 1990s was either the worst or near the worst in the nation.[42] Predictably, whites in particular were disgusted. A poll taken by the *Washington Post* in 1990, after the mayor was caught on tape smoking crack cocaine, showed that more than 70 percent of Washington's white population wanted Barry to step down. Most blacks also felt he should resign, but they simultaneously believed that federal investigators had targeted Barry only because he was African American.[43]

As we have seen, even after his arrest, and in spite of his public humiliation, Barry was determined to hold on, at least to his hard-core supporters. So he repackaged himself. After serving six months in prison, Barry recast himself as the prodigal son, linking his own recovery and resurrection to the recovery and resurrection of the African American community more generally: "Here's Marion Barry," he would say, "who was internationally embarrassed, abandoned by his friends, and he has come back to be better than he was before he went down."[44]

To a degree, the tactic worked. Barry went on to win a fourth term as mayor, and at rallies organized on his behalf, blacks were heard to shout things such as, "The white folks want their city back. That's why they took down our mayor."[45] What Barry seemed to know, perhaps intuitively as well as intellectually, was that his new persona was in keeping with black tradition. As one observer put it, "African-American vernacular culture permits the redemption of a person both in religious and social terms and therefore permits it politically."[46]

Barras provides a similar explanation of why Barry was elected a fourth time, continuing against all odds to appeal to black voters. In effect, he was seen both as a victim of white supremacy and as a good guy in his own right, one who helped the poor when whites and wealthy African Americans had turned way. Therefore, instead of being excoriated and exiled for his transgressions, Barry "was hoisted on the shoulders of the community, celebrated and supported as if he were Jesus entering Nazareth."[47]

Washington had changed during the years Barry was in office, and Washingtonians had changed as well. But one thing that had hardly changed at all was the nature of Barry's inner circle, the women and men who constituted his closest followers. The cast of characters did not remain exactly the same, but with few exceptions, the members of Barry's inner circle never served him especially well. They did not protect him from crime and corruption. Nor did they shield him from his own inner demons, from the excesses to which he had always been prone and which became more extreme as time went on.

This is not to lay the blame for the lapses of the leader at the doorstep of the followers. Rather, it is to point out that more than a few of those who were Barry's political associates, and more than a few of those with whom Barry had close personal relationships, were enablers. They were coconspirators in the corruption and decline with which Barry's mayoralty will forever be associated, and in the wrongdoing specifically related to his addictions to sex and drugs.

Effie Cowell Barry, Marion Barry's wife during the worst of his troubles, provides some insight into how those around Barry tolerated and therefore enabled his lack of self-control. She was married to him for more than a decade; obviously, therefore, she had long known he was a notorious philanderer and used illegal drugs. Still, when asked about her husband by a local television reporter, she chose not to sidestep the question but to stand by her man in no uncertain terms: "My husband is an honest man, an arrogant person, and you expect him to be. He has a right to be. His arrogance goes along with his charisma. It's the street dude in him."[48]

The Web

This chapter begins by observing that no type of bad leadership seems as unnecessary, as careless and wasteful, as intemperate leadership. If self-control is a personal obligation, as Bennett's homilies on the virtues of moderation seem to suggest, then those who ignore the instruction "nothing overmuch" are, presumably, morally fallible. This might be said particularly to pertain to leaders whose bad behavior in private has a bad effect on the public.

The focus on individual responsibility makes intemperate leadership appear rather a personal matter, one that is most easily understood at the level of the leader rather than the led. For example, Ronald Heifetz and Marty Linsky write about how leaders must learn to "manage their hungers."[49] They address the temptations of sex, to which Gary Hart, Jesse Jackson, Jim Bakker, Henry Lyons, and Marion Barry all succumbed—as have many others, of course, who are not named here. But there is a difference between being slightly intemperate and being very intemperate, particularly perhaps in matters pertaining to sex. In retrospect, Gary Hart's indiscretion with Donna Rice might seem more silly than sinful. And in the end, the main reason Jim Bakker and Henry Lyons fell from grace was not their large appetite for women but rather their large appetite for money.

As mayor of Washington, D.C., Marion Barry Jr. was at the far end of the spectrum. He was not a little bit intemperate; he was over the top. He was unable to manage his hungers, nor to keep them confined to his private life. Moreover, his use of drugs was, in addition to being personally and politically destructive, illegal.

Many people now consider addiction to be not a sin but an illness, and it can be said of the four-time Washington mayor that for a long time he was simply not well. But his affliction, however personal a calamity, had serious public repercussions. When leaders are badly impaired for whatever reason, their followers pay a price.

But perhaps the most interesting thing about the story of Marion Barry is that it's counterintuitive. It makes clear that intemperate leadership is not only about failure at the individual level but also, equally, about failure at the collective level. Barry's well-known weakness for sex and drugs affected his capacity to govern effectively because the governed did not intervene.

Most of the leaders discussed in this chapter—Hart, Jackson, Bakker, Lyons, and Bennett—paid for their mistakes soon after they were publicly disclosed. Only Marion Barry Jr., the most intemperate of the lot, was able to go on for a long time even though many people knew what was going on.

He might not have lasted anywhere else. We have seen that the city of Washington provided fertile soil for a leader like Barry to take root. The city had no history of self-government, no traditional governing class, no broad economic base, and no culture of accommodation among the classes and between the two races. It therefore had too few individuals and too few institutions that were prepared to recognize and finally resist a governor, a government, that was going wrong.

Of course, the District was itself embedded in a larger context, in a country in which race relations, often bitter and fiercely divisive, were the subtext of its domestic politics from the start. More than anything else, it was the politics of race that made Marion Barry possible. During his first years as mayor he was the great black hope for whites as well as for blacks. During his last years as mayor he remained the great black hope, but only for a dwindling if still sizable black electorate. As Ronald Walters put it, "Because of our situation . . . we've respected those [black] people who can stand up to the system, and Marion has told almost everybody in this town where to get off."[50]

In the end, then, Marion Barry was caught in a web collectively spun. First, his mayoralty was a wasted opportunity because too many times over too many years the mayor was incapacitated. Second, Barry's dysfunctional behavior coincided with Washington's dysfunctional history and political culture. Third, many of Barry's intimates—family and close associates—colluded in his bad behavior. They became his enablers, either providing him with easy access to sex and drugs or protecting him from public scrutiny. Finally, those followers who were at a greater remove—largely black voters who, remarkably, elected him even to a fourth term—were so angry, so bitter, and so resentful that they chose to do themselves in rather than sacrifice one of their own on the altar of the white establishment.

The Benefit of Hindsight

In this story of bad leadership, arguably the followers were more responsible for what happened than the leader. Residents of the District who repeatedly voted for Barry, even after his addictions and transgressions became well known, were as culpable as the mayor himself. Moreover, Barry's family and close political associates also bear some of the blame; either directly or indirectly, they too further weakened an already weak civil society. If Marion Barry Jr. was guilty of steering Washington into "an abyss," so were all those who propped him up long after he should have stepped down.

Barry began strong. He might have been a rare bird: a twentieth-century politician able to bridge the divides of race and class. But as it turned out, he lost his way, and everything went wrong.

Given a personal problem such as Barry's, what is a leader to do? What could the mayor have done to preclude such a long period of bad leadership? Most important, all leaders—particularly those, like Barry, who have something of a checkered past and who know they are vulnerable in particular ways—*must* surround themselves with at least some people who can be relied on to tell truth to power. These people might be close aides or political associates. Or they might be friends, or family. Someone, in any case, must be ready, willing, and able to tell it like it is.

In a perfect world Marion Barry would never have had a problem in the first place. In a less perfect world, he would have known enough, been just healthy and courageous enough, to seek help on his own. In the world in which we live, one in which Barry was unable to take care of either himself or his constituents, it's up to others to provide tough love.

But no one did. None of Barry's intimates took the situation in hand. As they saw it, their loyalty to the mayor meant that they had to cover his tracks. And so they left him alone and thus became his enablers. Those at a greater remove were also culpable. Leaders of the black community, especially church and civic leaders, were reluctant to take on one of their own, even one so deeply flawed and obviously ill. They could not have been oblivious of Barry's deficits, but their priority was to have this man be mayor. This brings us finally to the voters: the men and women of Washington who four times preferred to put him, rather than any of his opponents, into the mayor's office. These followers, these voters, knew enough to know better. Still, they voted, freely, for Barry. Still, they voted, freely, for four more years of bad leadership.

To leaders who might have it in them to be intemperate we would advise, "Know thyself." To followers who might have it in them to be enablers, we should advise the same.

CHAPTER SEVEN

CALLOUS
AL DUNLAP

*Callous Leadership—the leader and at least some
followers are uncaring or unkind. Ignored or discounted
are the needs, wants, and wishes of most members of the
group or organization, especially subordinates.*

I N A PERFECT WORLD, which is the world depicted in
much contemporary leadership literature, leadership
"is an influence relationship among leaders and followers who intend real changes that reflect their mutual purposes."[1] This definition implies that the exchange is based on influence rather than
coercion and that it is multidirectional, with followers influencing
leaders and vice versa. It further implies that the mutual purposes
are arrived at through negotiation, in which followers voice their
preferences and leaders really listen.

But even in the real and imperfect world, according to the basic
tenets of democratic theory, leaders should, at a minimum, consider

the preferences of their followers. This obligation has become increasingly applicable to the private sector as well. In the past half century, workers in developed countries have come to expect some degree of participation in decisions made by management. Words now in fashion—for example, *power-sharing* and *team-building*—further suggest that even if employers and employees are not presumed to have equal influence, employees should expect to work alongside, rather than merely under, their employers.

The good part about all this is that leaders who fail to be sensitive to and considerate of their followers sometimes run into trouble. The bad part is that too often leaders still get away with callousness toward the very people whose well-being they are supposed to enhance as well as protect.

Brief Examples

Rudolph Giuliani

Since September 11, 2001, former New York mayor Rudolph Giuliani has been lionized. Considered a hero who, in the immediate aftermath of the attacks on the World Trade Center, was a model of exemplary leadership in a time of crisis, Giuliani has since been viewed as a man for all seasons—the best America has to offer.

But for all his accomplishments, and they were significant before as well as after 9/11, some of his constituents felt not only that he was unresponsive as a leader but also that he came across as distant, cold, and callous. To members of New York City's minority communities—in particular, African Americans—Giuliani was never considered a hero or even a friend. He was considered an antagonist.

Giuliani became mayor of New York City in 1994, and for most of his two terms in office, he alienated black (non-Hispanic) New Yorkers, who constituted nearly 25 percent of the city's total population. As far as they were concerned, what mattered was that he refused to build bridges to the city's black and also Hispanic neighborhoods, that he avoided meeting with black leaders, that he "gloried in every Police Department triumph and belittled complaints against the force, and [that] he exuded a my-way-or-the-highway style of governance."[2] Members of the black community used the mayor's greatest claim to success—the steep drop in the crime rate—against him. African Americans felt that the mayor's triumph came at their expense because the police were targeting young black men unfairly and in a way that bred police brutality.

The mayor's continuing refusal to meet with leaders of the African American community was particularly irksome. As the *New York Times* put it, "From the moment he took office in 1994, Mr. Guiliani's relationship with various black leaders has been complicated, even dysfunctional."[3] Unlike his predecessors, Giuliani had no liaisons between his office and the various minority communities. And for years he rebuffed even New York's most prominent black leaders, such as State Comptroller H. Carl McCall and Manhattan Borough President C. Virginia Fields. When McCall finally met with the mayor in 1999 he claimed to welcome the opportunity, but he told Giuliani bitterly, "Since our last meeting at City Hall at 4:30 P.M. on Wednesday, Nov. 30, 1994 [the day of Giuliani's inauguration as mayor], you have rejected every request for a meeting."[4] And when the mayor finally met with Borough President Fields, New York City's highest elected black official, their joint appearance seemed to observers to be "awkward" and "contrived."[5]

The antipathy between the mayor and his African American constituency came to a head after the shooting death of Amadou Diallo, an unarmed twenty-two-year-old West African immigrant. Four police officers fired forty-one rounds at Diallo in the doorway of his apartment building in the Bronx, leaving in their wake not only Diallo's corpse but also a minority community convinced that this single incident symbolized a mayor and a police force that for nearly five years had been biased against them.

Giuliani's immediate response to the tragedy was judged to be weak. "It obviously troubles both the Police Commissioner and me that 41 shots were fired," he said. "We don't know the reason for it at this point, but that is what the investigation is all about."[6]

There were no heartfelt expressions of sympathy from the mayor, nor much apparent empathy for the large numbers of his constituents who chafed under his leadership, convinced that he considered them second-class citizens.

Within days after Diallo's death, anger erupted: African Americans took to the streets to protest what they considered Giuliani's disrespect and lack of real consideration for their feelings of anger and hurt. One such rally drew more than a thousand people to the federal courthouse in New York City's Foley Square, where protesters chanted for more than two hours, denouncing the mayor and demanding that the federal government take over the investigation into Diallo's death. Said the Reverend Al Sharpton, who led the demonstrations, "They can shoot everyone 41 times. It may start with blacks and Latinos, but it can go everywhere." Added another angry man, a lawyer from Crown Heights who said he'd never before taken to the streets, "I've sat back for too long while this kind of thing happens time and time again. I feel that as black people, we have not done enough to show Mayor Giuliani that we will not tolerate this."[7]

Before it was over, more than one thousand people, including the state comptroller, had been arrested for participating in demonstrations in the wake of Diallo's death. Belatedly, the mayor got the message; finally, he reached out and tried to make amends. McCall was invited to the mayor's Gracie Mansion residence for a breakfast of lox, bagels, and fruit, and Giuliani went to Brooklyn for lunch with a group assembled by Priscilla Wooten, a black Republican city councilwoman. When he was asked what he had learned during his recent meetings with black and Hispanic leaders, the mayor replied, "The only change that actually works in human society is mutual change."[8]

But it was difficult if not impossible for the mayor to change his stripes, and memories were long. In the past he had responded with sarcasm to suggestions for improving community-police relations, and so whatever gestures he did make in the Diallo case, including overtures to the dead man's family, appeared to some as insincere.[9] Moreover, he did not exactly enhance his reputation among African Americans when he dismissed the daily demonstrations led by Sharpton as "silly" and "highly partisan."[10]

Perhaps the most persuasive attack on Giuliani's apparent disregard for the black community came from John Lewis, who was, as we have seen, one of the civil rights movement's greatest leaders and now a Democratic congressman from Georgia. Wrote Lewis in a *New York Times* Op-Ed piece about two months after Diallo's death, "More than a thousand men and women have been arrested for protesting police misconduct and brutality in the case of Amadou Diallo. . . . Some critics, including Mayor Rudolph Giuliani, have ridiculed the daily demonstrations at New York's Police Headquarters as a publicity stunt. Hearing this brings to mind the white politicians who stood in our way in the 1960's, when we in the civil rights movement used sit-ins, freedom rides, mass meetings and marches as a form of protest in the South. . . ."[11]

Whatever Mayor Giuliani's legacy as a result of 9/11, his callous attitude toward African American New Yorkers is part of the package. Were it not for the World Trade Center catastrophe, his mayoralty would likely have been judged to be divisive as well as flawed. A poll taken in April 2000 showed that only 32 percent of New York City residents approved of the way Giuliani was handling his job. It further indicated that more than two thirds of blacks felt that police brutality was widespread, compared with 23 percent of whites, and that his standing among black voters, which had never been strong, was weaker than ever. Indeed his approval rating among black voters "was so low as to be virtually unmeasurable."[12]

Leona Helmsley

Leona Helmsley had more than fifteen minutes of fame. Born in 1919—although she never admitted to being more than fifty-nine—she had a somewhat difficult and checkered history until she found her true calling: real estate. Leona Roberts, as she was then named, turned out to be such a natural at selling high-end

New York apartments that she soon was in a position to buy and lavishly furnish her own penthouse as well as travel in some of the city's best circles.

These circles included Harry Helmsley, one of New York's richest and most successful real estate magnates. Helmsley, then in his sixties, was inconveniently married, but he fell madly in love with Leona, then in her fifties, who was as capricious and brash as Harry's wife, Eve, was quiet and reserved.[13] And so Harry was divorced from Eve, leaving him free to marry the redoubtable Leona.

It was a match made in heaven. The Helmsleys were truly in love, isolated from everyone else, and passionately dedicated to expanding still further their impressive real estate empire. Leona Helmsley became increasingly involved in Harry Helmsley's business, a process that reached its apex in the late 1970s when he successfully negotiated to transform one of New York City's architectural treasures, the Villard Houses, into one of New York City's best hotels. Situated on Madison Avenue and originally built between 1882 and 1886, the Villard Houses consisted of six brownstone mansions arranged in a U around an interior courtyard. The city turned down Harry Helmsley's original plans, but in 1978, after he revised them to accord with the demand for historic preservation, the city's Landmarks Commission approved his plans for a hotel with fifty-one stories and one thousand rooms. The Helmsley Palace was to be the best hotel in the world.

It was said that during the two and a half years of construction, Leona Helmsley would "emerge from the shadows to take her place as a power in her own right, a queen, on the throne beside her husband."[14] Still restless and ambitious, Helmsley wanted her own domain. When the Helmsley Palace—promoted as "the most magnificent hotel to open in New York in a century"—opened for business in 1980, she ran it or, better put, ruled it.

In part as the result of a hugely successful advertising campaign in which Leona was presented as a queen and her hotel presented as "the only Palace in the world where the Queen stands guard," her reputation for exercising absolute authority became entrenched. Indeed Leona Helmsley demanded perfection from those who served her, and nearly without exception she "treated people like garbage."[15] The fact that she was widely, and ridiculously, advertised as queenly did little to dispel her image as a corporate despot.

Still, the ads made Leona Helmsley famous, and her hotels a success. By 1983 she had become a formidable corporate leader in her own right. She was president of Helmsley Hotels, Inc., a subsidiary of the Helmsley organization, which put her in charge of a company that controlled nearly $1 billion in hotel rooms and employed more than three thousand people.[16]

With all the wealth and power of Harry's empire now at her command, Leona Helmsley's darker side, apparently part of her disposition all along, emerged. Her leadership style became increasingly tyrannical; her behavior toward her employees was offensive to the point of being abusive. She "relished venting her power and instilling fear," and stories about her exploits become part of her lore.

- "Leona, on an unexpected inspection tour enters a room, spots a crease on a bedspread, a piece of lint on the floor or dresser, a crooked lampshade, anything. She screams imprecations, obscenities: 'The maid's a slob. Get her out of here. Out! Out!' "

- "Leona marches into the hotel dining room or kitchen, notices a busboy, a waiter, an assistant chef, anyone, turns violent and shouts, 'You, with the dirty fingernails, you're fired.'"

- "Leona, hearing that a secretary who had spilled something on her dress had dared send it to the Helmsley Palace dry cleaner, raged that the woman had cheated her, and fired her on the spot, though she had worked for the Helmsley organization for eight years."[17]

It is said of Leona Helmsley that in the end she got what she deserved. Disgruntled employees and contractors turned over to the *New York Post* records that led to the investigation of the Helmsleys' finances. The newspaper's revelations touched off federal and state investigations that led to charges against the couple, including tax evasion, falsified records, kickbacks, and extortion. Harry's age and frail health saved him from jail, but Leona ended up serving twenty-one months.

The final indignity was the making of a TV biopic—Leona was portrayed by Suzanne Pleshette—that included many of the notorious details, right down to her infamous crack that "only the little people pay taxes."[18] The name of the movie? *Leona Helmsley: The Queen of Mean.*

Howell Raines

In recent years, perhaps no American leader has fallen farther faster than Howell Raines, former executive editor of the *New York Times*. Although under his stewardship the *Times* had won a record seven Pulitzer Prizes in one year, Raines was fired after only twenty-one months on the job.

The conventional wisdom was that Raines had to go because on his watch reporter Jayson Blair's multiple and finally egregious transgressions had gone unnoticed and unpunished for too long. But insiders claimed that Raines would likely have survived had he not already earned a reputation for being high-handed and callous. As the scandal surrounding Blair unfolded, we learned not only that Raines had mismanaged this particular situation but also that he was neither loved nor even liked by most of those who worked under him. Moreover he was very nearly detested by several key players, who judged him an autocrat.

Like Rudolph Giuliani, Raines was very smart and highly accomplished. He would not have been offered the most prestigious job in American journalism had he not been a prodigiously gifted newspaperman. Raines had experience and expertise (he had been with the *Times* since 1978 and had won a Pulitzer Prize for writing), drive and vision (in Ken Auletta's words, Raines was determined to "quicken the pulse of the *Times*"), a strong reputation for competence and capacity, and a stunning record of getting things done. According to Auletta, under Raines's leadership, in the immediate aftermath of September 11, 2001, the *Times* "deployed some three hundred reporters, thirty staff photographers and two dozen freelance photographers. Eighty-two thousand five hundred words were devoted to the attacks on the World Trade Center and the Pentagon; there were seventy-four bylines accompanying sixty-seven stories, filling thirty-three pages of a ninety-six page paper."[19]

Given this striking record of achievement and the honors bestowed on the *Times* under his leadership, what went so wrong so quickly for Raines? It appears that for all of Raines's cognitive intelligence and talent for journalism, emotional intelligence was not part of the package, at least not during his brief tenure as executive editor. In fact, his callousness toward many of those who worked under him was so offensive that certain adjectives soon stuck to Raines "like lint." Epithets included "arrogant, autocratic, dictatorial, patronizing and peremptory."[20]

Raines got off on the wrong foot, conveying to his subordinates immediately after becoming executive editor that he was dissatisfied with, even contemptuous of, the old way of doing things. He was intent on shaking things up and on revving up the "competitive metabolism" of the *Times*.[21] The implication—that those who had previously worked for the *Times*, including reporters and desk heads, had grown lazy and lethargic—was offensive. As one person put it, "We all felt that our metabolism was pretty fucking high. And some of us had ex wives to show for it."[22]

Raines's insensitivity seemed to seep into nearly everything he did. He rode herd over reporters in out-of-town bureaus, ordering them to "get out more, write more, collect more datelines."[23] He centralized power, sharing it with only two other editors, who soon became equally well known for their "contemptuous, dismissive, sarcastic" ways. He insulted managers who dated back to the time of his predecessor, letting it be known publicly that he was dissatisfied with their performance. He took on key players in the Washington bureau, tough infighters who were based at an outpost with a long-standing reputation for fierce independence from the New York office. He killed stories by top reporters without adequate reason or explanation, including some written by Tim Golden, who had twice shared in Pulitzer Prizes. And Raines could be personally offensive: During a bitter exchange with metropolitan editor Jonathan Landman, Raines accused him of being "emotionally labile." Reportedly it was not the first time Raines had suggested to a subordinate that he or she had psychological problems.

Perhaps even more telling than Raines's many missteps as executive editor of the *New York Times* was that he was unable or unwilling to read the handwriting on the wall. The article by Ken Auletta mentioned earlier, which appeared in the *New Yorker* a year before Raines was forced to resign, made clear that his leadership style was causing dissention and distress.

Given that the complaints against him were aired long before the Blair scandal, the question is why Raines didn't take them to heart while he still had time. As Warren Bennis has observed, Raines should have known that his infamous morning masthead meetings were a disaster waiting to happen. And he should have realized that dividing his staff, as he did, into stars and also-rans, would result both in a plunge in morale and in a decline in the quality and quantity of information he received. But Raines did not learn any lessons, including those suggested in Auletta's detailed critique of his leadership.[24]

Howell Raines was by no means the first autocrat to serve as executive editor of the *New York Times*. In fact, one of his predecessors, A. M. Rosenthal, who served in the same capacity for about ten years during the 1970s and 1980s, was also notoriously difficult and dictatorial, especially toward the end of his tenure. But that was then. Styles of leadership have changed, organizational cultures have changed, and how much followers are willing to put up with has also changed.

This is not to suggest that Raines would have been toppled had the Blair affair never happened. Rather, it is to point out that this is no longer a time, nor is the *Times* any longer a place, in which leaders can count on getting away with being mean and nasty. When Raines ran into trouble, his callousness—a consequence of which was that few at the *Times* liked him—was a prime factor in his unhappy fate as executive editor.

Al Dunlap: "Chainsaw Al"

The Prologue

In July 1996 the board of Sunbeam Corporation brought in Albert J. Dunlap to serve as the company's chief executive officer. Dunlap's reputation preceded him. Known as the "poster child of corporate restructuring," with all that this implied, Dunlap was hired to effect at Sunbeam the same kinds of changes he had wrought at his previous post at Scott Paper.[25]

Dunlap's modus operandi was no mystery. The fact that his so-called successes came at great cost to the working people he led was well known. During his brief (twenty-month) tenure as CEO of Scott, more than eleven thousand people had been fired—some 35 percent of all the employees and 71 percent of the corporate staff. Shareholders, on the other hand, were amply rewarded. Under Dunlap's leadership, Scott's stock price rose from $38 to $120 a share; and the deal he crafted in which Scott merged with (was sold to) Kimberly-Clark provided shareholders with a $6 billion gain.[26] Indeed Dunlap's reputation as a turnaround specialist was so strong that the day Sunbeam announced that he had been named CEO, the company's stock price jumped 49 percent.

In essence, Dunlap's restructuring strategy involved an egregious kind of callousness. Without ceremony or second-guessing, he pitted the company's stakeholders, including its employees, against the company's stockholders. In the past this approach had paid off, at least insofar as the stock price was concerned, but at Sunbeam Dunlap's tenure was in every way a fiasco. His knee-jerk, short-term response to the immediate situation, which was to lay off 40 percent of the company's work force, did little over the long term to shore up investor confidence. In the end, Dunlap failed to produce the shareholder value he had ruthlessly pursued; in fact, he vanished from Sunbeam before even two years had elapsed. The reaction of one of the many thousands sacrificed on Dunlap's altar was succinct: "I'm just happy the son of a bitch is fired."[27]

The Context

The modern incarnation of Sunbeam Corporation dated to 1990, when two fund managers and one independent investor purchased the company after it declared bankruptcy. Although they were hoping for a quick turnaround, the three men were fully aware that the prize was of dubious value. Rather than thriving, as it had during the postwar era, Sunbeam was now a "decayed and neglected enterprise that sorely needed rejuvenation."[28] Its physical plant was old, and its product line, items such as blenders, irons, and can openers, was similarly dated.

It soon became clear, however, that the investment was a good one—a very good one. As John Byrne put it in his excellent biography of Dunlap, "Among the rot was enormous opportunity."[29] Soon the three original investors revived the near moribund operation and made a killing. In 1991, one year after they bought Sunbeam, operating earnings hit $91 million, a dramatic reversal from the company's loss of $95.3 million only one year earlier; and in 1992, they took the company public.

But by 1993 the three original investors had had a falling out and the company was in turmoil, largely because of bad leadership. The decision was made to bring in a new chief executive officer, this time Roger Schipke, who from 1981 to 1989 had successfully run General Electric's $5 billion appliance business.

Initially there was optimism. Schipke's extensive experience was in sharp contrast to his predecessor's, and his low-key manner brought calm to a company only recently roiling. But Schipke and Sunbeam turned out to be a mismatch.

Schipke concluded early on that in contrast to General Electric, things at Sunbeam were done on the cheap. As far as he could determine, the company had second-rate manufacturing, unsophisticated financial procedures, virtually no marketing, and a deeply flawed senior management team. Moreover, Sunbeam's backers appeared "none too eager to invest in the future."[30]

Sunbeam's board was becoming similarly disenchanted. By early 1995, when earnings began to disappoint, board members started to see Schipke as "indecisive and ineffective," and by 1996 three of the company's five directors had come to believe it was time to get Schipke out. A change of guard quickly ensued, but there was blood on the floor. Schipke himself was eased out rather quietly, but he left behind a company in big trouble and a board rife with dissension.

Many had now come to believe that Sunbeam was a dying brand. It had failed to keep up with competitors such as Black & Decker, attract new customers, restore its physical plant, and update its information systems. In addition, costs had spiraled out of control and the company was suffering from political conflict. Finally, its management was weak. In 1994 the magazine *Chief Executive* voted Sunbeam's board of directors one of the worst in America.[31] Clearly the company badly needed a new, permanent boss—a leader who was powerful and forceful and an expert at turnarounds. So when Al Dunlap arrived, he was viewed as "Sunbeam's corporate savior."[32]

Dunlap brought with him what has been described as a "well-established record for 'rescuing' ailing companies."[33] In other words, he had been successful in the past, if success is measured, as it usually is, in terms of market value. The deal in which Scott had merged with Kimberly-Clark saved the former from its role as a "stodgy, tired underperformer" and created a $12 billion global consumer-products company whose stock, under Dunlap's leadership, went up 225 percent.[34]

Nor did Al Dunlap neglect his own interests. After less than two years on the job, he walked away from Scott $100 million richer than when he arrived. In the most lucrative noncompete agreement ever crafted in American business, Dunlap got $20 million just for promising not to work for one of Kimberly-Clark's competitors until five years had elapsed.

Along with his reputation for being effective, Dunlap brought to Sunbeam a similarly strong reputation for being callous to the point of ruthlessness. Within months of arriving at Scott he had drafted a job-cutting plan so extreme that it amounted to a "brutal prescription" for anyone who worked there. Said one executive who had been with Scott for more than a quarter century, Dunlap "put the fear of God into a lot of people." [35]

On the basis of his track record as the ultimate corporate tough guy, Dunlap negotiated with Sunbeam a $1 million annual salary, $2.5 million in stock options, and one million shares of restricted stock worth $12.25 million. He also received six weeks' vacation, a new car along with a chauffeur and a bodyguard, a virtually unlimited expense account, and other perks and compensations valued at additional hundreds of thousands of dollars. Obviously Dunlap was going to cost Sunbeam a lot of money. But for a "corporate savior," he was presumed to be a good buy.

The Leader

Although Al Dunlap liked to picture himself as a poor boy who made good, in fact he was born in July 1937 to a New Jersey family that was comfortably well off. His childhood was secure, and he went on to do so well in high school, as both a student and an athlete, that he became the first young man in his town ever to get into West Point. Although he did not flourish in the academy's less supportive and more competitive environment, his hard work and perseverance got him through; Dunlap graduated 537th of 550 in his cadet class. One year later, at the age of twenty-four, he married Gwyn Donnelly, a woman of nineteen. The daughter of a plumber, she was tall and slender and worked as a manufacturer's model in New York.

As Byrne makes clear, a theme of anger and resentment ran through Dunlap's life from an early age. His sister, Denise, recalled that as a child he was short-tempered and obstinate and prone to fits of rage. And Dunlap's high school football coach said, "He sure did have a temper, an aggressive one. If someone knocked him on his butt in a game, he was going to knock the guy back twice." [36]

As Dunlap matured, he seemed to harden further. According to a divorce complaint filed later by his first wife, the marriage was full of "wretchedness and misery." She said that Dunlap was physically as well as emotionally abusive, and before the marriage ended, one son later, he had thrown her to the floor and threatened her with a kitchen knife.[37]

A few years later Dunlap remarried, but by then he had become estranged from his family. His parents were not invited to his second wedding (this marriage appears to have been successful); nor, years later, did he attend the funeral of his mother or that of his father. His relationship with his only child, a son named Troy, was also poor or, more precisely, nonexistent. After his remarriage when Troy was two, Dunlap had no further contact with him for almost two decades. Only when Troy Dunlap turned twenty-one did he see his father again, on his own initiative and at his own expense. The reunion was later described by Troy as "unemotional."[38]

After serving his mandatory three years in the military, Dunlap went straight into business. From the start of his career, he was known to work long and hard and to thrive in "messy situations that demanded tough, decisive actions."[39] These actions nearly always involved handing a lot of people pink slips, a task at which Dunlap seemed to excel. At Lily-Tulip, Inc., he got rid of one-fifth of the salaried employees and half of the managers. At Crown-Zellerbach, Diamond International, and of course later at Scott, Dunlap proved a "faithful and effective hatchet man, cutting and slashing his way to success."[40] Again he was handsomely rewarded. After a two-year stint in Australia, working for a billionaire whose TV and magazine empire was in financial trouble, Dunlap returned to the United States in 1993, some $40 million richer.

Al Dunlap's book, *Mean Business: How I Save Bad Companies and Make Good Companies Great*, was published the same year he joined Sunbeam. He said he wrote *Mean Business* so that others might learn from his experiences, so that, like him, they could "plan for success in some of the toughest times business has ever known." The title of the book was intended to promote Dunlap's image as the toughest and meanest of America's corporate leaders. As Dunlap wrote, "You're not in business to be liked. Neither am I. We're here to succeed. If you want a friend, get a dog. I'm not taking any chances; I've got two dogs."[41]

At Scott, Dunlap had overseen the largest proportionate restructuring of a major corporation in U.S. history, making it clear that he believed that implementing change, especially unwelcome change, was easier if it was rapid rather than prolonged. Like Machiavelli, Dunlap apparently was persuaded that when nasty work must be done, it must be done quickly: "You have a window of one year, and I passionately believe at the end of a year the window comes down like a steel door."[42] So when he arrived at Sunbeam, he hit the ground running; he did what he thought he had to do to increase shareholder value.

Even though critics had accused Dunlap of "heartlessness" with regard to the sudden, massive layoffs at Scott—in addition to their impact on individual workers, they had left "tangible holes in the civil and social fabric" of several communities—two days after taking charge at Sunbeam, he reverted to form. Dunlap presided over a conference call with company analysts, in part to express contempt for members of Sunbeam's former management team, who, he said, he "would have hung."[43] And in keeping with the way he had practiced restructuring before, Dunlap moved immediately not only to fire many of Sunbeam's senior executives but also, again, to plan for massive layoffs. Within five months of becoming CEO, Dunlap announced the details of a turnaround strategy that called for eliminating half the company's total workforce (six thousand employees), closing eighteen of twenty-six factories and thirty-seven of sixty-one warehouses, and consolidating six regional offices into a single headquarters in Florida.[44]

Sunbeam's board of directors, which had been briefed on the plan only hours before it was made public, fell promptly into line. But not everyone was supportive. Dunlap's draconian proposals made even some Wall Street analysts uneasy, especially when they learned that after only one month on the job, Dunlap had lost or fired three of the top four operating executives, who had a combined total of forty years of company experience and had been responsible for at least 90 percent of Sunbeam's revenues.

Uncertain about the efficacy of a plan that called for so many job cuts in such a short time and appalled by the callousness with which Sunbeam was proposing to treat its employees, critics voiced reservations about the company in general and Dunlap in particular. Even Secretary of Labor Robert Reich weighed in: "There is no excuse for treating employees as if they are disposable pieces of equipment."[45]

Dunlap was not to be deterred. He had made clear from the moment he arrived at Sunbeam that he intended to uphold his reputation. He told his associates, "I don't want people to think I've lost my touch. I want big numbers [of cuts]."[46] He was serious. Byrne writes that although Dunlap claimed to despise being called "Chainsaw Al," in fact he liked to joke that the epithet made him sound like a serial killer. He also loved "Rambo in Pinstripes," a tag given him by his mentor, the British magnate Sir James Goldsmith. The nickname referred to the movie character John Rambo (played by Sylvester Stallone), a deranged Vietnam veteran who was famous for his extreme, often violent, behavior. According to Byrne, Dunlap also liked being called simply Rambo. He considered it a compliment; if anything, the name seemed to have made him even more determined to live up to his own reputation for savagely attacking costs and people. Byrne wrote, "On downsizing, Dunlap's underlying belief was profoundly simple: like a street fighter with a sharp blade, he always cut big, deep, and a little wild."

Dunlap was an equal opportunity s.o.b., indifferent to the welfare not only of salaried employees but also of those with whom he worked directly, members of his own management team. The pressure on them was brutal, the hours exhausting, and the casualties high. He intimidated those who reported to him, and they passed that intimidation down the line. "Dunlap created a culture of misery, an environment of moral ambiguity, indifferent to everything except the stock price. He did not lead by intellect or by vision, but by fear and intimidation. . . . The pressure was beyond tough. It was barbarous."[47]

But for all the stakeholder misery Dunlap imposed in the interest of boosting stockholder wealth, this time around the "Dunlap effect" did not take hold.[48] Although the price of Sunbeam stock initially went up, the lofty level was not sustained.

In late 1997 Chainsaw Al declared victory in the Sunbeam turnaround. Many observers responded positively, including *Fortune*, which insisted that Dunlap was much more than a mere cost-cutter, predicting that when Sunbeam announced its year-end results, "people would see that sales, not just profits, rose dramatically."[49]

But Dunlap's moment of triumph was brief. A few months after he declared the miracle accomplished, Sunbeam's stock dropped 50 percent in a little more than sixty days (March to May 1998). "The turnaround hasn't turned and isn't likely to," forecast *Forbes*.[50] The reason: fiscal hanky-panky or, in any case, enough uncertainty about Sunbeam's numbers to give Wall Street the jitters.

When Dunlap took over Sunbeam, it had a relatively clean balance sheet. But less than two years later, the company was more than $2 billion in debt. Moreover, after zeroing out Dunlap's accounting tricks—more evidence of behavior both unethical and ineffective—Sunbeam had a negative cash flow. In a damaging article that caused considerable upset at company headquarters, *Forbes* pointed out that because Sunbeam's net worth had dropped from $500 million to a negative $600 million, this time around it was not only the employees who "got a taste of Al's chainsaw." Shareholders and debenture holders also would likely bleed.[51]

By June things had gone from bad to very bad. An article in *Barron's* took Dunlap to task: "Sunbeam's financials under Dunlap look like an exercise in high-energy physics, in which time and space seem to fuse and bend. They are a veritable cloud chamber." Sunbeam's CEO was furious. "This is scurrilous," Dunlap said. "We've got to do something about it."[52] But after the cascade of criticism began, it was impossible to stop. Dunlap's days as CEO of Sunbeam were numbered.

Soon it was apparent that the real truth was worse than any of the Sunbeam board members had imagined. Dunlap had driven the company into the ground. The estimate of the second-quarter shortfall ballooned from $80.9 million to $200 million; more ominous was the fact that if the company's banks had chosen to call in a recently extended $1.7 billion loan, Sunbeam would have been forced to declare bankruptcy. Al Dunlap's refusal to tell his own directors that the situation was dire meant that he was either delusional or hiding the truth. Either way the situation was untenable.

Dunlap was fired over the phone. During a hastily arranged conference call, a member of the board read from a script: "Al, the outside directors have considered the options . . . and have decided that your departure from the company is necessary." Dunlap remained calm and requested an explanation. But within moments the hookup went dead and he was gone.[53]

Given Dunlap's behavior, the response to his fate was predictable. Former employees "nearly danced" in the streets. Former colleagues now felt free to describe him as a man without values or ethics. His son said he was glad his father "fell on his ass." And Dunlap's sister declared that her brother got "exactly what he deserved."[54]

The Followers

Al Dunlap behaved so badly to so many people for so long that it's a wonder he lasted as long as he did. On the surface his durability is easy to explain: He was a "corporate savior," an expert at company turnarounds and at increasing, sometimes greatly increasing, shareholder value. But he was not the only man in American business to be so accomplished; others had achieved similar successes without inflicting so much pain. Thus a question arises: How did Dunlap get away with being so bad for so long?

The answer is at once simple and complex. On the one hand, he had several groups of followers, all of whom, for reasons that will become clear, chose to go along even with a leader as uncaring and unkind as Dunlap. On the other hand, given how extraordinarily difficult it was to work under him, even alongside him, the outside observer cannot help wondering why so many were so willing to tolerate so much abuse.

It helps to think of Dunlap's constituencies as concentric circles, with him in the middle. The one at the furthest remove from him personally was the one he considered most important: the large if inchoate group of investors who held shares of Sunbeam stock. They, of course, had every interest in seeing him succeed; they generally were uninterested in how he did so. Dunlap was a colorful figure—Chainsaw Al and Rambo in Pinstripes rolled into one—who promised that he would do for Sunbeam what he had done for Scott: increase shareholder value. So, for many months, Sunbeam's stockholders looked happily on the bright side, willing to buy Dunlap's bill of goods, unwilling carefully to examine the mounting evidence that his magic was based on questionable accounting. Sunbeam's investors could have taken the time to question what was being presented as fact, but most did not.[55]

To be sure, the average investor was misled by another group of followers, those in the next circle: financial analysts. Not every Wall Street guru was in thrall to Dunlap—by mid-1997, some of them foresaw trouble—but most experts were content to follow Dunlap's lead. He kept them in tow by cultivating the relationship and hyping his product. Despite the chaos inside Sunbeam, for the benefit of outsiders its CEO "kept up a steady drumbeat of optimistic sales and earnings forecasts, promises of tantalizing new products, and assurances that the Dunlap magic was working."[56] Analyst Andrew Shore has described what it was like to be taken in by "Al's PR machine." After visiting Sunbeam headquarters and meeting with its chief executive, and in spite of what he later conceded might have been his better judgment, Shore declared Dunlap "not a CEO you want to bet against."[57]

Closer to Chainsaw Al was the next circle of followers: his employees. By the time Dunlap joined Sunbeam, everyone with any interest knew that during his career he had thrown a lot of people out of a lot of jobs. But even those most directly affected typically had no recourse.

For example, because one-third of Sunbeam's total work force was located in one of six Sunbeam factories in Mississippi, the governor tried to stave off disaster by offering financial incentives and tax credits if the company would agree to remain in the state. But his effort was largely in vain. When Dunlap announced the largest restructuring in Sunbeam's history, Mississippi was not spared. Not Shubata, Mississippi, where Sunbeam employed 350 people out of 577 residents; nor Bay Springs, Mississippi, where Sunbeam employed 300 out of a total population of 2,200; nor, for that matter, Coushatta, Louisiana, where 500 out of 2,300 locals made Sunbeam irons and toasters. Political pressure occasionally compelled Dunlap to relent slightly; for example, the mayor of Bay Springs was able to extract from the company added benefits including six weeks' pay and six months of medical coverage. But by and large, employees were powerless, or any in any case they felt powerless, to stop their employer from laying them off. Like most large businesses, Sunbeam was a corporate hierarchy in which those at the bottom typically felt they had no recourse to change decisions made by those at the top.

Of course, Sunbeam was not the only company to restructure. A changing global economy and competition from abroad necessitated change at home. Still, the callousness with which Dunlap cut his work force was singular. John Byrne writes that at the same time that the last few workers were filing out of the plant in Bay Springs, Mississippi, Dunlap was cutting into a steak in a Florida restaurant and negotiating his new contract. The contract would later be valued conservatively at $46.5 million. Writes Byrne, "It was enough money to employ 620 workers for three years at an average salary of $25,000 per year, a sum more than most of the employees made at the Bay Springs plant."[58]

In the next circle of followers were members of Sunbeam's board. All boards of directors are charged with exercising independent judgment. How else can they perform oversight, especially of leaders and managers? Although we know that there is often a gap between what should happen and what does happen, in this case the problem was pronounced.

Dunlap's original contract gave him the right to immediately select three new board members and eventually to replace nearly every director with one of his own choosing. Consequently, until nearly the end of his reign, the majority of board members supported him; they were not overly curious, nor did they seek to interfere with the way he ran the business. Sunbeam's board unanimously approved his plans for restructuring, no matter its draconian measures. And whatever their personal reservations, board members continued nearly for the duration to acquiesce in what Dunlap wanted when he wanted it. When the time came for Dunlap to negotiate a new contract, some directors found the numbers so obnoxiously high that they initially balked. But when Dunlap pushed back, hard, they caved in. Whatever their reservations, Dunlap seduced and bullied board members into approving "the biggest of a long string of oversize compensation packages he had ever received."[59]

On paper, Sunbeam's board of directors, like all boards of directors, was officially in charge, but in fact, it was not. By empowering Dunlap to do what he wanted when he wanted, board members became followers, even groupies.

In the next concentric circle were those who constituted his management team. Let's be clear here. It was largely because of money that they came and stayed, in spite of working conditions that included personal abuse, brutal hours, and organizational chaos. Dunlap promised his managers that if they were loyal and did good work, they, like their predecessors at Scott, would soon be so rich they'd never again have to work a day in their lives.

Some, like Russell Kersh, Dunlap's most trusted aide, remained virtually to the end. Kersh was viewed as the most extreme of Dunlap's sycophants.[60] Other members of Dunlap's inner circle, such as lawyer David Fannin, were marginally more independent. Fannin is an interesting case because on the surface it's hard to explain his continuing allegiance to a man so different from himself, and whom Fannin later described as a "capricious and egotistical hothead." Still, although he often toyed with the idea of quitting, Fannin stayed on, unwilling to forfeit big money and fearful of Dunlap's vindictiveness. Fannin later explained his behavior: "It was like being in an abusive relationship. You just didn't know how to get out of it."[61]

Not every member of Dunlap's team obeyed his every order without objection. Donald Uzzi, a gifted, experienced, and credentialed manager, was worried about Dunlap's drastic cutbacks. He said so to Dunlap's face and, from time to time, quietly countermanded his orders. Still, in the larger scheme of things, Uzzi's occasional resistance did not amount to much. Those who worked under him considered him just another one of Dunlap's henchmen, another toady who failed to use his "fuck you" money effectively to stand up to his boss. Said one executive, Uzzi "had the money to stand up to Al, and he didn't do it because he wanted more."[62] Said Uzzi later, "The environment was so abusive, yet so fraught with opportunity for success, that you became subverted by it. You got the stink of this guy on you from working with him."[63]

In the circle of followers that was closest to Al Dunlap stood one man: Michael Price. Price was one of the three original investors who had bought Sunbeam in 1990, and he remained throughout Dunlap's time with the company the single most important player. When negotiations with Dunlap began, Price wanted him so badly as CEO that he acceded to all of Dunlap's demands. It was an omen. Even though ostensibly Dunlap was accountable to Price, this initial exchange, in which Dunlap called the shots, set the tone for their relationship until the day Dunlap was fired.

Even as Sunbeam turned sour, Price continued to play cheerleader. He defended the massive layoffs as necessary to the company's survival; and when the stock dropped, he insisted it was only a matter of time before it would rebound. At one inauspicious moment Price was so desperate to keep Dunlap that he doubled his base salary to $2 million and handed him additional shares worth $11 million, with options to buy 3.75 million more shares. In other words, in spite of Sunbeam's growing troubles, Price bestowed on Dunlap one of the most lucrative such packages ever awarded.

Price had a problem: His financial fate was inextricably bound to Sunbeam's. Consequently, he felt he had no choice except to

continue to back his horse. To admit making a mistake with regard to Chainsaw Al would mean not only being publicly humili-
ated but also losing, personally and as a fund manager, hundreds
of millions of dollars. In the end, of course, Price was able to save
neither Dunlap nor himself. By permitting Dunlap to dominate,
Price saw the value of his investment in Sunbeam drop nearly
$850 million. In addition, the performance of his mutual funds
took a serious hit, and his own reputation as a savvy investor was
badly damaged.[64]

The Web

Rudolph Giuliani, Leona Helmsley, Howell Raines, and Al
Dunlap differ in many ways. One was elected; three were appointed. One was in the public sector, three in the private sector.
One had followers consisting primarily of political constituents;
three had followers who worked for them. Two became leaders
because they were motivated mainly by money; the other two became leaders because their greater interest was in public service.

But the similarities among them are striking. They are alike in
that all of them were callous. As far as many or most of their followers were concerned, they were uncaring and unkind and dismissive of others' needs, wants, and wishes. More to the point,
perhaps, is that all four shared a lack of empathy and an inability
to realize that in late twentieth and early twenty-first century
America, the leader's capacity to empathize matters. Because followers are generally less intimidated than they once were, and because the media is generally more intrusive than it was, callousness is not likely to be tolerated for long. Put another way, there
was a reason Bill Clinton kept repeating that he felt our pain.

Because the definition of what constitutes callousness is to a
degree culturally determined, I deliberately dug each case of callous leadership out of American soil. This is not to say that in
another time and another place Leona Helmsley's or Al Dunlap's
erratic and abusive behavior would have gone unnoticed. Rather,
it is to argue that at this moment in this place, leaders who are

consistently callous put themselves in peril, especially if they are highly visible.

It is impossible to know what Guiliani's political future would have been had 9/11 not intervened. We do know that a year earlier his standing among blacks was "so low as to be virtually unmeasurable," and we also know that the early polls had him lagging behind Hillary Clinton in the race for the U.S. Senate. As to the other three, their callousness led to their comeuppance. Helmsley was done in by some of her victims. Raines was brought down by Jayson Blair and by those he'd disrespected. And Dunlap, mean and nasty without fail, was hoisted by his own petard. In the end he failed to do even the single thing he was hired to do: increase shareholder value.

Given these outcomes, given that leaders who treat followers badly put themselves at risk, we can speculate that the callous leaders to whom I referred were either self-destructive or lacked emotional intelligence. It doesn't cost leaders much to be at least minimally respectful of their followers. So if they cannot bring themselves to do even this, the reason likely falls into one of these two categories.

Giuliani and Raines, it seems, just didn't get it or didn't want to get it. Neither stupid nor crazy, both men seem to have concluded that being callous was integral to their leadership style and that the costs of such behavior would be outweighed by the benefits. Helmsley and Dunlap are another matter. In both of these cases a screw seems loose; there was callousness so consistent and considerable as to suggest personalities that were more than passing strange.

The saga of Sunbeam also says something about how in this day and age as callous a leader as Alfred Dunlap can hold sway for so long. It's a matter of two things: fear and greed.

The narrow context was a company in trouble, but the broader context was similar to the one described in chapter 5, in the case of Mary Meeker. Dunlap reigned when the economy was booming and markets were soaring. So much dot-com money was being made by so many so fast that some leaders of some old economy companies such as Scott and Sunbeam were desperate to be part of the action. The context became a culture in which shareholder interests became paramount, much more important in any case than stakeholder interests. What counted more than before was the money to be made; what counted less than before were virtues such as loyalty to long-time employees or the security of the communities in which they lived.

Dunlap was hired to do for Sunbeam what he had done for Scott. His leadership style and the direction he would take were known even before he walked in the door. What's clear, then, is that those who recruited Al Dunlap struck a Faustian bargain: In exchange for satisfying their desire for more money, they would satisfy his desire for complete control.

Greed is easy to explain and understand. Fear is more complicated. What was everyone around Dunlap afraid of? How did he hold people tight in his grip for so long, even after it became apparent that things were going downhill? Of course, most Sunbeam employees were scared simply of losing their jobs. What, though, can we say about the board? And what can we say about members of Dunlap's management team? Why did no one fight back? Why was there no organized resistance to a man clearly out of control—a man who, in addition to everything else, turned out to have cooked the books?

Dunlap cut a menacing figure. He threatened not only the unnamed workers toiling in plants far from company headquarters, but also those he knew personally. His tirades were legendary, his rages so extreme that his chest puffed out, his face flushed a bright red, and saliva sputtered from his lips.[65] Fighting with Dunlap was not simply scary. It was so deeply unsettling as to be avoided at all costs.

After Dunlap left Sunbeam, the company had to restate its profits, and in September 2002 he was compelled to agree to the demand by the Securities and Exchange Commission that he "would never again serve as officer or director of another public company."[66] Dunlap also had to pay $500,000 to close the government's civil case against him, as well as $15 million to settle a shareholder class action.

But his ignoble end does not dim the memory. What other corporate leader would take public pleasure in monikers such as Chainsaw and Rambo? And what other corporate leader would eagerly pose for a picture with a wide black bandana around his head, a leather strap crisscrossing his chest holding dozens of bullets, and a firearm cocked in each hand?[67]

The Benefit of Hindsight

Alfred Dunlap's career is an example of bad leadership that tells us a lot about what the followers might have done differently, but virtually nothing about the man himself. Dunlap was what he was: mean and nasty nearly his whole life. His short tenure at Sunbeam was a textbook case of callous leadership as exhibited by other "spectacularly unsuccessful" chief executive officers. He dominated his environment. He thought he had all the right answers, and he squelched anyone he thought might undermine him.[68] His personal abusiveness in face-to-face situations distanced Dunlap from the very people who should have been his closest allies.

The main problem was that key players who were supposed to behave like Sunbeam leaders behaved instead like Sunbeam followers. Enticed by the sweet smell of success, they were in thrall to Dunlap and his tough guy persona. Members of the small group that recruited him to Sunbeam established the precedent. Their judgment impaired by ambition and greed, they mistakenly assumed that Dunlap's past was his future. In fact, so eager were they to hire him as corporate savior that they acquiesced to every one of his extravagant demands for pay and perks.

Members of Sunbeam's Dunlap-picked board were similarly pliant, in good part because their guiding philosophy was the same as his: shareholders first. Apparently persuaded that he would lead them to the Promised Land, board members essentially stood by and did nothing while he proceeded to eviscerate the company. In particular, the board surrendered its right to independent oversight; it was mute on the subject of Dunlap's style of leadership and management, even as his notoriously bad behavior traumatized employees at every layer of the organization; and no matter how miserable Dunlap's performance, the board continued to surrender to virtually all of his increasingly outrageous demands for still higher salaries, still bigger bonuses, and still greater benefits.

Among Dunlap's close associates, not one had the fortitude to provide him regular, reliable information and relentlessly honest feedback. Not one had the fortitude to call him privately to account, either as chief executive of a company in trouble, or as leader of an enterprise on which many thousands depended for their livelihoods. And not one had the fortitude to take a public stand by resigning in protest.

At Sunbeam, the bottom line was the bottom line. As long as the major players believed he would make them rich, Chainsaw Al got away with being Chainsaw Al—callous to the core. As a result, by the time they fired him it was too late. Sunbeam was already in deep trouble.

CHAPTER EIGHT

CORRUPT

WILLIAM ARAMONY

Corrupt Leadership—the leader and at least some followers lie, cheat, or steal. To a degree that exceeds the norm, they put self-interest ahead of the public interest.

L IKE A VIRUS that easily insinuates itself, corrupt leaders, and those who follow them, are everywhere. No place is immune: not churches or charities, not banking or biotech, not small towns or large cities, not North America or South America or, for that matter, any other place on the planet. For example, a recent survey confirms that corporate America is infected with corruption: More than one-third of companies polled had been victimized by fraud and other kinds of economic crime.[1]

The temptations are great, and for leaders in particular the paths to lying, cheating, and stealing are easy to follow. Elected officials lie every time they promise what they know they can never deliver; corporate executives lie every time they pump up the good news to pump up the company's stock price. Cheating and stealing usually involve money—money to stick under a mattress, money to buy things with, and money to feel good. The lure of money leads leaders astray and it can explain followers who become corrupt as well—some of the time followers profit from the wrongdoing. We are told not to lie, not to cheat, and not to steal. But leaders and followers do lie, and they do cheat, and they do steal.

Brief Examples

Vincent (Buddy) Cianci Jr.

Buddy Cianci was first elected mayor of Providence, Rhode Island, in 1974. Seven years later he survived a U.S. attorney's office investigation without being penalized, but thirty members of his administration were indicted on charges of extortion, larceny, and conspiracy. Ultimately, twenty-one were convicted, and sixteen went to jail.

In 1983, after holding captive a man who was dating his ex-wife, Cianci was indicted by a grand jury on six counts, including kidnapping and assault with a dangerous weapon. He was charged with hurling an ashtray at the man's head, swinging at him with a fireplace log, burning his eyelid with a lit cigarette, demanding from him five hundred thousand dollars, and threatening him with murder.[2]

Cianci was convicted on a felony charge and forced to quit City Hall. Still, he remained popular with the people of Providence. On the day he left office, hundreds of supporters gathered to see him off. "You'll be back," they chanted.[3]

Less than a year later Cianci had reinvented himself, this time as a talk show host. He was a hit, and when he reentered politics in 1990 to run again for mayor, he won. By 1998, when Cianci was reelected mayor of Providence for the last time, his popularity was so high that no one bothered to challenge him.

But in 2001 Cianci and four of his close associates were indicted on charges of federal racketeering for demanding bribes and campaign contributions in exchange for jobs and city permits. Cianci was convicted on one count of racketeering conspiracy, sentenced to five years and four months in jail, fined $100,000, and required to put in one hundred fifty hours of community service.

Still his constituents were undeterred. On the evening after he was convicted, Cianci attended graduation ceremonies at a Providence high school. When he appeared before the crowd, a couple of thousand people stood up to cheer and chant, "Bud-dee, Bud-dee."[4]

Cianci was not the only member of his administration to be convicted of being on the take. For example, top aide Frank Corrente, known as the mayor's errand boy, was found guilty of racketeering conspiracy.

How can we explain Cianci's continuing popularity, even after he and several close associates were sentenced in federal court for lying, cheating, and stealing?

First, Cianci was ingratiating, even charming. In 1996 *Rhode Island Monthly* reported that even though Cianci looked "like a crook," he was the man whom the women of Rhode Island most wanted to date. He worked at being adorable. As mayor of Providence he made more public appearances in a day than most politicians do in a week. And he exuded the "game, absurdist cheer of a man who knows that one can get away with a great deal in this world, a man who lives by his own rules and is not averse to making up those rules as he goes."[5]

Second, Cianci had a strong record of accomplishment. Although on the one hand he was corrupt, on the other hand he was an extraordinarily effective mayor. During his time in office, Providence had changed from a city in severe decline to a thriving New England metropolis, designated by *Money* magazine as one of America's ten best places to live. Even his critics applauded the mayor for the transformation of Providence, which in recent years had become postcard-pretty.[6]

Finally, Cianci's continuing popularity can be explained in part by the context in which he operated. Rhode Island is tolerant of its public servants.[7] As Philip Gourevitch put it, "Political corruption is to Rhode Islanders as smog is to people who live in Los Angeles: nobody complains of its absence, but when it rolls around everyone feels right at home."[8] In other words, to the good people of Providence Cianci's corruption was not, by itself, a sin sufficient to disqualify him as mayor. As far as most of them were concerned, his personality and political effectiveness compensated for his moral failings. Thus Buddy Cianci, as much as anyone in this book, is an exemplar of one of the paradoxes of leadership. It is possible to be both effective and unethical.

Mario Villanueva

After a two-year search, in 2001 Mexican officials arrested Mario Villanueva on the Caribbean coast of the Yucatan peninsula. Among other things, the six-year (1993–1999) governor of the Mexican state of Quintana Roo was charged with facilitating the shipment of cocaine to the United States, drug trafficking, criminal association with drug cartels, and money laundering.

In June 2002, the U.S. attorney's office for the Southern District of New York unsealed two federal indictments charging Villanueva and his associates with narcotics conspiracy, racketeering, and money laundering. The claim was that he had helped smuggle into the United States two hundred tons of cocaine, a quantity worth $2 billion wholesale and perhaps ten times that much on the street. A formal request for extradition was submitted to the Mexican government.

Villanueva was the highest-ranking Latin American leader to face cocaine charges in a U.S. courtroom since Panamanian dictator Manuel Noriega (1989). According to Mexican and American investigators, under Villanueva's governorship cocaine moved freely through airports, highways, and marinas en route from Mexico to the United States. Arriving on jets and speedboats, the coke was loaded onto light planes and trailer trucks, ending up on the streets and in the suburbs of New York, Philadelphia, Chicago, Detroit, Atlanta, Houston, San Antonio, and Los Angeles.[9]

The smuggling would have been impossible had Villanueva operated alone, but he did not. The governor had close followers, accomplices such as Barnard College graduate Consuela Marquez, along with Jose Chejin, Quintana Roo's onetime finance minister. Prosecutors contended that Marquez, who had been hired in 1996 by Lehman Brothers to work as a broker, used her good offices to set up a web of shell companies and offshore accounts so that Villanueva's millions might conveniently be laundered.[10] And they contended that Chejin was Villanueva's "trusted bagman," whose primary responsibility was also to help him launder the drug money, in this case through a Salomon Smith Barney brokerage account located in Miami.[11]

As of mid-2003 Villanueva remained at large. Although the request for his extradition from Mexico to the United States was still pending, the prospects were not good. Mexico and the United States have had an extradition treaty since 1978, but since then only a small number of criminals have been turned over.[12] Meanwhile, in some circles in Mexico, Villanueva is a folk hero—while his relatives and friends worry that if he is ever extradited to the United States, "he might never return alive."[13]

Andrew Fastow

Americans are accustomed to corruption in the public sector. But in recent years our attention has shifted from corrupt political leaders to corrupt business leaders. Since the infamous collapse of Enron in 2001, scores of executives have been indicted for financial fraud, and many have been found guilty. As noted by the *New York Times*, it now "takes a scorecard to keep up with corporate scandals in America."[14]

Executives at HealthSouth, the nation's largest chain of rehabilitation hospitals and clinics, pleaded guilty to fraudulent accounting practices dating back to the company's founding in the mid-1980s. Top officers at Tyco International were charged with looting the company of almost $600 million. In what may be the largest accounting fraud in American business history, WorldCom executives were charged with having intentionally misclassified as much as $11 billion in expenses as capital investments. The founder of Adelphia Communications, along with two of his sons and two other executives of America's sixth-largest cable company, were charged with stealing more than $1 billion from the company and misleading investors and regulators to cover up their actions. The founder and former CEO of ImClone was twice convicted of criminal charges in one year, and in June 2003 was sentenced to seven years in prison after pleading guilty to two charges of conspiracy and wire fraud in connection with a purchase of fine art. The chairwoman of Martha Stewart Living Omnimedia was found guilty on four counts related to lying about the reasons she sold shares of ImClone stock. And the chairman of the Royal Dutch/Shell Group was forced to resign after it was revealed the company had overstated its oil and natural gas reserves by twenty percent.

The subsequent scandals notwithstanding, it is still the first of the big corporate calamities, the sudden and stunning collapse of Enron, that remains the archetype. In just a few weeks, the Houston-based energy trader was transformed from the seventh-ranked company on the *Fortune* 500 to a bankrupt shell of its former self. Some of the consequences of this appalling turn of events became clear within months. By the middle of 2002, four thousand five hundred Enron employees had been laid off, and the pensions of thousands more wiped out.[15]

Founded in 1985, only a few years later Enron boasted the largest natural-gas transmission network and the most extensive physical assets in the United States. Enron had also become a developer of power plants, a finance company, and a risk-management company—all the while developing a go-go organizational culture perfectly in keeping with the heady times.[16] Known for its impassioned embrace of deregulation, its risk taking, and its quick adoption of hot new ideas, Enron became the epitome of entrepreneurial success.[17]

Virtually without exception, Enron's top executives mirrored its mission. Driving and ambitious, they were the realization of the original dream of CEO Kenneth Lay: "to get a superstar in every key position."[18] Arguably, none was a greater superstar than Andrew S. Fastow, Enron's former chief financial officer, who turned out to be a whiz at, among other things, wrongdoing.

Fastow joined Enron in 1990. Over the next decade his star rose steadily, and he grew close to Jeffrey Skilling, who in 1997 became Enron's president and chief operating officer. Fastow deeply admired Skilling and tried to please him; Skilling, in turn, relied on Fastow to protect the value of the company at all costs.

For his efforts, Fastow was handsomely rewarded. He made a lot of money, owned a lot of real estate, and along with his wife, Lea, began to dabble in art. In October 1999, *CFO* magazine rated Fastow the "Finest in Finance"—one of the best CFOs in the country.[19]

But to please Skilling and to get as rich as possible as quickly as possible, Fastow crafted a series of deals so crooked that they finally cracked Enron apart. When Enron's chief financial officer was arrested on October 2, 2002, he was charged with fraud, money laundering, and conspiracy; a month later, he was accused of obstruction of justice. It was alleged that Fastow had arranged a series of fraudulent deals between Enron and its numerous off-balance-sheet partnerships—deals that had enabled Enron to hide about $1 billion in losses.[20] It was further charged that Fastow and a few close associates profited from investing in the partnerships, sometimes to the disadvantage of Enron itself. Fastow also was accused of reaping $31 million in illegal gains.

Fastow did not act alone. To the contrary, Fastow is perhaps best viewed as the leader of a small group of men, each of whom for his own venal reasons conspired in the corruption. This group included Michael Kopper, who, before turning against Fastow in court, had been his protégé, a brilliant lieutenant willing to go along with his boss even if it meant breaking the law.[21] Kopper eventually pleaded guilty to charges of conspiracy to commit wire fraud and money laundering, and he agreed to turn over to the government $12 million obtained through what he now admitted was criminal activity.

Insider followers also included men such as Richard Causey and Richard Buy, both former Enron executives who for their own reasons apparently turned a blind eye to, or even facilitated, Fastow's wrongdoing. As well, among Fastow's close followers were individuals from outside the company—for example, Schuyler Tilney, a managing director at Merrill Lynch, who apparently had a "special relationship with Enron." Tilney dealt with Enron professionally. He was Fastow's personal friend. And Tilney invested some of his own money in one of the off-balance-sheet partnerships Fastow had crafted on Enron's behalf. When Tilney was brought to Washington to appear before a Senate committee investigating the ties between Merrill and Enron, he refused to testify.[22]

But perhaps the most important point is that Andy Fastow had many more followers than the small numbers of his intimates would seem to suggest. It's safe to say that more than a few of the men and women who worked at Enron had at least some idea that Fastow was up to no good. In spite of the famous cautionary memo to Ken Lay sent by Sherron Watkins (who at the time reported to Fastow), the real question is why someone inside Enron didn't blow the whistle sooner. The answer is that nay-sayers and second guessers are frowned on in most corporate cultures, and Enron was no exception. "At Enron raising a red flag was a ticket to exile."[23]

The phenomenon of the whistle-blower, or the would-be whistle-blower, is more interesting than we generally imagine. Enron was typical of large organizations in that there was a lot of pressure to ignore the wrongdoing and little incentive to expose it. The pressure comes from inside an organization: from the hierarchical structures that characterize large enterprises, and from peers who prefer not to be personally discomforted or professionally jeopardized. And it comes from outside the organization—for example, from families of employees who rely on regular paychecks. Above all it's worth remembering that the tendency to ignore wrongdoing is natural. It's human nature. I write in chapter 2 of our basic needs for safety, simplicity, and certainty and also of our need to belong. To become a whistle-blower is to put all of these at risk.

And so Fastow's followers included more than a few insiders and more than a few outsiders, all of whom were happy to follow Fastow's path as long as it was paved with gold. One Houston banker estimated that before Enron's house came tumbling down Fastow controlled some $80 million to $100 million in annual fees for a variety of banking and investment banking services. If someone asked too many questions, Fastow would simply threaten to withhold future business.[24] For their part, Wall Street analysts who followed the company were content to go along with Enron's complicated and even mysterious accounting practices because until the company went bust, it delivered what investors wanted: smoothly growing earnings.[25]

To prop up Enron while at the same time lining his own pockets, Andy Fastow struck deals that cost a lot of people a lot of money. But there would have been no Fastow without Lay and Skilling, and there would have been no Fastow without followers who colluded in the corruption.

Skilling was eventually charged with conspiring to conceal Enron's true balance sheet while profiting from sales of stock inflated by false earnings reports. And Fastow finally pleaded guilty to two felonies—with 96 counts against him still remaining on the books. Even Lea Fastow was ultimately embroiled. She pleaded guilty to one tax felony stemming from her effort to hide income from one of her husband's secret deals. To those who lost jobs and money on account of Enron's collapse, nailing the guilty is likely cold comfort. On the one hand justice is served. But on the other the costs of corruption are not easily repaid.

Aramony as a Corrupt Leader: Charity Began at Home

The Prologue

We tend to think that leaders of nonprofit organizations, especially of charities, are different from people who head for-profit companies. We tend to think that the former take the high road and are somehow exempt from being venal. In a study conducted in 1989, 95 percent of Americans who gave to charitable organizations said that they trusted that their contributions would be put to good use. Some 98 percent added that if they learned that a charity they supported was in any way dishonest, they would stop giving.[26] In other words, with regard to charitable organizations, expectations are high and tolerance of bad behavior is low. Charities are held to a higher moral standard than their public and private sector counterparts.

So it was shocking when William Aramony, head of the United Way of America (UWA), arguably America's best-known charitable association, was forced to resign after a furor arose about his accounting and management practices. Aramony had been named president of the UWA in 1970. His resignation twenty-two years later, and his conviction three years after that on twenty-five counts—including conspiracy to defraud, mail fraud, wire fraud, transportation of fraudulently acquired property, engaging in monetary transactions in unlawful activity, filing false tax returns, and aiding in the filing of false tax returns—confirmed that leaders who worked for charitable organizations were not necessarily different from leaders who worked for other kinds of organizations. They too were capable of being corrupt.[27]

Of course, Aramony was not the only leader of a charitable organization to disappoint. For example, in 1990, Father Bruce Ritter, president of Covenant House, a home for troubled youth in New York City, was forced to resign after allegations of sexual misconduct. But because Aramony was associated with the UWA, a huge and highly visible charity thought to be as American as apple pie, his mistakes were especially costly—to the UWA and to American charities generally, which were tainted by Aramony's brush.

The Context

The first modern Community Chest was established in 1913. Streamlining giving to better meet community needs was clearly an idea whose time had come: By 1929 there were more than three hundred fifty Community Chests, and by the mid-1940s it was common practice for American workers to contribute to such charities through payroll deductions.

The modern United Way of America is a descendant of these Community Chests. The UWA is a national association with about one thousand four hundred autonomous members and affiliates, each one run by local volunteers. These local officials decide whether their United Way group should pay dues to the national association for services such as training programs and advertising.[28]

Although the community-based United Ways retain their independent decision-making authority, the UWA has considerable clout. A fund-raising campaign launched in 2000 pulled in $3.9 billion, enabling the UWA to continue to make significant contributions to causes related to health and human services, such as the American Cancer Society, Big Brothers/Big Sisters, Catholic Charities, Girl Scouts and Boy Scouts, and the Salvation Army.[29]

William Aramony became CEO of the UWA on the basis of his strong record as an insider who was an innovative thinker and effective development officer. It was anticipated that under his leadership the national UWA would "be revived and once again become a relevant and major force in American life."[30] Because the hundreds of United Ways across the United States lacked coherence and a strong common identity, thousands of United Way workers, staff, and volunteers eagerly embraced the man who promised to lead them to a new and better place.[31]

During the first few months of his tenure, Aramony produced the "most impressive and far-reaching changes in the United Way since its inception."[32] He developed a new national staff. He sent a new and more coherent message. And he encouraged local United Ways to recruit business leaders to serve on their boards and help them develop sound management practices.[33] In other words, Aramony wanted the national UWA, as well as its members and affiliates, to be run with the presumed efficiency of a profit-making enterprise.

Aramony quickly secured board of directors' approval of several major changes, including a revised charter and bylaws, and a reduction in the size of the board from an unwieldy sixty-two to a more manageable thirty-two.[34] Above all, Aramony was a leader with a vision; he was determined to energize and centralize the United Way movement. To this end he inspired his staff, developed a thirteen-point program to make the UWA more efficient and businesslike, mustered the requisite political support by meeting with hundreds of local United Way officials from across the country, and reached out to constituents who previously had been ignored, such as young people and members of minority groups.

A fitting climax to Aramony's initial burst of activity was the approval he secured to move the association from New York to Washington and into new national headquarters. Although some derided the new United Way building for its opulence—it was tagged the Taj Mahal—it nevertheless was tangible evidence that as national leader of the United Way of America, William Aramony got what he wanted.

The Leader

Bill Aramony was the first-generation son of Lebanese parents and the youngest of four children. He graduated from Clark University, went on to earn a master's degree in social work, and then joined the Army. A subsequent stint in the family clothing business convinced him that he wanted something different, and so he took a job with the United Way, a charity network that would over time define his professional life.[35]

Aramony served in communities around the country, including Miami, Florida; South Bend, Indiana; and Columbia, South Carolina. From the start he was viewed as ambitious, hard-working, and politically skilled. After hitting his stride in Florida, turning in an outstanding performance, he became the obvious choice to head the national association.

Aramony's early success as CEO of the United Way of America was a predictor. John Glaser, a one-time insider who later wrote a book about Aramony and the United Way, observed that for most of his twenty-two years as CEO, Aramony was highly accomplished and widely admired. Glaser described Aramony's contributions as prodigious by any standard, concluding that it was "inconceivable that any more could have been tried or accomplished."[36] Glaser was not alone in his assessment. Aramony was credited with professionalizing the UWA, expanding its reach, upgrading its services to affiliates, and, with the help of his increasingly prestigious and powerful board, launching a series of ambitious and successful fund-raising drives.[37]

How then did all this end in "the biggest charity scandal of them all"?[38] How did Aramony fall so far so fast?

On February 16, 1992, a story appeared in the *Washington Post* that broke the scandal. Headlined "Perks, Privileges, and Power in a Nonprofit World: Head of United Way of America Praised, Criticized for Running It Like a Fortune 500 Company" and written by Charles E. Shepard, the article depicted an ostensibly charitable organization in which charity began at home. The blame for the questionable policies and practices was laid squarely at Aramony's doorstep.[39]

Although stating for the record that Aramony's colleagues considered him "brilliant and creative," Shepard charged that the UWA's chief executive officer had significant problems. First, Shepard criticized Aramony's management style, claiming that he exercised "power much as he pleased" while the organization for which he was responsible was in constant flux and under a lot of stress. Indeed, reorganizations and executive departures were said to be so routine that some local United Ways complained that they could not "keep track of whom to talk to in the national office."

Second, there was the matter of money. Shepard pointed out that in 1991 Aramony had been paid $463,000, on top of which he enjoyed benefits and perks "more in keeping with a large corporation than a publicly supported charity."

Third, Shepard claimed that Aramony's friends and relatives were given UWA-related jobs in ways that smacked of nepotism and cronyism. For example, although Aramony insisted that he had "nothing to do" with the process, one of his sons had worked for three UWA spin-offs and ultimately became president of a fourth.

Finally, the *Post* took on Partnership Umbrella, Inc., one of the spin-off companies. Partnership Umbrella was given $900,000 seed money by UWA, but some of the $900,000 was used to "buy and decorate a condominium apartment on New York's Upper East Side, primarily for Aramony's use on his frequent business trips to Manhattan."

Within a few days the article was followed by another piece that was even more sensational. This one appeared in *Regardies*, then a popular chronicle of life in Washington, and it further contributed to what was fast becoming a feeding frenzy. But it was the *Post* that kept the story front and center. On February 20 a *Post* editorial raised questions about Aramony's effectiveness in helping the local United Ways raise money. And on February 24 it delivered the "coup de grace."[40] Two other articles reiterated and further detailed some of the earlier charges; and this time Partnership Umbrella came under special scrutiny for questionable spending and accounting practices.

Aramony's fate was sealed. Well-known philanthropist Walter Annenberg, a major contributor to UWA, called for Aramony's removal to prevent "destructive fallout" that could be "fatal to the local United Way" organizations. He added that if reports about Aramony were true, it was "indecent and disgusting" and that "an immediate decision must be made" to remove him from office.[41] Even more damaging was the reaction across America. Before February was over, more than thirty local United Ways, including several based in cities as large as Philadelphia and San Francisco, declared that they would withhold their dues until the UWA's house was put in order.

On February 27, during a video teleconference with United Way officials from around the country, Aramony announced his retirement. In response to a request from one local official for a formal apology, Aramony replied, "I do apologize for any problems my lack of sensitivity to perceptions has caused this movement."[42]

But it was too little too late. Although he first insisted that he would stay in office until his successor was named, Aramony's situation fast became untenable. One day later he resigned effective immediately.

When something this good goes this bad, the reasons are multiple. Obviously, Aramony had suffered the equivalent of a moral breakdown. The longer his time in office, the more problematic became his style of leadership and management. By the time Shepard wrote his piece, Aramony was described as exercising power almost at will. Glaser, who had worked with Aramony for years, went further. He concluded that by the end of his long reign, Aramony felt a need to control everything and everyone and thought himself immune to criticism. He had become increasingly distrustful of anyone outside his immediate circle; he was playing to the handful who had the most power and influence; and he was exhibiting a "barely disguised contempt" for many of his United Way colleagues.[43] In sum, whatever his early virtues, it's clear that Aramony stayed on too long. After twenty-two years in office his capacity to manage and lead was badly diminished.

The story of William Aramony does not end with his resignation. By 1995 prosecutors had enough evidence of fiscal wrongdoing to persuade a federal jury to find Aramony guilty of having stolen hundreds of thousands of dollars from the UWA and spending it on himself and his girlfriends.[44]

The trial was not about infractions that were merely offensive, such as excessive salaries and perks, including chauffeurs, flights on the *Concorde*, and a Florida condo. It was about infractions that were illegal—in particular, fraud. Indirectly the trial was also about Aramony's personal proclivities, especially as they pertained to teenage girls and young women. The Upper East Side apartment was described during the proceedings as a "love nest" for Aramony and Lori Villasor, who was seventeen when they met (Aramony was then married and fifty-nine), just "out of high school and desperate to escape the squalid Macclenny, Florida trailer park where she grew up with her mother and three siblings."[45] Although members of the jury later claimed that Aramony's sexual practices did not influence their guilty verdict, his behavior in this regard presumably did not make him more endearing as a defendant.

The federal judge who presided over the case was in any event hard-nosed. For conspiracy, fraud, money laundering, and filing false income tax returns, he sentenced Aramony to seven years in prison and an additional three years' probation. It was February 2002 before William Aramony was released from the federal prison camp at Seymour Johnson Air Force base in Goldsboro, North Carolina.[46]

The Followers

On the road to perdition, Aramony had a little help from his friends. He could not have done wrong without followers who facilitated or at least tolerated the corruption. They fell into one of two groups: those who actively facilitated Aramony's wrongdoing, and those who passively tolerated it.

Most prominent among the first group were Stephen J. Paulachak and Thomas J. Merlo. Paulachak was chief financial officer of the United Way of America from 1979 to 1983; Merlo served in the same capacity from 1989 to 1992, when he was forced to resign. Both men had known and worked with Aramony for many years. Paulachak joined the UWA in 1971, just after Aramony's move into the top job, and he remained deeply involved with the UWA, serving as "senior vice president for special initiatives" long after he quit as chief financial officer. Merlo first met Aramony in the 1960s, when he was a volunteer at the United Way in Miami, which Aramony then led.

Merlo's relationship with Aramony was especially close. They were good friends and together played poker and gin rummy and visited the racetrack. During the 1980s Aramony relied on Merlo for spot projects, choosing to ignore the fact that Merlo's character did not seem to be entirely upstanding. During the late 1970s Merlo got into trouble more than once. For example, he grossly overcharged the city of Sunrise, Florida, for accounting work on bond issues; and his firm was alleged to have billed Medicare excessive fees for services to home health care agencies.

Of particular note is that Aramony offered Merlo the job of UWA's chief financial officer at a time when Merlo was in trouble. In the late 1980s his pizza takeout business was late paying bills. His development company was about to lose its headquarters to foreclosure. And a bank whose board he chaired was struggling.[47]

When Aramony was indicted (1994), Paulachak and Merlo were indicted along with him. Also named as a defendant was Partnership Umbrella, the UWA spin-off company that was headed by Paulachak. The original indictment charged Aramony with fifty-three felony counts, Paulachak and Merlo with thirty-five each, and Partnership Umbrella with twenty-four. The bottom line was that, along with Aramony, Paulachak and Merlo were accused of defrauding the United Way of America and of filing false personal and corporate income tax returns. (Merlo was also charged with perjury.)

As the investigation unfolded, it became clear that Aramony's criminal behavior was aided and abetted by Paulachak and Merlo. Both men not only defrauded the UWA along with Aramony, but they were also the ones who made it possible for him to satisfy his sexual appetites at the partial expense of the UWA.

Among the specifics of the indictment were the following:

> Merlo was paid $320,000 between 1989 and 1991 by the Partnership company and he routed nearly $80,000 of the money to Aramony's girlfriend. United Way and Partnership paid thousands of dollars in chauffeuring fees for Aramony and his girlfriend in Atlantic City and for Aramony in New York. Aramony and Paulachak used $383,000 in Partnership funds—most diverted from the UWA—to buy an apartment in New York City for Aramony's exclusive use. They spent another $72,000 to decorate the apartment, which was used by the girlfriend as her New York residence during more than 15 trips to the city. . . . Aramony and Paulachak

used United Way, Partnership and United Way International Funds to pay nearly $10,000 for an Egyptian
and London vacation for Aramony and his girlfriend;
Partnership paid for a $2,330 Nile cruise and other ex-
penses. Aramony and Paulachak used the funds of another charity to pay a $4,500 personal chauffeuring
charge, which included a tour of the English countryside for Aramony and his girlfriend. Paulachak used
$6,100 in Partnership money to pay for a Hawaii vaca-
tion for himself and his family; $9,600 for a London
vacation for himself and his wife; and $80,200 for a
lifetime, nonrefundable, nontransferable American Air-
lines travel pass.[48]

Paulachak and Merlo were the most loyal of bad followers:
They made it possible for Aramony to be a bad leader. They enabled him to carry out his plan to divert at least $2.74 million in
corporate contributions from the United Way into a for-profit corporation, Partnership Umbrella. Then, in accordance with Aramony's preferences and proclivities, they siphoned funds from
Partnership for their personal pleasures, concealing the scheme by
keeping two sets of books and creating phony accounts.[49]

But they were not alone. The damage could not have been done
without other collaborators, particularly members of the UWA
board. As Glaser pointed out, the executive committee or the
board had always approved Aramony's salary, expenses, and virtually everything else. With one exception they had also approved
the establishment of the spin-offs.[50]

After Aramony's troubles became known in the media, the
board took action. The perception created by Aramony's poor
judgment was "damaging to the institution," said United Way of
America board member Robert E. Allen, CEO of AT&T.[51] Other
board members were similarly eager to assure the public, particularly potential donors, that the board was now in charge and that
Aramony's mess was being cleaned up.

But the mess was ultimately the board's responsibility. It was
a curious, if not entirely surprising, lapse by a string of board

members who were otherwise highly accomplished. They included the CEOs of Microsoft, Exxon, Johnson & Johnson, JC Penney, and Sears; the chairman of IBM; the presidents of several unions; and the commissioner of the National Football League.[52]

But in this particular drama most members of the UWA board were bit players. Much like the boards of many other organizations, the UWA board was populated by well-intentioned but overextended executives, lawyers, and financiers who had neither the time nor the inclination to exercise meaningful oversight. It was Aramony who was the protagonist, and board members, being otherwise engaged, were reduced to following his lead. Board meetings, which took place three or four times a year, were marked not by close attention to detail but rather "by good meals, a self-congratulatory sense of philanthropy, and a cursory review of the books and major issues."[53] As one critic put it, "Basically it was Aramony's board. He put it together for his buddies."[54]

Just as I have divided Aramony's most important followers into two groups—close aides who actively facilitated, and board members who passively tolerated his corruption—so did the law. Stephen Paulachak was sentenced to thirty months in prison and one year's probation on eight counts; and Thomas Merlo was given fifty-five months in prison and three years' probation on seventeen counts. Even though by law the members of UWA's board were ultimately responsible for the corruption that occurred on their watch, none of them was ever held to account.

The Web

Charitable organizations are different from other organizations. Although we have come to expect a certain amount of lying, cheating, and stealing in the private and public sectors, in the court of public opinion, the nonprofit sector, and especially charities, are held to a higher standard.

We expect leaders of charitable associations such as the United Way of America to be, at least in comparison with their corporate counterparts, altruistic in their professional lives, modest in their personal tastes, and generally decent. It can fairly be argued that to these organizations having a leader who has a first-class character is, or should be, as important as having a leader who is a first-class administrator.

The case of William Aramony is complicated in that for many years he was highly effective as both a leader and a manager. For at least the first decade of his tenure, he took the UWA exactly where it wanted to go. But after a long time in office he gradually changed. Increasingly he equated the organization with himself, believing that what was good for him was good for the UWA. During his last several years in office, helping himself became more important to Aramony than helping others.

Those who staff charitable organizations generally are presumed to be good and to do good, a presumption that complicates the task of oversight. Aramony, Paulachak, and Merlo could never have escaped detection without the presumption, held both by the board and by the public at large, that the United Way of America's leadership team was honorable as well as competent. For a long time, no one, inside or outside the organization, was willing, indeed able, to imagine wrongdoing at the top.

After many years in office, Aramony knew that he could count on board members to leave him alone. From where they sat, they had good reason to trust him. He had been in place since 1970 and had been in most ways effective. He was a skilled pitchman who was able to divert their attention away from management and toward the exciting philanthropic initiatives that had motivated them to become board members in the first place.

As to the protagonists themselves, we cannot know exactly what makes them corrupt. However, based on the cases of Cianci, Villanueva, Fastow, and Aramony, and given what we know about human nature, we can make three safe assumptions.

First, because the temptations are great, corrupt leaders are likely to be more prevalent and persistent than we know. For all the cases of lying, cheating, and stealing that come to light, countless others doubtless remain hidden from view, largely because we have neither the inclination nor the resources to fight corruption at every turn.

Second, corrupt leaders have corrupt followers—people such as Frank Corrente, Jose Chejin, Michael Kopper, and Thomas

Merlo—who for reasons of their own join in the wrongdoing. Corruption is often a collective activity from which more than one person usually stands to benefit. Although the most obvious rewards are the material ones, followers get other rewards as well, including proximity to power and membership in an in-group that is powerful in its own right.

Third, although corrupt leaders (and corrupt followers) are obviously risk-takers, consciously they're betting that their crimes will go undetected. Cianci, Villanueva, Fastow, and Aramony were not stupid or crazy. All of them apparently calculated that the likely rewards of their bad behavior outweighed the likely price.

Among the many bad habits to which humans are prone, greed is one of the more functional. From the time we lived as a "primal horde," it has stood us in good stead to accumulate for ourselves and for our progeny as much as we possibly can. So although the tasks associated with finding food and shelter are no longer primitive, the impulse to hunt and gather remains. In this sense corrupt leadership is a deeply human impulse; greed begets power and status, and power and status, in turn, beget greed.

The Benefit of Hindsight

For most of his professional life, William Aramony was presumed to be a man of integrity. There is no evidence that early in his tenure as CEO of the UWA he was anything else. But over time his moral compass was shattered. He changed, while the UWA's inclination to exercise oversight did not. Until the end, Aramony was left alone, free to operate more or less as he saw fit and free, therefore, to go bad.

Wrongdoing by officers and directors of charities is not as rare as we would like to believe. While the exact extent of corruption in similar nonprofit organizations is difficult to determine, Aramony was not alone in putting his hand in the till. During the years 1995–2002, some $177 million was stolen or diverted from charities—a large sum in the abstract, if rather modest in comparison with the $2 trillion in assets estimated to be held by American charitable organizations in total.[55]

What exactly happened to Aramony over the two decades he served as the head of the UWA will never be clear. From a distance it can be diagnosed simply as a moral breakdown in which the normal constraints against stealing from the sick and the poor were lost. The fact that Aramony went so far astray—he not only stole but used the money in part to support an extramarital relationship with a woman some forty years his junior—suggests that his capacity for impulse control was, at least at this point in his life, near zero. Put another way, it appears Aramony could have been stopped from wrongdoing only by outside interference.

This should have happened in two ways: through institutional controls or individual intervention. The UWA should have had policies and procedures in place that would have made conspiracy and fraud by a top officer virtually impossible. And one or more of those who were responsible for governance should have recognized the wrongdoing early on and intervened to bring it to a halt.

Similarly, no one was prepared to blow the whistle—either because they were afraid or because they were ignorant. Until the bad news became public knowledge, Aramony's leadership of the UWA was not openly challenged by anyone from within the organization, nor by the board that was charged with overseeing it. Members of his management team were apparently more loyal to Aramony than they were to the mission and purpose of the UWA. And members of the board were too busy and distracted, and too easily seduced by Aramony, to take as seriously as they should have their responsibility to what was arguably America's most venerable charitable association.

This is a case of corrupt leadership that is especially offensive. For the many hundreds of thousands who supported the UWA over the years it was a serious breach of trust. But, given human fallibility, and the sloppy management practices that had beset the UWA for too long, it comes as no surprise. Clearly institutional constraints and controls are indispensable—even in situations in which the road to wrongdoing is paved with good intentions.

CHAPTER NINE

INSULAR

BILL CLINTON

Insular Leadership—the leader and at least some followers minimize or disregard the health and welfare of "the other"—that is, those outside the group or organization for which they are directly responsible.

I NSULAR LEADERS ESTABLISH BOUNDARIES between themselves and their followers on the one side, and everyone else on the other. To insular leaders, human rights in general are less important than the rights, and even the needs and wants, of their specific constituencies.

To a degree this is simply human nature. My group—my family, my tribe, my country—competes with your group for scarce resources, and it comes first in every other way as well. Still, leaders could decide differently. They could decide to promote intergroup relations characterized by collaboration and cooperation rather than by competition and conflict. In today's small world the idea of what constitutes the common good is different from what it was before. It is more inclusive. No longer can we make a distinction between self-interest and the common interest.

The information revolution has made it impossible for leaders (and usually also for followers) to claim innocence on the grounds of ignorance. Leaders who do not know that bad things are happening to groups other than their own do not want to know. Of course, leaders who do know but choose not to act are equally culpable.

Brief Examples

Lee Raymond

In 1993, Lee Raymond, president of Exxon Corporation, the largest energy company in the United States, was named chairman and chief executive officer. He had helped the previous CEO navigate the company's worst environmental and public relations crisis: the 1989 *Exxon Valdez* oil spill off the coast of Alaska. Raymond had a reputation as a blunt cost-cutter and technician. In an age when business leaders mimicked political leaders in their focus on public relations, Raymond avoided attention and was impatient with questions he considered redundant or stupid. "I'm not interested in your views of how we ought to deal with the FTC," he told one reporter.[1]

As CEO Raymond is not loved, but he is widely respected. He presided over Exxon's purchase of Mobil, which made Exxon Mobil the world's largest corporation; and he was a notably aggressive executive—for example, in the areas of deepwater oil and gas exploration. To industry observers it was no surprise that under Raymond's leadership Exxon Mobil's profits are huge, as is his salary. In 2000 he took home close to $39 million.

But Raymond is not endowed with a strong social conscience. It is not that he is ignorant of the issues. Rather, he refuses to engage in them so as to demonstrate concern for anyone outside the world of Exxon Mobil.

For example, Lee Raymond was arguably the most outspoken oil industry executive against the effort to contain global warming. Lobbying against the multinational agreement reached in Kyoto (but not signed by the United States) to cut the emissions of greenhouse gases, Raymond said that costly restrictions were a bad idea, especially when "their need has yet to be proven, their total impact undefined, and when nations are not prepared to act in concert."[2] He also questioned the science behind global warming and declared that in part the greenhouse effect was triggered by natural sources.

A second example concerns repressive regimes. As *Forbes* put it, Lee Raymond is "unapologetic about making deals with regimes that lean toward the diabolical."[3] Under Raymond's leadership Exxon Mobil gave hundreds of millions of dollars to a corrupt regime in Angola, thereby helping to prolong the country's ruinous civil war. Under Raymond's leadership Exxon Mobil courted Chad, whose president promptly siphoned off millions to purchase arms for a war against northern rebels. Under Raymond's leadership, human rights activists charged Exxon Mobil with supporting a repressive regime in Indonesia. And under Raymond's leadership, Exxon Mobil wrought changes in the Russian tax law primarily for the benefit of Exxon Mobil.

To an extent, Raymond's way is the way of the oil business generally. Moreover, he could not have done what he did without the support of followers who were willing and eager to follow his lead. During a 2001 shareholder meeting in Dallas, a few dissidents staged a protest against company policies. But the large majority of those present sat quietly through the proceedings and then, at the end, when Raymond announced a two-for-one stock split and an extra two-cent per share dividend, "roared" their approval.[4]

But if protestors such as those in Dallas failed to score a short-term victory, they had at least a modest long-term impact. One year later, Robert Monks, a well-known shareholder activist, spearheaded a shareholder resolution aimed at reducing Raymond's duties as chairman and CEO. Monks sought to mitigate what he saw as the damaging effects—on the company, among others—of Raymond's view that global warming was not a problem. Monks's resolution got 20 percent of the vote, a number that was considered surprisingly strong.[5]

It's important to note that some of Raymond's peers took an approach quite different from his. In December 2001 five oil companies joined with human rights groups and agreed to examine and, if possible, to investigate any allegations of human rights abuses in their overseas operations. And Exxon Mobil's European rivals, companies such as the Royal Dutch/Shell Group, came out in support of the global warming principles that had been adopted in Kyoto.[6]

Raymond is in many ways an extraordinarily effective chief executive and a leading figure in the oil industry worldwide. In fact, in 2001 the board of Exxon Mobil extended his contract. But his refusal to confront at least two of the most urgent issues of the day—global warming and human rights—is indicative. His inability or unwillingness to see into the distance, to consider any interests, no matter how vital, other than those of Exxon Mobil, can reasonably be considered a moral flaw: promoting the interests of a very few at the expense of the very many.

Raymond once said, "Everyone at this company works for the general good—and I am the general of that general good."[7] Of course, he missed the point. What's good for Exxon Mobil is not necessarily the same as the general good. Thus, Raymond is typical of insular leaders: He actively looks out for his own well-being while willfully ignoring the well-being of others.

James W. Johnston

British researchers first published evidence of a link between cigarette smoking and lung cancer in 1952, more than half a century ago. Twelve years later, the surgeon general of the United States issued a landmark report that declared smoking to be a definite "health hazard." And nine years after that, Arizona became the first state to restrict smoking in some public buildings.

But even though the damning evidence continued to pile up, in 1994 top executives of the seven largest American tobacco companies appeared before Congress to testify that they did not believe cigarettes to be addictive. Although they admitted it was possible that cigarettes caused lung cancer and confessed to knowing about a twice-suppressed Philip Morris study that suggested animals could become addicted to nicotine, they continued to maintain that the evidence was inconclusive.

Of the seven presidents and CEOs, none was more staunch a defender of the tobacco industry than James W. Johnston, chief executive of R.J. Reynolds. A 1994 article in *Science News* describes how the battle lines were drawn between government officials on the one hand, and industry executives, Johnston in particular, on the other. Food and Drug Administration Commissioner David Kessler had earlier asked why cigarette manufacturers fortified low-tar brands with nicotine if not to create and sustain a nation of tobacco addicts. At a congressional hearing, Representative Henry Waxman, a California Democrat, followed Kessler's lead, warning the tobacco companies that times had changed and that relations between Congress and the tobacco companies were changing: "The old rules are out. The standards that apply to every other company are in."[8]

Johnston took on all comers. Serving as the most passionate defender of the industry with which he had come to identify, he set about trying to refute the charge that smoking was addictive. He contended that when the 1988 report of the Surgeon General called tobacco habit-forming, it merely "altered the definition [of addiction] to fit the existing data on smoking."[9] In essence, Johnston insisted, "the Surgeon General moved the goalposts after he located the ball on the field." Smoking, he went on, was "no more addictive than coffee, tea, or Twinkies." Finally, Johnston tried to stave off any intrusive legislation. He declared that "forcing manufacturers to produce products that smokers find unsatisfying and unacceptable," such as nicotine-free cigarettes, would be "backdoor prohibition." While otherwise a leader known to be nimble, on this one issue, Johnston was adamant.

But the heyday of the industry was over. After Jeffrey Wigand, who was vice president for research and development at Brown and Williamson, another leading tobacco company, blew the whistle on the TV news program *60 Minutes*, the position of industry executives such as Johnston became increasingly untenable. Wigand's testimony suggested that the lot of them had known for years that tobacco was addictive and that, being more interested in sales than science, they had knowingly continued to deceive the public. Wigand accused his ex-boss at Brown and Williamson, former CEO Thomas E. Sandefur Jr., of lying under oath to Congress about his views on nicotine addiction. Wigand further charged his former colleagues with hiding or altering evidence that might have a negative impact on the company's bottom line.[10]

Of the seven tobacco executives who testified at that 1994 Congressional hearing, Johnston was the last to quit the industry. It is impossible to know whether his decision to retire at the age of fifty had to do with the fact that he, along with his fellow executives, was being investigated for perjury. Johnston maintained that he wanted a break to spend time with his family while he was "still young enough to fully appreciate the experience."[11] But Cliff Douglas, an antitobacco lawyer, had another explanation. Referring to the hasty departures of cigarette company executives more generally, Douglas said that "the events of recent times involving multiple criminal investigations and litigation and regulatory attacks [had] taken [their] toll on the leaders of the tobacco industry."[12]

Bill Clinton: America First

The Prologue

The Tutsi constituted only about 15 percent of the total population of the African nation of Rwanda. But because they were more Western in appearance than the majority Hutu, they were favored by the colonial powers. The Belgians, in particular, considered the Tutsi more capable than the Hutu and therefore gave them better positions in the local hierarchy and a better shot at gaining an education. But beginning in about 1959, during the years of transition to independence, there was a shift: With the blessings of the Belgians, who had belatedly recognized the need for change, the Hutu seized power from the Tutsi. For the next few decades Rwanda managed to sustain an uneasy and precarious semblance of peace.

But in the early 1990s the situation became unstable, and by 1994 it had deteriorated to the point of war. In a little more than three months, the Hutu killed so many Tutsi that the calamity amounted to genocide.

When Rwanda began to unravel, the United States was inevitably drawn into the drama. On the one hand, there were pleas from Rwanda for the Americans, under the leadership of President Bill Clinton, to intervene to try to prevent a disaster in the making. But on the other hand, the United States was reluctant to become involved in any foreign conflict in which there was no clear and present danger to its own national security.

After the massacres began, the president's choices became stark. To intervene in some way would probably save many African lives, at the probable cost of some American ones. But for Bill Clinton to decide not to intervene at all was bound to end in wide-scale murder and mayhem.

The Context

The dead of Rwanda accumulated at nearly three times the rate of Jewish dead during the Holocaust. It was the most efficient mass killing since atomic bombs fell on Hiroshima and Nagasaki a half century earlier.[13]

The story unfolded primarily on two continents and in two countries: Africa and North America, Rwanda and the United States.

RWANDA

In 1962, after nearly a half century under Belgian control (before World War I Rwanda-Urundi was a German colony), Rwanda gained its independence. At about the same time, the transfer of power from the minority Tutsi to the Hutu majority began in earnest, and by the mid-1960s the transition was virtually complete. Although there was a semblance of national stability, relations between the two groups remained hostile. In retaliation for the insults that had been directed against them for so long, the Hutu systematically discriminated against the Tutsi, even subjecting them to occasional waves of killing and ethnic cleansing. In turn, Tutsi who had recently fled Rwanda kept returning and invading, hoping to regain their previous positions of power. However, between 1975 and 1990, the large-scale violence largely subsided.[14]

During the years after its transition to independence, Rwanda, a small, landlocked, east central African country about the size of Vermont, was one of the poorest in the world. Its population survived on subsistence farming, but land was extremely scarce, and thus per capita income extremely low. Rwandans were living in abject poverty and in a precarious political situation. In 1990 this fragile balance was upset. A rebel force comprising mainly Tutsi expatriates invaded northern Rwanda, and there they remained. By 1993 they had managed to make substantial inroads against the Hutu-dominated Rwandan armed forces.

Tensions between the Hutu and the Tutsi continued to increase in spite of some good faith attempts at conflict resolution. It was at this point that the United Nations became involved. Peacekeepers were sent to the area under the command of Romeo Dallaire, then a major general in the Canadian army. He was charged with overseeing the newly crafted Arusha accords, an agreement in which the Rwandan government committed itself to sharing power with both the Hutu opposition parties and the Tutsi minority. In addition to overseeing the peace process, UN forces were to patrol a cease-fire and provide a secure environment for exiled Tutsi to return home.

However, Hutu president Juvenal Habyarimana resisted the UN's efforts. The extremist wing of his Hutu clique viewed the Arusha accords as tantamount to surrender. The Tutsi, they feared, would "seize the spoils of rule and seek retribution."[15] At about the same time, about six months before the massacres began in earnest, there were already signs of an impending calamity. In late 1993 several thousand Rwandans were killed, and some nine thousand detained. Guns, grenades, and machetes began arriving in the region by the planeload. And two international commissions "warned explicitly of possible genocide." [16]

Just when it appeared as if Habyarimana might succumb to international pressure and implement the Arusha accords, his plane was shot down. This incident was the match that lit the fire: Large-scale violence started the next day, April 7, 1994. Radio stations urged the Hutu to take vengeance against the Tutsi for the alleged murder of their president, and the Hutu began to rob, rape, and murder the Tutsi.[17] (Later it came out that Habyarimana might well have been murdered by extremists from his own side. The debate over who did what to whom has not been settled.) But the majority of Hutu were poorly armed, and this first phase of the conflict was not deadly. Most Tutsi were able to flee from their homes and seek refuge in gathering places such as churches, schools, and hospitals. Within a few days, most of Rwanda's Tutsi had congregated at centralized sites scattered throughout the country.

At first, this concentration of people gave the Tutsi an advantage. The Hutu were armed mostly with swords, spears, and machetes or with their traditional weapons: large clubs studded with nails. But when better-armed Hutu reinforcements were brought in, equipped with rifles, grenades, and machine guns, the situation changed. Alan Kuperman writes, "They would typically toss a few grenades on the Tutsi and follow with light-arms fire. Survivors who attempted to flee were usually mowed down by gunfire or caught and killed by the surrounding mob. Militia-led Hutu would then enter the site, hacking to death those still alive. Some Tutsi escaped in the initial mayhem or avoided death by hiding beneath their dead compatriots, but many were later caught at roadblocks and killed on the spot, or taken to other central sites to face a similar ordeal." [18]

Perhaps the most striking aspect of the slaughter was its speed. An estimated eight hundred thousand Tutsi and Hutu sympathizers

were killed within one hundred days, almost a quarter million in
a little more than two weeks. Reporter Philip Gourevitch calculated that this was three hundred thirty-three and one-third murders per hour, or five and a half lives every minute.[19]

THE UNITED STATES

The calamity in Rwanda took place during the first half of President Bill Clinton's first term. Although the Clinton White House
was known initially for its youthful exuberance and hard work at
all hours, neither it nor the president distinguished himself in leadership and management.[20] Rather, the administration was an "adhocracy" that minimized reliance on systematic decision making,
depending instead on the president to micromanage. Debate and
dissent were discouraged, inconsistency was endemic, and critical
data were lost in translation—or merely lost.[21]

Like his administration more generally, the president was energetic, curious, and smart. But he was not a strong administrator.
Among his managerial deficits, Bill Clinton was easily distracted
and overly busy. Very little time was left to set priorities and focus
on what was most important.[22]

The situation in Rwanda unfolded not only in the context of the
first years of Clinton's first term but also in the context of American
foreign policy generally. In this regard, let me make four points.

First, unlike his predecessor, George H. W. Bush, during the
campaign Clinton had promoted himself as a domestic rather than
a foreign policy leader. The former governor of Arkansas had little experience in foreign affairs, and so his inclination, especially
early in his presidency, was to fend off rather than solicit engage-
ments far from home.

Second, in spite of his preferences and promises, by the time of
the tragedy in Rwanda, Clinton had already been beset by foreign
policy crises in Bosnia, Somalia, and Haiti.[23] None had been successfully resolved. The Balkans presented a chronic, increasingly
urgent set of problems, with no obvious immediate solution. The
Somalia crisis had ended on the streets of Mogadishu with the
tragic and humiliating loss of eighteen American lives, along with

seventy-three wounded. And for all the good intentions, there was as yet no clear evidence that the U.S. intervention in Haiti had yielded much of a result.

Third, the collapse of the Soviet Union, the fall of the Berlin wall, and the demise of what for nearly a half century had been considered the Communist threat were still new. The United States was only a few years into this brave new world; it had yet to reach even modest consensus on where it stood in relation to an international system only recently transformed.

Finally, Rwanda is in Africa. Unlike the European continent, the focus of U.S. concern since its founding, Africa was never uppermost on American minds nor at the top of any president's agenda. Africa was distant—the heart of darkness—and considered nearly irrelevant to America's military or economic interests.

It was against this background that the drama of Rwanda was played out. Although there is disagreement about which member of the Clinton administration should have known what when, I would venture the following.

- The quality of the information coming from Rwanda was poor.

- There was little likelihood that the information that did exist would reach the right people.

- The level of knowledge was equally low. For example, Secretary of State Warren Christopher knew little about Africa. During a meeting with his top advisers that took place shortly after Habyarimana's plane was shot down, Christopher pulled an atlas off the shelf to help him locate Rwanda.[24]

- The level of confusion was high. For example, American policymakers had difficulty distinguishing between civil war and mass murder.

- The administration's attitude toward peacekeeping missions in general was ambivalent at best. Neither Clinton nor any of his top foreign policy advisers were enthusiastic about peacekeeping efforts per se or about the United Nations, the organization generally charged with carrying them out. In October 1993 the United States had voted, reluctantly, to support Dallaire's mission, but it made clear that it would not send troops to Rwanda. Given what had happened in Somalia and Haiti, multinational initiatives for humanitarian purposes were now presumed likely to bring the United States no gain.[25]

Whatever the problems, little or nothing was done to address them. Neither the president nor any of his top foreign policy aides sought to improve the quality of the information coming from Rwanda; to make certain that any available information reached the right people; to educate themselves about the country and the region; to sort out what was happening on the ground; nor to analyze the possible differences between the situation in Rwanda, which led in the end to genocide, and other peacekeeping challenges.

The Leader

Even at an early age, Bill Clinton was ambitious. A high school teacher remembered that he "set his goals and *never* deviated from them." A friend from college recalls that Clinton exhibited "all the signs of someone who was on the way to somewhere else and in a hurry to get there."[26]

On one level, then, it is surprising that in foreign affairs Clinton was diffident and circumspect, especially during the first years of his first administration. After all, since the end of World War II no American president had been spared deep involvement in international politics. And because accomplishments abroad are often considered more significant than accomplishments at home, one might have expected Clinton's ambitions to extend to the idea of shaping the new post–Cold War world.

But in the early 1990s his interests and intentions were almost exclusively domestic. In fact, had it been possible, Clinton would likely have been content to stay clear of foreign entanglements altogether.

Because he had avoided service in the Vietnam war, the president was unable to claim exposure to or experience with the military. In addition, by largely limiting his public service to being governor of Arkansas, he had ensured that however long his list of political credentials, it was rooted at home rather than abroad. Journalist Elizabeth Drew claimed that Clinton's real problem was that he "had trouble defining [foreign] policy, even in a given case, and seemed not very interested in foreign policy. He seemed uncomfortable talking about it." It was revealing, Drew wrote, that, "unlike every president since Truman, Clinton had no regularly scheduled meetings with his foreign policy team."[27] Given Robert Kagan's observation that if you are the president of the United States, somehow foreign policy finds you, for Clinton to operate as a foreign policy ostrich was bound to cause trouble.[28]

In fairness, it must have come as a shock to the nation's forty-second president to find himself quickly and deeply immersed in international crises such as Bosnia, Somalia, and Haiti, none of which had been widely predicted. In any case, there is no question that as the massacres in Rwanda began to unfold, President Clinton was ill prepared—emotionally, experientially, and even intellectually—to respond. And so it was that "when a small country in the center of Africa imploded into genocidal conflict, the United States stood on the sidelines."[29] Put bluntly, neither Clinton nor virtually anyone else in his administration wanted to play a part in the tragedy.

Some of the evidence of Clinton's neglect of this calamity is circumstantial. Even Samantha Power's powerful book, *"A Problem from Hell": America and the Age of Genocide*, does not tell us exactly what the president knew and when he knew it.[30] It's easy to skirt the question of the president's personal responsibility because, as is often the case when foreign affairs are examined, the question becomes abstract. Thus Powers, who is as blunt and straightforward about these matters as anyone, asks not when or what President Clinton knew, but rather, "Just when did *Washington* [italics added] know of the sinister Hutu designs on Rwanda's Tutsi?"[31]

We can, however, piece together the following.

In December 1993 President Clinton met Rwandan human rights activist Monique Mujawamariya. Struck by her boldness and bravery, he singled her out for attention. "Your courage is an inspiration to all of us," he told her. Some four months later, on April 8, 1994—two days after Habyarimana's plane was shot down and after the massacres in Rwanda had begun—Mujawamariya was feared lost. Power writes that word of her disappearance got the president's attention, and he repeatedly inquired about her whereabouts. "I can't tell you how much time we spent trying to find Monique," an American official has since recalled. "Sometimes it felt as though she was the only Rwandan in danger." It turned out that Mujawamariya was safe. But after her rescue became known, "the president apparently lost his personal interest in events in Rwanda."[32]

Two other pieces of evidence confirm that Clinton knew about the massacres virtually as soon as they started. In his weekly radio address on April 9, he said he was "deeply concerned about the continuing violence."[33] And as soon as the mass killings began, on April 9 and 10, the U.S. ambassador and two hundred fifty other Americans were evacuated from the country. They were part of a larger convoy in which some four thousand persons were shipped out of Rwanda in only three days—the same three days during which twenty thousand Rwandans were killed. We can be sure that President Bill Clinton and First Lady Hillary Clinton were aware of this general circumstance because after the American evacuees were safely out and the U.S. embassy was closed, they visited the U.S. officials who had manned the emergency operations room at the State Department to offer their congratulations on a "job well done."[34]

It cannot therefore be said of the American president that he did not know. Quite the opposite. Clearly, Clinton did know that there were mass killings in Rwanda the day after they began. Small wonder Power writes, "It is shocking to note that during the entire three months of the genocide, Clinton never assembled his top policy advisers to discuss the killings."[35]

When he was asked about Rwanda, on at least one occasion Clinton was evasive. Rather than seize the moment to lead the American (and even the international) community, he used it to justify American passivity in the face of a humanitarian disaster. To the question, the president replied, "Lesson number one is, don't go into one of these things and say, as the U.S. said when we started in Somalia, 'Maybe we'll be done in a month because it's a humanitarian crisis.'... Because there are almost always political problems and sometime military conflicts, which bring about these crises."[36]

Toward the end, when the worst of the genocidal rampage was over, Clinton did make some token amends. He ordered Rwanda's embassy in Washington closed and its assets frozen. And in late July he requested from Congress $320 million in emergency relief funds (the Senate ended up authorizing only $170 million), dispatched four thousand troops to neighboring Zaire to aid Rwandan refugees, and sent two hundred U.S. troops to Rwanda's capital, Kigali, to secure emergency relief. But America's chief executive never wavered from the position he had taken at the start. On July 29, 1994, Clinton said, "Any deployment of United States troops inside Rwanda would be for the immediate and sole purpose of humanitarian relief, not for peacekeeping." Lest anyone doubt his determination to keep the United States out of the line of fire, he added, "Mission creep is not a problem here."[37]

Four years after the fact, in 1998, when he was traveling through Africa, Clinton visited Kigali to apologize for the failure to stop the genocide: "The international community, together with nations in Africa, ... did not act quickly enough after the killing began. ... We did not immediately call these crimes by their rightful name: genocide. It may seem strange to you here, especially the many of you who lost members of your family, but all over the world there were people like me sitting in offices, day after day after day, who did not fully appreciate the depth and the speed with which you were being engulfed by this unimaginable terror."[38]

But Clinton's apology received mixed reviews. Although some saw it as better than nothing, others thought it offensive. The late, great journalist Michael Kelly called Clinton's effort a "profound blasphemy." As Kelly saw it, Clinton lied when he said "people like me" did not "appreciate" what was happening. Kelly wrote, "The truth is that the president knew about the massacres as they were occurring, knew that first hundreds, then thousands, then tens of thousands, then hundreds of thousands of people were being killed. The truth is that the President was told that the massacres amounted to genocide and that the United States, under international law, was obligated to stop the genocide."[39]

The Followers

Three months before the massacres started, Romeo Dallaire sent a fax, later known as "the genocide fax," to UN peacekeeping headquarters in New York. The fax reported in "startling detail" the preparations then under way to carry out an extermination campaign.[40] This is not to claim that members of the Clinton administration had easy access to Dallaire's memo, but had they pursued the relevant information with any diligence, they would have discovered that more was available earlier than is widely appreciated.

In general, it can be said of Clinton's foreign policy team that on the matter of Rwanda, they played the soldiers to his commander in chief. As we would expect, they followed his implicit if not explicit lead and did their best to avoid involving the United States in "mission creep." As far as we now know, even in private none of Clinton's top foreign policy advisers took strong exception to the president's position.

Secretary of State Warren Christopher's extreme caution was perhaps most vividly demonstrated with regard to the question of whether the events in Rwanda could, or should, be called "genocide." Semantics mattered because, as Kelly suggested, if the massacres had been labeled genocide, the United States would have been obliged, under the terms of the 1948 genocide convention, to try to stop the atrocities. In addition, and this is a point Power makes, American officials "also believed, and rightly, that it

would harm U.S. credibility to name the crime and then do nothing to stop it."[41] And so Christopher, taking his cue from the president, opposed the use of the word, although his efforts to avoid
it were awkward and unconvincing. On May 24, one month after
Human Rights Watch called the killings genocide, Christopher
was willing to concede only that "acts of genocide" had occurred
or that "genocide has occurred in Rwanda." He was not willing,
in other words, to agree to any formulation that would indicate
that "all killings in Rwanda are genocide."[42]

National security adviser Anthony Lake also conformed to the
rule, which was simple: After the Americans were evacuated,
Rwanda largely dropped off the administration's radar screen.[43]
Unlike most of his government colleagues, Lake actually knew
something about Africa. Still, he recalls that during this period
he was "obsessed with Haiti and Bosnia," so Rwanda quickly
"became a sideshow, or, worse, a no-show."[44] Lake delegated
the matter of Rwanda almost entirely to one of his subordinates;
he confined himself to a single major public statement on the
matter, which simply called on Rwandan leaders to do what they
could to end the violence immediately.

Predictably, Defense Department officials were not disposed to
differ. Neither Secretary of Defense William Perry nor any of his
top aides were inclined to become involved in Rwanda, nor "even
to make financial sacrifices to stop the killing."[45] As to the military, in the absence of leadership from the White House, it followed what had been its natural impulse at least since Vietnam,
which was to avoid a war far from home and in every way uncertain. As Lieutenant General Wesley Clark put it later, "The Pentagon is always going to be the last to want to intervene. It is up to
the civilians to tell us they want to do something and we'll figure
it out."[46]

Madeleine Albright, then U.S. ambassador to the United Nations, was generally more of an interventionist than Christopher,
Lake, or Perry. Albright was more likely to favor the use of
American power even when the national interest was not obviously at stake; she argued for American intervention in the

Balkans and supported maintaining a meaningful United Nations presence in Rwanda. But there was stiff opposition from other high-ranking members of the administration, who continued to resist the idea of even a UN military presence in Rwanda because it would have involved at least some American troops. In the face of this, Albright remained a team player.[47] In late April, when the UN Security Council voted to slash the UN force in Rwanda to two hundred seventy, Madeleine Albright fell into line, commenting that a "small skeletal" operation would be left in Kigali to "show the will of the international community."[48] When she testified some weeks later before the House Foreign Affairs Committee, she said that it would have been "folly" for the UN to rush into the "maelstrom" in central Africa and that "we want to be confident that when we do turn to the U.N., the U.N. will be able to do the job."[49]

To be sure, a few members of the Clinton administration, most of them in the State Department, saw things differently. They wanted the United States to do more to stop the killings. But they were not positioned at the highest levels. For example, Prudence Bushnell, the principal deputy assistant secretary of state for African affairs, did her best to warn her superiors, including Christopher, that the death of Habyarimana was likely to produce widespread violence.[50] Moreover Bushnell, along with George Moose, her immediate superior and assistant secretary of state for African affairs, and Arlene Render, another bureau colleague, reportedly "argued fiercely" for a stronger mandate and an increase in UN troops, as well as for diplomatic measures to "isolate and stigmatize" the Rwandan government.[51] Moose and three other State Department officials also pressed Christopher publicly to use the word *genocide*.[52] But without support from anyone higher on the bureaucratic ladder, their cause was lost.

On the matter of Rwanda, even the opposition was content to follow Clinton's lead. Republican Senate minority leader Bob Dole, who at that moment was supporting American intervention in Bosnia, stayed out of the way on Rwanda. "I don't think we have any national interest there," Dole said on April 10. "The

Americans are out, and as far as I'm concerned, in Rwanda that ought to be the end of it."[53]

Of course, like Clinton, Dole was doing no more and no less than reflecting—that is, following—American public opinion. Those in Congress who cared enough to comment at all counseled the administration not to repeat in Rwanda the mistake of Somalia. After Somalia, Clinton had to fear a public backlash only if he sanctioned another African operation, but not if he did nothing.[54] Without leadership at the highest level, there would be no popular mandate anywhere in the world, certainly not in the United States, to stop the Hutu from massacring the Tutsi.

The Web

The humanitarian disaster in Rwanda raised, yet again, the following question: Which individual or institution is charged with, and equipped to, lead at the international level? Although Rwanda was in dire need of a humanitarian intervention, the president of the United States was not the only major world leader to beg off. No other head of state raised a major public outcry, nor even tried to forge a coalition that might effectively have intervened.

At least as striking was the ineffectiveness of the United Nations, in particular of Secretary-General Boutros Boutros-Ghali Broadly speaking, on the matter of Rwanda, Boutros-Ghali mirrored Clinton. In his case, as in the case of the American president, there are claims and counterclaims—for example, on the question of what Boutros-Ghali knew and when he knew it, and of what precisely his position was on this matter.

We know that the secretary-general did not cut short a tour of Europe to preside over the crisis. We know that he did not educate himself in any serious way about what was happening in Rwanda while the massacres were taking place. And we know that throughout the period he remained remarkably detached even though he claimed to be "a friend of Africa and an advocate for intervention" and even though the small peacekeeping force that remained in place was under UN command.[55] Moreover, Kofi

Annan, who at the time was in charge of UN peacekeeping efforts and who subsequently became Boutros-Ghali's successor, was no more effective in response to the genocide than was anyone else.[56]

The refusal—or, if you prefer, the inability—of UN officials to take the lead in trying first to prevent and then to stop the genocide in Rwanda confirms what we already know: that since the fall of the Berlin wall and the demise of the Soviet Union, it is the United States to whom the world turns for help. The United States is so overwhelmingly rich and powerful that it is expected to lend a hand whenever it is needed. This is the price America pays for being the world's only remaining superpower. This is the price everyone else pays for the lack of a viable alternative.

In fairness, Americans are damned if they do and damned if they don't. When the United States does intervene, it is considered intrusive. But when it refuses to become involved, especially when human lives are at stake, it is judged to be indifferent. Arguably, however, this puts more rather than less responsibility on Americans to do what is right in spite of the political pressure.

American presidents, then, end up between a rock and a hard place. What are the criteria by which they should decide when to intervene and when to hold back? Every time the commander in chief involves the American people in a foreign war, there is a cost. If troops are sent, as opposed to only money and materials, this cost is likely to include American lives. It is easy to understand why most presidents, not only Clinton, are inclined to hold back and not to intervene unless they conclude that intervention is in the overwhelming national interest. Still, it is impossible to read the story of Rwanda, of eight hundred thousand murders in only a few months, without thinking that there *must* be a better way. If the American president had been less worried about what might happen in his own backyard, might he have developed a more creative response?

We have seen that even the idea of becoming involved in Rwanda put off nearly everyone who was important in American politics: most Republicans as well as Democrats, most legislators as well as members of the executive branch, most military officers and civilian officials alike. In the wake of their recent history, especially in Somalia, the American people were not disposed to intervene in Africa again. The consequence of this widespread disinclination to get involved—to put at risk even one American life—was a lack of political pressure on President Clinton to do anything other than what he did, which was nearly nothing.

And so he led by not leading, by making clear both directly and indirectly, particularly through his secretary of state and national security adviser, that whatever the African body count, the Americans planned to sit this one out. The UN, and the international community more generally, would do little without U.S. backing, which was withheld. Given this, it is not too much to say that even if the political calculus of Clinton's position is understandable, it as much as sealed the fate of hundreds of thousands.

The Benefit of Hindsight

Responsibility for what happened in Rwanda is clearly not the president's alone. A range of other players—UN officials, other heads of state, most members of Congress, and most members of the Clinton administration—also abdicated responsibility. Moreover, globalization notwithstanding, the American body politic continues to send the same message it has sent from the start: America first.

But if the failure to prevent genocide in Rwanda seems nearly inevitable—the political, military, organizational, and psychological factors working against effective intervention were *that* potent—it was not foreordained. Strong leadership by the American president might have resulted in a different outcome.[57]

Insular leadership divides the led group from every other group. Consequently, as we saw with Lee Raymond and James Johnston as well as with Bill Clinton, a strong group cohesiveness develops that precludes challenging the leader's priorities. If anyone inside Exxon Mobil seriously questioned Raymond's position on global warming, there is no evidence of it. If anyone inside R.J. Reynolds seriously questioned Johnston's position on the question of whether cigarettes were addictive, there is no evidence of it. And, as we have seen in some detail, of 270 million Americans, only a handful took issue with the president's position on Rwanda.

For most of human history, it was possible to justify insular leadership. Leaders and their followers knew little about what was happening to groups other than their own, and the information they did have was often unreliable and late in coming. But things have changed. Raymond did know. Johnston did know. And Clinton did know. So did a number of their followers, who were part and parcel of the tacit, and at times explicit, understanding that "well enough" should be left alone.

The planet has shrunk, and so the rules of engagement must change. Just as we have some measure of responsibility for people other than members of our own family and for people other than members of our own group, so, too, do we have some measure of responsibility for people other than citizens of our own country. Standing by and doing nearly nothing while eight hundred thousand people are being slaughtered in three months' time is not acceptable—even when the killing fields are far from home.

CHAPTER TEN

EVIL

RADOVAN KARADZIC

Evil Leadership—The leader and at least some followers commit atrocities. They use pain as an instrument of power. The harm done to men, women, and children is severe rather than slight. The harm can be physical, psychological, or both.

W E ARE FAMILIAR with the idea that evil is a political force to be reckoned with. Only a few decades ago, Ronald Reagan described the Soviet Union as an "evil empire." And even more recently George W. Bush labeled Osama bin Laden an "evildoer," and later went on to identify an "axis of evil"—Iraq, Iran, and North Korea. As far as Bush was concerned, America's mission was clear: to root out evil at the individual level (bin Laden, Saddam Hussein), and at the collective one (the regime in Iraq).

It is frightening to think that really bad people can be, even for a moment, all-powerful. So is the notion that evil is, in Hannah

Arendt's memorable, if controversial, term, "banal." But evil, like everything else, is relative. Ron Rosenbaum, who is an authority on Hitler, distinguishes among degrees of evil leadership by looking at two variables: consciousness of the crime and scale of the crime. The first raises a qualitative question: Was bin Laden convinced of his own rectitude when he committed mass murder? And the second raises a quantitative question: How many were murdered? It assumes that there is difference between, say, Hitler's six million and bin Laden's three thousand—and that the former is worse than the latter.[1]

Debates about moral relativism are important and interesting, but when leaders are evil, it is understanding the followers that presents the greatest challenge.[2] How can we make sense of those who tolerate, enable, and even actively support leaders who are widely viewed as wicked? How does it happen that evil leaders hold sway, in some cases for many years? Why are they not more often done in, literally, by their own constituents, who are often the victims? Or by others, outsiders, who are outraged by what they see? (I presume for the purpose of this discussion that to see evil and do nothing is to be a follower.)

The answers to such questions differ, depending on the circumstances. Nevertheless we can make two important assumptions. First, when leaders commit atrocities and still stay in power for years on end, their followers are anesthetized, inflamed, or terrorized—or they are in some way rewarded. Second, when leaders are evil, at least some followers are also evil.

Brief Examples

Saddam Hussein

In recent years the most vilified national leader, at least in the United States, has been Saddam Hussein.[3] As documented in Kenneth Pollack's influential book *The Threatening Storm*, Hussein was a despot in the image of Stalin, whom he revered.[4] Hussein was guilty of murder and torture; of genocide and ethnic cleansing; of using chemical weapons, even on his own people; and of refusing for years to allow inspections for weapons of mass destruction, despite the costs to Iraqis, which ranged from a long and costly international embargo to war.[5]

It is the sadism of leaders such as Hussein that is the most unsettling. Under his rule, Iraq had a gulag of prisons, dungeons, and torture chambers. It had overlapping secret police agencies and a culture of betrayal. So-called enemies of the state were eliminated, and their spouses, adult children, and even cousins were often tortured and killed along with them. John F. Burns, a correspondent for the *New York Times* in Iraq, pointed out that even before the war that toppled Hussein, this terror was self-compounding, "with the state's power reinforced by stories that relatives of the victims pale to tell—of fingernail-extracting, eye-gouging, genital shocking and bucket-drowning. Secret police rape prisoners' wives and daughters to force confessions and denunciations. There are assassinations, in Iraq and abroad, and, ultimately, the gallows, the firing squads and the pistol shots to the head."[6]

To be sure, this story, like most such stories, is not simple. Just as the Americans were wartime allies of Josef Stalin, only to acknowledge years later that all along he was an evil tyrant, so there was a time, not long ago, when the United States was friendly to the Baathist regime of Saddam Hussein. In the 1980s, during the Iran-Iraq war, the United States supported the Iraqi secularists against the Iranian fundamentalists; the Americans ditched Hussein only when he invaded Kuwait. Even then, President George H. W. Bush chose not to have U.S. troops march into Baghdad, a decision that left Hussein in control of Iraq.

Exactly why the second president Bush decided to topple the dictator whom the first president Bush decided to let stay will be the subject of debate for many years. But there is no doubt that the man who ruled Iraq for more than two decades committed atrocities that are nearly beyond our capacity to comprehend.

Pol Pot

The bloody excesses of Hitler, Stalin, and Saddam Hussein are by now well known and thoroughly documented. But even in the recent past, there have been other, less familiar figures who are equally malicious and murderous.

Pol Pot was the Cambodian leader who in the 1970s used the Khmer Rouge army to effect the most radical Communist revolution in history.[7] To this end, and in his name, crimes were committed that included repression, slavery, torture, starvation, execution, and, ultimately, genocide.[8]

Under Pol Pot, violent deaths were more common than deaths by natural causes. Although he was in control for only three years, he and his black-clad followers conducted a rule of terror that led to the deaths of more than 1.7 million people—one-third of Cambodia's population.

Pol Pot was elusive, a shadowy figure with a smiling face and a quiet manner, whose trajectory to tyranny remains something of a mystery.[9] As a young man he was described as sensitive and timid, a teacher loved by his students and a great admirer of French poetry. Even much later he cut an elegant figure, with an attractive appearance and good manners. But in his role as national leader, Pol Pot was something else entirely: a man apparently afflicted by deep-seated, extreme paranoia that, in turn, had calamitous consequences.

In 1960 Pol Pot helped found Cambodia's own Communist Party, and within two years he became its leader. For most of the next decade he lived in hiding, but he was able to assemble an army that grew from three thousand men in 1970 to seventy thousand by the time of its triumphant entry into Phnom Penh in 1975. But his success neither mollified nor satisfied him. Pol Pot's fear of treachery continued to motivate much of his behavior, and by the end he held the kind of absolute power that Stalin had in the Soviet Union. As Cambodia was being destroyed and his regime was collapsing—the end came when Vietnamese troops invaded Cambodia and overthrew its leader—Pol Pot became even more brutal. Suspected enemies were arrested in every corner, including old friends and former comrades-in-arms. Nor were such prisoners exempt from what had become a ghastly routine: Pol Pot personally sanctioned their torture, ignored their pleas for mercy, and finally had them killed.

How murderous leaders like Pol Pot get others to follow them remains a puzzle that only in-depth analyses of individual cases can begin to solve. But one fact applies nearly across the board: Evil leaders typically acquire their most loyal followers early on, before the onset of the murder and mayhem. Pol Pot could not have killed old friends without having made friends in the first place. Similarly, in his younger days, Saddam Hussein was seen as articulate and open-minded, a good enough chap who "seemed to enjoy engaging in genuine give-and-take discussions with others [and who] took many significant steps to improve the quality of life for the Iraqi people."[10]

Jim Jones and David Koresh

Some evil leaders do their dirty work without formal authority and on a rather small scale. Jim Jones and David Koresh were both petty dictators—"petty" in the sense that their domains were small. Still, they were totalitarian rulers who caused or at least strongly contributed to the deaths of nearly all of their most loyal followers.

Anthony Storr, who studied both men, describes them as "gurus." Although ostensibly their message was not political but religious, nevertheless Jones and Koresh were tyrants. Like their overtly political counterparts, they thrived on adulation, ended up with no real intimates, attempted to exert total control, and were inclined to paranoia.[11]

Jones and Koresh were remarkably similar. As boys, both were isolated and had few friends. Both became eloquent, fluent preachers who battered their audiences into submission with a constant torrent of words. Both were unscrupulous sexually— Jim Jones with both sexes, David Koresh with children as well as with adults. Both inflicted vicious punishments on followers they judged guilty of breaking their arbitrary rules. And both did all they could to prevent their followers from leaving the group by "undermining family ties, by threatening dire punishments, and by posting armed guards who were as much concerned with keeping people in as with protecting the enclosures from intruders, although very few disciples wanted to leave."[12]

Like Saddam and Pol Pot, Jones and Koresh were sadists, using cruel and inhuman punishments as instruments of control. Jones generally disciplined in public, on the stage of his church. A three-foot-long paddle was used for beatings; some lasted a half hour. Children who had soiled their pants had to wear them on their heads, and they were forbidden to eat. Other punitive measures included confinement in crates too small to permit standing, and shocks administered by a machine called "Big Foot."

Koresh punished with equal severity and depravity. He taught that children as young as eight months old should be hit if they misbehaved, and he warned mothers that they would burn in hell if they failed to oblige. He immersed offenders of all ages in sewage and then forbade them to bathe. Like Pol Pot, Koresh used starvation as a means of control, and on arbitrary occasions he woke his followers in the middle of the night to listen to his protracted ramblings on the Bible, some of which would last fifteen hours. Moreover Koresh routinely slept with girls as young as twelve and thirteen, even those who were still slight and immature.[13]

Storr tells us that on November 18, 1978, "over nine hundred people, including two hundred and sixty children, drank or were injected with cyanide in Jonestown, Guyana. This self-annihilation of the members of the People's Temple was ordered by [Jones], who himself died of a gunshot wound to the head." While the circumstances under which eighty-six people, including twenty-two children, perished in the flames of the Ranch Apocalypse, Waco, Texas, on April 19, 1993, are more controversial, Koresh, who died on that day of a gunshot wound to the head, in any case bore major responsibility for the calamity.[14]

Again, it strains credulity that either of these quasi-religious leaders could have retained the allegiance of his followers for so long. Indeed, when the mothers of small children had a chance to escape with their offspring from Ranch Apocalypse, none chose to do so. Koresh's followers, like those of Jim Jones, were "true believers." They believed in and were utterly devoted to their leaders. But at the same time they were so terrorized that rational choice became impossible.

The scale of these crimes seems to us to make a difference: Being responsible for eighty-six deaths, or even nine hundred, is intuitively different from being responsible for six million or even three thousand. But the dynamic is the same. In all cases of evil leadership the leader inflicts or threatens to inflict pain; and in all cases of evil leadership the purpose of the pain is first to get and then to maintain total power and complete control.

Radovan Karadzic: "No Longer the Person I Had Once Known"

The Prologue

On November 14, 1995, Richard J. Goldstone, prosecutor of the international criminal tribunal for the former Yugoslavia, presented to the tribunal an indictment against Radovan Karadzic and his top general, Ratko Mladic. It charged both men with "genocide, crimes against humanity, and violations of the laws or customs of war."[15]

In 1992, Karadzic, a poet and psychiatrist who had morphed into the "Most Wanted Man in the World," became the first president of the Bosnian Serb administration. In this capacity he had formal, constitutional responsibility for commanding the Bosnian Serb army and for appointing, promoting, and discharging its officers. In addition, Karadzic was authorized to supervise the Bosnian Serb territory and to issue orders to mobilize the police in the case of war, immediate threat, or other emergencies. In short, he was ultimately responsible for upholding the law and maintaining order.

Karadzic failed utterly to uphold his constitutional responsibilities. Moreover, he permitted, indeed encouraged, the widespread rape, pillage, and murder of Bosnian Muslims. Thus Goldstone charged that Karadzic was "individually responsible" for these crimes and also "criminally responsible as a commander for the acts of his subordinates."

Under Karadzic's leadership the Bosnian Serbs became perhaps most notorious for their crimes against women, but Karadzic was an equal opportunity perpetrator of evil. The atrocities committed under his jurisdiction and command left no group unharmed.

The Context

"Once upon a time," wrote Timothy Garton Ash in 1999, "there was a country called Yugoslavia." Ash described a republic that although still rather new—it was established only in 1918—worked quite well. This medium-sized nation, situated in southeast Europe, was inhabited by twenty-five million people of different religions, ethnicities, and nationalities, all of whom coexisted in relative peace. Held together by a powerful "king called Tito," Yugoslavia was not rich, but its children thought of themselves as Yugoslavs, and it was, as Ash noted, at least "a country."[16]

In the last decade of the twentieth century Yugoslavia came asunder. Between one hundred fifty thousand and two hundred fifty thousand men, women, and children died in the process. As Ash recalled it, they died "with their eyes gouged out or their throats cut with rusty knives, women after deliberate ethnic rape, men with their own severed genitalia stuffed into their mouths. . . . In this former country, the grotesque spectacle of a whole village burned, looted, and trashed [became] an entirely normal sight. . . . The killing, burning, plundering and expelling went on throughout the summer of 1998, even as West Europeans took their holidays just a few miles away."

Yugoslavia had a problem from the start. On the one hand, Serbs thought their centuries-old dream had finally come true; Yugoslavia, they imagined, would be Greater Serbia, a single state under their control. But on the other hand, those who were not Serbs had a different conception. They thought that in Yugoslavia the different groups were all supposed to be equal, none more powerful than any of the others.

Under charismatic strongman Josip Broz Tito, who took power in 1945 and held it until his death in 1980, it was this second conception that prevailed. Yugoslavia evolved into a communist federation of six republics and two provinces. Each of them was autonomous and corresponded roughly to the religious and ethnic groups who lived there.

But what Tito put together, only Tito could hold together. As soon as he was gone, Yugoslavia began to break apart.

During the late 1980s changes at home and abroad threatened the fragile state. Yugoslavia went into a severe economic decline, and communism collapsed. By 1991, two of the six Yugoslav republics—Slovenia and Croatia—had already declared their independence, and Slobodan Milosevic, president of Serbia since 1987, was fanning the flames of the old concept of Greater Serbia. Serbian nationalists blamed the weak economy on the fragmentation of power; they insisted that Serbs were oppressed in republics in which they were not a majority and claimed that Yugoslavia had denied them their special place in Balkan history.

Milosevic aggressively encouraged and exploited the growing xenophobia. Between 1988 and 1990 he organized antigovernment rallies throughout Yugoslavia in which hundreds of thousands of Serbian nationalists participated.[17] Warren Zimmerman, the last U.S. ambassador to Yugoslavia, witnessed the gathering storm. Although he considered the Serbs talented and ebullient, in his view they also had a "tragic defect": They were obsessed with their own history.[18]

More than anything else, it was this zealous Serbian nationalism that was responsible for the Balkan bloodbath. In a state as tenuous and complicated as Yugoslavia, with different religious, ethnic, and national minorities dispersed throughout, the late-twentieth-century idea that one group, the Serbs, had a right to dominate the rest was bound to meet strong resistance.

Bosnia was the most diverse of the Yugoslav republics, and that made it particularly vulnerable to Serbia's growing appetite. No group of Bosnians had a majority. Forty-four percent were Muslims, thirty-three percent were Serbs, and about eighteen percent were Croats. The Serbs were mainly in the north, far from Serbia, and the Muslims were mainly in the east, near Serbia. Thus, during the forty-five years of Tito's regime, and indeed for centuries before, the various Bosnian groups had lived together more or less in peace. In Sarajevo, people from one group did business with people from other groups, and almost everyone participated in the lives of those from different ethnic, religious, and national backgrounds.

Throughout the 1980s most Bosnians continued to support a unified Yugoslavia on the condition that it maintain its existing political balance. But when Slovenia and Croatia declared their independence, this precarious balance was immediately imperiled. So even though Bosnian Serbs were content to stay in a Yugoslavia that would be dominated by Serbia, Bosnian Muslims and Bosnian Croats were not.[19]

By 1990 positions had hardened. The Serbian Democratic Party (SDS), led by Radovan Karadzic, was fiercely opposed to the declaration of Bosnia as an independent state. In fact, Bosnia's Serbs, who occupied 70 percent of Bosnia's land, were now determined at all costs to stake what they considered their historic claim to all of Bosnia.[20]

In 1991 Bosnia's legitimately elected president, Alija Izetbegovic, scurried through Europe and the United States hoping to gain their active support and thereby avert Serbia's grab for Bosnia. Zimmerman recalled that during the first months of 1992, events in Bosnia careered down two parallel tracks. On the one, the Izetbegovic government was preparing for independence; on the other, Bosnian Serbs, under the leadership of Karadzic, were preparing for secession and war.

During this period Zimmerman met with Karadzic several times. He described Karadzic as "a large man with flamboyant hair, an outwardly friendly manner, and in the unlikely profession of psychiatry." Zimmerman was struck by Karadzic's stubbornness, by his "deep-seated hostility to Muslims, Croats, and any other non-Serb ethnic group in his neighborhood." As Karadzic put it to Zimmerman, "Serbs have a right to territory not only where they're now living but also where they're buried, since the earth they lie in was taken unjustly from them."[21]

All along, Karadzic and Milosevic were partners in crime. With Milosevic's enthusiastic support, Karadzic declared three autonomous Bosnian Serb regions; secured arms from the Yugoslav army; established artillery positions around Sarajevo; created a Bosnian Serb military force; established a Bosnian parliament; attempted a putsch in March 1992; and finally declared a "Serbian Republic."

In April 1992, the United States and the other NATO countries made a last-ditch effort to avoid war: They recognized Bosnia as an independent state. But it was too little too late. By then Serbs were already attacking towns with large Muslim majorities, and the atrocities had begun. Even early in the conflict, Serbian marauders were crossing into Bosnia to rape and murder Muslim villagers.[22]

A few weeks before he was recalled as American ambassador in protest against the Serbian aggression, Zimmerman had a final meeting with Karadzic. He found Karadzic determined to secure a separation of Serbs from Muslims so strict that Sarajevo, perhaps the most diverse of all European cities, would be "like Berlin when the wall was still standing." Karadzic tried to explain: "You have to understand Serbs, Mr. Zimmerman. They have been betrayed for centuries. Today they cannot live with other nations. They must have their own separate existence. They are a warrior race and they can trust only themselves to take by force what is their due."[23]

The Leader

Radovan Karadzic was born in Montenegro in June 1945. A friend recalls the Karadzic family as "poor and primitive," having "a village mentality." But Radovan grew into a tall, wild-haired adolescent with a broad, sad face who was exceptionally clever. At the age of fifteen, he was sent to Sarajevo to finish his schooling.[24]

From his late twenties to his early forties, Karadzic lived the life of a European cosmopolitan. He resided primarily in Sarajevo and Belgrade, received his degree in medicine, married a medical school classmate, and learned English. He went on to study psychiatry in New York, where he became a specialist in depression, eventually returning to Yugoslavia to become a practicing psychiatrist.

Karadzic was also a poet. In fact, he was a well-known member of Sarajevo's cultural elite, eventually publishing four volumes of poetry. Tellingly, all of them have recurring themes of exile, destruction, death, and return to a forsaken homeland.

> I hear misfortune walking
> Vacant entourages passing through the city
> Units of armed white poplars
> Marching through the skies.
> (1970)[25]

Like Pol Pot and Saddam Hussein, during his early adulthood Karadzic showed no strong signs of his later paranoia and malevolence. Although some of his contemporaries recall bad behavior of various sorts, others remember a "peace-loving and good-natured fellow," extroverted and convivial. Reported one acquaintance, "It wasn't easy to detect bitterness. . . . The hatred so evident in his early poetry just slipped by."[26]

Whatever his underlying character, during his twenties and thirties Karadzic behaved in ways that were unethical as well as illegal. He was reputed to have been an informer for the Communist government during its crackdown on loyalty; he earned extra income by selling fraudulent medical certificates to those seeking to avoid military service; and by the time he turned forty he had been sentenced to three years in prison and fined for embezzlement and fraud. (He served eleven months.)

As if to signal his split personality—poet and psychiatrist on the one hand, informer and embezzler on the other—in 1990 Karadzic underwent a dramatic transformation: He entered politics. He founded the Green Party, which was like Green parties in the rest of Europe. It stood for peace and not war, protection rather than desecration of the environment, and other policies generally considered left-wing. Not surprisingly, it was not a good fit. Karadzic soon quit to join the newly formed Serbian Democratic Party, which was committed to the strong support of Slobodan Milosevic.

However difficult it is to explain Karadzic's metamorphosis during this period—from bohemian psychiatrist to rabid politician—it seems to have been fundamental. Although he had practiced psychiatry for years, in jobs ranging from consultant to the Red Star soccer team in Belgrade to staff physician in the psychiatric clinic at Sarajevo's Kosovo Hospital, he now left medicine forever to enter politics. An acquaintance recalled, "His expression turned wild and he was no longer the person I had once known. His unassuming look evaporated, like the soul leaving the body of a dead man."[27] Nearly overnight Karadzic had become a political figure of major consequence—the leader of the increasingly inflamed Bosnian Serbs.

In his new incarnation Karadzic was a fanatic, an extreme partisan whose public behavior was bellicose and increasingly malignant. In October 1991 he delivered a speech to Parliament in which he openly threatened Bosnian Muslims. And in April 1992, in direct opposition to President Izetbegovic, he proclaimed an independent Serbian Republic and declared Sarajevo the capital and himself head of state.

In his new role Karadzic further stoked the fears of Bosnian Serbs, particularly in rural areas, where the growing resentment against Sarajevo's urbanites fed into long-standing grievances against local Muslims. By recklessly predicting that if Izetbegovic were to head an independent state, Serbs would soon be living under a fundamentalist Muslim regime, Karadzic gained tighter control over the growing number of his anxious and bellicose followers.

The establishment of Bosnia as an independent state does not explain the carnage that became the Bosnian War. But it did provide former Yugoslav army units, Serb militias, and Karadzic himself with an excuse to start a war and to initiate ethnic cleansing.[28] Zimmerman has observed that it was during this period that even in Karadzic's casual conversations, he repeatedly used words such as "war," "genocide," and "hell."[29]

Although Karadzic predicted that Serb forces would triumph within six days, one month into the fighting it was clear the war would not end soon. General Ratko Mladic was appointed commander of the Bosnian Serb Army (BSA), a telling choice. Mladic was ruthlessly committed to ethnic cleansing, to ridding large swaths of Bosnia of all its Muslim men, women, and children. Widely considered "sadistic and extremely dangerous," Mladic had an extreme hatred for Muslims.[30]

In short order Karadzic's army began to pound Sarajevo with heavy artillery; it also set up detention camps and gained control of nearly 70 percent of Bosnia's territory. By the summer of 1992, most of Bosnia was aflame, with Karadzic himself in the thick of it.[31] He traveled often to the front, meeting with troops. He would recite to them blood-curdling passages from ancient epics, all the while assuring them that the war would lead not only to victory but also to redemption.

Fueled now by nationalist passions, Serb fighters demolished mosques, forced hundreds of thousands of Muslims from their homes, and killed or injured tens of thousands of others. By every account Karadzic unleashed the worst humanitarian crisis in Europe since the Second World War.

The war in Bosnia was reminiscent of the war in Rwanda in that it was motivated mainly by ethnic hatred, by the fierce determination to destroy the "other" that typifies the genocidal mind. Serbs felt about the Muslims among them in the same way that the Hutu felt about the Tutsi among them or, for that matter, how the Nazis had felt about the Jews among them: They had to be exterminated. The term "ethnic cleansing" is reminiscent of the German word *judenrein*, which literally meant clearing, cleansing, or ridding Germany of all its Jews, by whatever means necessary.

Under Karadzic ethnic cleansing became unofficial Serb policy. This was not an impetuous response to the recent war, even though spontaneous outbreaks of irrational violence were common. Unlike what happened in Rwanda, this was the implementation of a strategy that was carefully conceived and planned well in advance. Its basic objective was to establish Bosnian apartheid: the complete separation of Serbs from Muslims, with Serbs in permanent control of most of Bosnia's land.

Ethnic cleansing unfolded as follows.

> Non-Serbs were isolated, forced to wear white armbands and subjected to abuse and attacks by local Serbs, who were given to understand they could prey on their neighbors with impunity. Over six thousand Non-Serbs incarcerated in the Omarska concentration camp experienced beatings, hunger and killings. Most woman and children were expelled, but some were interned in the Trnopolje camp, where rape and other abuses were common. The Serbs singled out Moslem Community leaders . . . for special attention. Mosques and Catholic Churches were destroyed to eliminate the physical traces of non-Serb culture, and over 47,000 homes belonging to non-Serbs were [also] destroyed. By June 1993, the total number of those killed or expelled in the Prijedor area reached 52,811. Virtually all of the Moslems and over half of the Croats who had lived in Prijedor were gone.[32]

Radovan Karadzic was ultimately responsible for all crimes committed against Bosnian Muslims by his regime. Two deserve to be singled out.

The first is rape. By August 1992 reports of rape of Muslim girls and women were so widespread that analysts began to suspect it was systematic Serb policy. Only months after the war began, large numbers of female Muslims in northern Bosnia were claiming to have been sexually attacked by Serbian forces.[33] There was evidence of a striking increase in abortions performed at six major hospitals serving largely Muslim populations. At one clinic in Sarajevo, the number of abortions more than doubled in late 1992, even though during this period the total number of patient visits declined by half.[34]

In January 1993 Amnesty International went public with the problem. Although the human rights organization stopped short of accusing Serbian leaders of using rape as a weapon of war, it declared that Bosnian women had suffered "horrifying violations—rape and sexual abuse—at the hands of the [Serbian] armed forces." It further charged that the assaults, considered a war crime under the Geneva Convention, had "been carried out in an organized and systematic way, with the deliberate detention of women for the purpose of rape and sexual abuse." Similarly, a separate investigation carried out under the auspices of the European Community found that incidents of organized rape "fit into the wider pattern of warfare, involving intimidation and abuses against Muslims and Croats."[35]

By 1995 the systematic sexual abuse by Bosnian Serbs against Muslims was well documented. Although some rapes were opportunistic, most were the result of an organized campaign of terror. Witnesses reported that the Luka camp, near the town of Banja Luka, had specific "rape rooms" and that in the Viktor Bubanj Yugoslav Army barracks near Sarajevo, rooms were divided for oral and vaginal sex attacks. Camp commanders, local police, military officials, civilians, and even local politicians were all said either to have participated in the assaults or to have been aware of them.[36]

The second crime of which Karadzic is guilty is murder in Sarajevo and Srebrenica. Sarajevo was a model of European cosmopolitanism, as well as Karadzic's long-time domicile. Still it became his favorite target—literally. For nearly two years his troops shelled the city. They destroyed the National Library and methodically reduced to ruin many of the city's other cultural treasures. They cut off electricity and water, forcing Sarajevans to chop down every tree in every park in search of wood. And from the hills that surrounded Sarajevo and the burned-out high-rise buildings that lined "sniper's alley," they shot to death twelve thousand men, women, and children.[37]

Whereas Sarajevo was the focus of Serb attention for many months, Srebrenica was dispatched more hastily. It was one of six Bosnian towns that had been designated by the United Nations as a safe area. But because neither the UN nor NATO saw fit to secure it, the Bosnian Serb army was allowed on the afternoon of July 10, 1995, to storm Srebrenica, where more than forty thousand Muslims had sought refuge. General Mladic ordered his men to execute every captured male, whether soldier or civilian. In all, more than seven thousand unarmed boys and men were killed.[38] It was Europe's greatest modern massacre.

Radovan Karadzic has denied responsibility for any and all crimes committed in association with the Bosnian war, including Srebrenica. In a 1997 interview with a Dutch journalist he insisted, "Ethnic cleansing was not a political target. War crimes were prohibited from the beginning, strictly prohibited. And I repeated that order many times." When asked point-blank whether he felt any responsibility for what happened, he replied, "Absolutely not. I repeat: The military authorities and the civil authorities did not condone any war crimes." With regard to Srebrenica in particular, Karadzic claimed that although Mladic did not provide him with a daily report of what was happening on the battlefield, no crimes could possibly have been committed under his command. "Mladic is a very strict man," Karadzic maintained. "I am sure that he would personally ruin a solder who was guilty of murder or rape. He . . . would never have allowed it."[39]

Proving beyond doubt the guilt of a man such as Karadzic is not easy. First, the responsibility for what happened is shared; alongside Karadzic were Milosevic and Mladic. And second, there is no smoking gun, no evidence that proves conclusively that Karadzic personally raped a Muslim woman or shot a Muslim man, or even that he gave direct orders to violate international codes such as the Geneva Conventions. But, as Eric Osterberg, prosecutor at the war crimes tribunal, stated in court, "It would be justified to say that the higher up the chain of command we go, the higher the degree of responsibility for the atrocities, which were ultimately executed by the common soldier on the ground."[40] This logic explains why the international court opened a special hearing against Karadzic and Mladic in 1996 and charged them with genocide, crimes against humanity, and the massacres in Srebrenica.

Obviously, the case would not be in court without good evidence, at least according to the standard that makes it a crime not only to commit or plan atrocities but also to fail to stop them and to refuse to punish those who carry them out. American intelligence agencies have electronic intercepts and satellite images of Serbian-run concentration camps dating back to 1991. The intercepts include conversations between Milosevic and Karadzic, as well as direct commands from Karadzic to generals in the field that clearly demonstrate his command and control role over the military. In addition Karadzic himself volunteered that so far as Srebrenica was concerned, "I gave my approval for the immediate task directly to the general staff."[41]

Finally, because Karadzic was a well-known figure, especially around Sarajevo, there were many who could testify personally to his cruelty. One example: "His utter and complete disdain for the lives of the people of Sarajevo was shown when he, like a proud father showing his son a new toy, invited the poet, Limonov, to fire a high-powered sniper weapon into the besieged city, and Limonov did so."[42]

From a psychological perspective, it is important to reiterate that those who had known Karadzic for many years were dumbfounded by his rapid and complete transformation from psychiatrist and poet to politician and leader. Said one old acquaintance, "It was strange to everyone, when he all of a sudden . . . had become head of the SDS."[43] Said another, a doctor who was Karadzic's superior in a Sarajevo hospital clinic, "It is impossible to understand him. . . . When he became leader of the political party, he changed his mind, he changed everything and went up the hills and with heavy artillery destroyed the town, destroyed this clinic, killed the people with whom he lived for more than twenty years."[44]

We are likely never to know how it happens that a healer is suddenly transformed into a leader who sanctions and even encourages atrocities. Robert Jay Lifton has written that Nazi doctors were able to do the work of Auschwitz by dividing themselves into two functioning wholes—the prior self and the Auschwitz self—and Karadzic has been described more than once as detached from reality. A journalist who interviewed Karadzic wrote that he "had mastered the fine art of constructing and delivering with great sincerity utterances that seemed so distant from demonstrable reality that he left no common ground on which to contradict him."[45] And a former associate recalled that when Karadzic was the psychologist of the Red Star soccer team he claimed he could make it the best in the world. "The point is that Karadzic really believed that. We all thought he was crazy, but he thought it was real. . . . He erected a wall between himself and the truth and he never dared to look at what is behind that wall. . . . He will die behind that wall believing he is a great man."[46] This is not to suggest that delusion, even self-delusion, is a necessary trait of those who commit crimes against humanity. Rather, it is to make clear that the forces of evil are not only political in their origins but also psychological.

The Followers

At the most fundamental level the followers of Radovan Karadzic were long-frustrated Bosnian Serbs now consumed by fear and loathing of the other—Bosnia's Muslims. As one American member of the Bosnia peacekeeping force put it, "When people are fighting for what they think are their lives, their culture, their traditions, yes, they will support that kind [Karadzic's] of leadership."[47] In any case it is clear that Karadzic's large physical presence, his capacity to evoke old hurts and stoke new fears, his credentials as an educated man, and his nationalist zeal all tapped into the Bosnian Serbs' desperate desire to secure their future by reclaiming their past. Karadzic did what every effective leader does: He united his followers in a common purpose.

But how can we answer more precisely the questions posed earlier in this chapter? How can we understand those who for more than four years tolerated, enabled, or actively supported Karadzic, a man who is now, and was then, considered by most people other than Bosnian Serbs to be evil? Why was he not in some way removed from office, either by his own constituents, convinced he was wicked, or by some individual, group, or organization on the outside, outraged by atrocities he sanctioned and even encouraged?

As indicated in chapter 2, to better understand those who follow evil leaders, and to better understand how leaders get followers to accept or even commit acts that testify to man's inhumanity to man, it helps to divide them into groups. In this case they are bystanders, egoists, and evildoers.

Bystanders present a difficult moral dilemma: How exactly should we judge them? They are not involved in the political process and, by definition, do nothing bad. But they are aware that evil is being perpetrated, and they do nothing to stop it. Arguably, more than anything else, it is the passivity of bystanders that enables evil to continue. Along with other followers, bystanders let evil leaders get away with murder.

Egoists follow evil leaders for their own benefit. For example, after Karadzic was in power, his party, the SDS, protected its supporters and provided them with favors, such as jobs or apartments. Thus many of Karadzic's followers followed because of a simple combination of fear on the one hand, and the promise of personal gain on the other.

Those in the West who chose not to intervene even after the atrocities became apparent also fall into this category. They were egoists who calculated that to them the likely costs of intervention would be greater than the benefits. For example, NATO stood by while Srebrenica was overrun, as did the United Nations, which had Dutch peacekeepers based in the endangered "safe area" pleading for help. As one British journalist later summarized this syndrome in The Hague, "I don't think that the Tribunal can begin to compensate for the hideous neutral compliance of the international community in the [Bosnian] violence. I find it grotesque that the diplomatic community was shaking the hand of Dr. Radovan Karadzic underneath the chandeliers of London and Geneva and New York while it was going on and while everybody knew it was going on."[48]

Evildoers were those among Karadzic's followers who actively supported his regime, including its policy of ethnic cleansing. They were the foot soldiers, sometimes literally. They did the heavy lifting.

Evildoers included individuals, groups, organizations, and institutions that went out of their way to facilitate Karadzic's work. Some argue that the Serbian Orthodox Church belongs in this category. After the collapse of communism, the church became politically involved; it strongly supported Bosnian Serb nationalism. To be sure, the church was not monolithic; nor was its position during this time (roughly 1990–1995) consistent or even clear. On the one hand, the church condemned the war and its attendant persecutions and atrocities. But on the other hand, it supported Karadzic well after the atrocities committed under his regime became an open secret. During an important meeting of the bishops' council in August 1994, the church reaffirmed its faith in Karadzic, declaring, "Just peace is the only lasting peace, while unjust peace is the source of all further suffering and renewed conflict."[49]

The evildoers most tightly held in Karadzic's grip were, of course, those who fought in the trenches, those directly tasked with carrying out his bloody orders. Drazen Erdemovic, an ethnic Croat who fought in the Bosnian Serb army, is typical. Convicted by the Yugoslav war crimes tribunal for his part in the massacre of Muslims at Srebrenica, Erdemovic, who looked no older than a teenager as he described for the court how his victims were killed, broke down in tears when he told how his Bosnian Serb commanders had given him no choice but to kill or be killed himself. "Your honor, I had to do this," Erdemovic said to the presiding judge. "If I had refused, I would have been killed together with the victims."[50]

Finally, it should be noted that although most evil leaders—for example, Hitler—have acolytes, who are deeply committed not only to their program but also to them personally, Karadzic to all appearances did not. He had close associates, General Mladic among them, who were willing to execute even his most radical and malignant orders, but there is no evidence that he had even a small circle of acolytes to whom he was closely bound.

The explanation for this deviation from the norm is simple. Most national leaders take a long time, years, to get to the top. Karadzic did not. The fact that nearly overnight he shed his old life as a psychiatrist and assumed a new one as a politician is the main reason he generally lacked acolytes as well as intimates.

Rob Siebelink, a Dutch journalist, secured a rare interview with Radovan Karadzic in 1997. He found him at home, in Pale, Bosnia, where he lived in an ordinary house, among other ordinary houses. Karadzic greeted Siebelink at the front door, his hair uncombed, wearing slippers and a vest. The man charged by the prosecutor of the international criminal tribunal with genocide, crimes against humanity, and violations of the laws or customs of war sat for nearly all of the five-hour interview with his three-month-old grandson, Nebosja, sound asleep on his big belly.[51]

The Web

I have argued that it is impossible to understand bad leadership without understanding bad followership and the context within which both operate. Nowhere does this dictum matter more than in the case of evil leadership. By definition, evil leadership entails the use of pain as an instrument of power. This brings special urgency to the task of better understanding the complex web in which this kind of inhumanity is ensnared.

By July 1995, when he and General Mladic were indicted for crimes against humanity, Radovan Karadzic had already become a pariah. One year later, Milosevic and Bosnian Serb leaders cut him loose. Karadzic was forced to resign as president of the SDS and to retreat from public life. In spite of rumors that he had fled to Russia, Greece, or Chechnya, Karadzic remained in Bosnia, in his house like other houses, supported not only by close relatives but also by a band of true believers who for years had followed his lead. In fact, the man, by then named Bosnia's most wanted criminal, not only "remained popular among Bosnia's suffering and impoverished Serbs but indeed became a legend."[52]

The fact that Karadzic continued to have a following even after his cause was lost, and even after he no longer had any power, is itself revealing. Even though he had been leader of the Bosnian Serbs for no more than about five or six years, so completely had he tapped into their fear and loathing that even after he was stripped of all authority he remained for many a hero.

It is impossible, by looking to Karadzic alone, to understand the beatings, the rapes, the hunger, the torture, and the killing that constituted the genocide and other crimes with which he was charged. We tend to take the easy way out. We tend to blame one man, one evil leader, for evil leadership. But if the story of Radovan Karadzic teaches anything, it teaches that evil leadership depends absolutely on some followers who are willing for whatever reasons to do the dirty work, and on other followers who are willing for whatever reasons not to intervene. In this critical sense evil leadership is a collective enterprise in which "the willing executioners" arguably play as important a role as the leader.[53]

Equally significant is the circumstance in which cruelty and even sadism are considered acceptable tactics. In the name of a cause that might be religious or political, or for the purpose of expunging the other, or in the interest of exercising greater control, it can become routine to inflict torture. The point is that this does not happen in a vacuum. The soil is previously prepared, made fertile for atrocity. The startling rapidity with which Karadzic assumed power, and the absolute degree to which he was able to exercise it for some five years, confirms that the time and the place were ripe. Bosnian Serbs were, in effect, waiting for Karadzic to lead them to a "Greater Serbia." They were waiting for him to make their dream come true long before he stood before them.

The word *evil* does not appear in the Old Testament until the second chapter of Genesis, when God plants in Eden the "tree of knowledge of good and evil," from which Adam and Eve eventually eat. Here begins the idea that evil entered the world of human experience through knowledge and freedom.[54] Here begins the idea that each of us is responsible for what we do.

In fact, the idea that we are all free to be evil is now a matter of law; it is in keeping with international jurisprudence since the Nuremberg trials. For more than fifty years we have rejected the principle that states are accountable for what they do but individuals are not. Soldiers who commit war crimes are now held responsible for their actions, no matter their intent or the orders they received. Similarly, their superiors, often passionless, dutiful bureaucrats of death, are accountable for war crimes committed by subordinates if they knew or should have known what was happening and made no effort to stop it.

It can reasonably be argued, then, that although Radovan Karadzic was guilty of crimes against humanity, so were the others who followed his lead, even if all they did was to do nothing. In this drama there was, in addition to Karadzic, an impressive cast that included Milosevic and Mladic, as well as bit players and extras who played lesser roles but were also part of the action. In addition, there were important characters off stage, such as those with decision-making responsibility at the United Nations, as well as the heads of the various NATO countries who, by refusing to intervene, contributed to the calamity.

In the end we return to Radovan Karadzic as the face of ethnic cleansing, atrocities committed primarily by Bosnian Serbs against Bosnian Muslims. The thousands of other players notwithstanding, it is, as we have seen, in our nature to look to the leader, in this case to the evil leader, for the most persuasive and powerful single explanation for what happened. The passion and skill with which Karadzic led the Bosnian Serbs was in any case one of the main reasons the war came to pass as it did.

Karadzic never did see his crusade in terms of good and evil. "The matter of morality belongs to literature. This is history," he was quoted as saying.[55] Moreover, from everything we know about Karadzic, whatever the legal judgment against him, he will remain persuaded that he is innocent. He will remain persuaded that the Serbs called on him to do a job and he just did it.

For the time being, the point remains moot. Nearly a decade after Richard J. Goldstone indicted Radovan Karadzic, he is still hiding—in plain sight. It is known that he is "shuffling about within a corridor of rugged terrain" in eastern Bosnia, but he continues for reasons not well understood to elude French and German NATO peacekeepers who are monitoring the area, and he continues for reasons rather better understood to be protected by an underground network of politicians, police, gangsters, peasants, and priests from the militant wing of the Serbian Orthodox Church.[56] So even though the West is morally as well as legally duty-bound to capture him, it has yet to happen. If this is not testimony to collective culpability, I do not know what is.

The Benefit of Hindsight

For all its complexities and extremes, this is a case of bad leadership that in hindsight is easy enough to understand. The lead actors were caught up in ancient rivalries freshly fueled by the death of Tito and the demise of European communism. And although what happened in Srebrenica was Europe's greatest mass murder in a half century, killing Muslims did not lead to public outrage, neither in the United States nor even in Europe. This freed top policymakers in all the NATO countries, and also in the United Nations, to intervene in the Balkans only after the deed was done.

In earlier chapters I write about what the leader might have done, and what the followers might have done, to stop or at least slow bad leadership. Evil leadership is a different matter. The idea of suggesting how Saddam Hussein, Pol Pot, and Radovan Karadzic might have changed their evil ways seems, on the face of it, ludicrous. Put another way, to suggest how a leader labeled a "malignant narcissist" might become benign is to suggest how a toad might become a prince. It's not going to happen, and so we turn to the followers.

There will always be leaders who have it in them to brutalize and even to kill for their own bad purpose. The only way—the *only* way—such leaders can be stopped or at least slowed is by followers who are willing to take them on.

In the Karadzic case the followers fell into three groups: bystanders, egoists, and evildoers. Earlier in this book I describe how

Hitler's followers also were different, one from the other; for example, he had followers who were acolytes. At the least, what we know now is this: For evil leadership to be realized, some followers must be willing to do nothing (bystanders), and other followers must be willing to do the dirty work (evildoers).

If the case of Radovan Karadzic does nothing else, it shines a cold light on the role of bystanders, those who were at a distance (policymakers in NATO and the United Nations) as well as those who were nearby. Clearly, to stand by and do nothing while evil is being perpetrated is to be complicit.

Arguably, the onus on bystanders is greater than on other kinds of followers. They have strength, at least potential strength, in numbers. And, unlike egoists, acolytes, and, especially, evildoers, all of whom have somehow already been co-opted or compelled, bystanders, by definition, are apart from the murder and mayhem. And so it is they who must intervene. To see no evil and hear no evil is to be certain that evil will be done.

PART THREE

FROM BAD TO BETTER

*All that is necessary for the triumph
of evil is that good men do nothing.*

—Edmund Burke (attributed)

CHAPTER ELEVEN

COSTS AND BENEFITS

A T THE BEGINNING of chapter 1 I wrote, "This book is about the dark side of the human condition. It is about leadership in shades of gray—and black." Now, all these pages later, we know much more about bad leadership than we did before, but still we gaze into the distance—not because bad leadership remains unfamiliar, but because it remains elusive. For all that's been learned, the heart of darkness remains remote.

Still, looking at bad leadership is important, and it is instructive. There is the text, which describes an aspect of the human condition. And there is the subtext, which implies the need for change in ways we've resisted since Eve led Adam to take a bite of the apple.

Throughout this book I make two main arguments. First, I claim that placing bad leadership along two different axes—ineffective and unethical—clarifies how the word *bad* is being used. Ideal leaders and followers are, at the same time, effective and ethical. But as we have seen, it's possible for leaders, and followers, to be simultaneously effective and unethical. Think of Buddy Cianci, who, although corrupt, nevertheless transformed Providence, Rhode Island, from a provincial backwater into one of New England's prettiest and liveliest cities. And it's also possible for leaders, and followers, to be simultaneously ethical and ineffective. Think of Robert Haas, who, although ethical, nevertheless failed adequately to consider the future of Levi Strauss within the context of the changing global marketplace. In other words, effective behavior and ethical behavior are not joined; nor is the distinction between them always crisp.[1]

Second, I claim that breaking the whole of bad leadership into seven types—incompetent, rigid, intemperate, callous, corrupt, insular, and evil—has, to echo Max Weber, "certain advantages which should not be minimized." To detect patterns of bad leadership is to make it easier to know and to render them.

By now it's clear that as it is used here, the word *type* does not signify personality type. People are too erratic and complex to be so pigeonholed. Rather, *type* refers to a pattern of leader and follower behavior that is sustained over time, that has a bad effect, and that is of consequence. In other words, in each of the seven long stories, the following apply:

- Short-term damage was done.
- Long-term damage was done.
- The damages were high.

Over time Juan Antonio Samaranch became incompetent, but his followers saw fit to leave him be, and so he bequeathed to the Olympic movement problems that persist to this day. Mary Meeker's rigid behavior also went unchecked, and that cost a lot of people a lot of money. As mayor of Washington, D.C., Marion Barry behaved in intemperate ways that were tolerated by family, friends, political associates, and local constituents, and this tolerance left him free to run down the nation's capital. The callousness with which Al Dunlap and his team led Sunbeam brought grief to thousands and finally ruined the company. William Aramony and some of his close aides turned out to be corrupt, and so the name of one of America's most venerable charities was sullied.

Bill Clinton and his top foreign policy advisers took a pass on genocide. And Radovan Karadzic morphed into an evil leader who, along with his henchmen, was responsible for the torture and murder of men, women, and children who in a previous life had been neighbors.

I harbor no illusions: To type human behavior is to invite argument. Still, it is precisely when the making of meaning is so difficult that typologies are especially useful. They constitute a tool with which to cut through the thicket.

Before turning to the question of how we can apply what has been learned, as I do in chapter 12, there are three areas on which I want to comment: costs, benefits, and ties that bind.

Costs

I argue from the start that to look at leadership through rose-colored glasses is a mistake for many reasons, not least because we tend to learn more from our failures than from our successes. So I welcome the still small but probably growing literature that focuses on bad, as opposed to good, leadership. As Sidney Finkel-stein wrote in a recent book on why smart executives fail, "[W]riting about 'worst practices' rather than the usual custom of best practices, and writing about failure rather than success, breaks the mold of most books on business."[2]

In fact, my own interest in bad leadership has been long-standing.[3] But now, prompted by publicity surrounding a series of spectacular corporate failures beginning with Enron in 2001, and further fueled by stark evidence of bad leadership in places previously thought inviolable, such as the Roman Catholic Church, I am joined by others who are turning to look at the dark side.

The study of bad leadership has been scant in part because the costs are difficult to calibrate. Exactly how much pain and suffering does bad leadership of different kinds inflict?

To be sure, sometimes the calculus is easy. Along with their followers, Stalin and Hitler were responsible for the deaths, respectively, of some twenty million Soviets and some six million Jews.

And, as *New York Times* writer Tina Rosenberg has observed, the costs of corruption are also now known, and "they are stunning." For example, Mexico's anticorruption czar claims that graft costs his country 9.5 percent of its gross domestic product (GDP). The Mexican experience further indicates that when the level of corruption is high, government spending is distorted. Countries known for having a culture of corruption spend less on health and education and more on public works, which are chosen for their "kickback potential." Moreover, corruption in one place can have a corrosive effect in others. Rosenberg notes that when the Bank of Credit and Commerce International went down in 1991, forty thousand depositors in Bangladesh lost their life savings.[4]

But if figures like these are helpful, the overall costs of bad leadership are impossible to calculate precisely. In addition to the pain and suffering of those directly victimized by bad leadership, there is the pain and suffering of those who are indirectly victimized, especially family and friends. How high was the total toll of the massacre at Srebrenica? Clearly, the costs were far greater than the actual body count—seven thousand boys and men.

Bad leadership incurs costs not only at the level of the individual but also at the level of the group. Samaranch and his cronies tarnished the entire Olympic movement and bestowed on the national Olympic committees worldwide a legacy of mismanagement and corruption. Meeker and her compatriots left a lot of people a lot poorer and damaged the reputation of Wall Street for years to come. With a little help from his friends, Barry did himself in, but he also "steered Washington into an abyss," leaving the city with deteriorating schools and public services, a shrinking tax base, and a culture in which drugs flowed freely and the murder rate soared. Dunlap and his fellow managers handed out pink slips by the tens of thousands, and they also brought down Sunbeam itself. With his cronies and board in tow, Aramony damaged one of America's best-known and most venerable charities, the United Way of America; and Clinton and his followers stood by and did almost nothing during the genocide in Rwanda. Finally, along with followers including bystanders, egoists, and evildoers, Karadzic not only abused the human rights of individual men, women, and children, but he also harmed national, ethnic, and religious groups, including Serbs, Croats, Bosnians, Christians, and Muslims.

The result of all this—of so much damage and such high costs—is that bad leadership has a ripple effect and also a lingering impact. Think of it as having multigenerational consequences. Bad leadership is not an evanescent phenomenon. It does not come and then go. It has a legacy that endures and is pernicious.

Benefits

Every story in this book tells about particular people in a particular place at a particular moment in time. Can we extrapolate from the specifics to arrive at more general conclusions about bad leadership? Can we develop types, even archetypes, based on a handful of cases? Or is the devil always in the details?

I pose these questions not merely as an intellectual exercise. They are important for several reasons, not the least of which is that they get at the mystery of why the study of leadership has been so meager. Although the impact of leadership, good and bad, is impossible to overestimate, as a field of inquiry leadership has been, until recently, only at the margins of the academy.

As far as bad leadership is concerned, the medical parallel again is useful. Medical researchers study disease in order to cure disease. Pathologists, virologists, and oncologists who decode cancer want to stop cancer or at least to slow its progression. The question that then arises, or should arise, is why there is no psychosocial analog. Why have there been highly concerted, generously funded, and well-publicized efforts to fight cancer, heart disease, and AIDS but *no* similar efforts to fight bad leadership, whose effects can be equally catastrophic? As far as I am concerned, our failure to develop psychosocial equivalents to medical cures constitutes a startling gap in the history of human achievement.

This neglect is a symptom of anxiety—performance anxiety. Twentieth- and early twenty-first-century scholars who might have chosen to study the role of human agency in human affairs have been intimidated. Knowing that the study of leadership is not easily amenable to the demands of rigor and reliability that are the established criteria of the modern social sciences, and knowing that they are more likely to be professionally punished than rewarded for intellectual idiosyncrasy, academicians have stayed away in droves. In other words, considering its obvious impact on the course of human affairs, even now leadership remains curiously undervalued and understudied.

The question then becomes how we can approach leadership in a way that is intellectually defensible but resists the pressure to make precise something that never can be precise. Clifford Geertz, whose seminal work was in cultural anthropology, faced exactly this problem. His task was first to interpret, and then to convey, phenomena so complex and abstruse that they resisted easy categorization or communication.[5] As Geertz recalled it, he had to figure out how to cut "the culture concept down to size" (as I had to figure out how to cut bad leadership down to size). He described what it was like to look at different structures and systems, which were superimposed on or knotted into one another, and that were "at once strange, irregular, and inexplicit." First he decoded and deciphered what he found. And then he painted a picture for others to see what he did. He did this through "thick description," a canvas of words that portrayed for the benefit of others the cultures to which he had been witness.[6]

Again, my task was much the same. First, I decoded and deciphered the various leadership structures and systems, and then I described what I saw. The device on which I settled was to follow three storylines: the context, the leader, and the followers. By providing a reasonably thick description of each, I outlined bad leadership in general and the seven types in particular.

Geertz provides another analog: that of the scholar who on the one hand is cautious about making assumptions but on the other hand does not shy from extrapolating from the evidence. Like Geertz, I do not claim a "science that does not exist." Analyzing

lea alyzing culture: It is "guessing at meanings, as-
se and drawing explanatory conclusions from
t At the same time each story about leadership
ut culture: It has strong elements of coher-
Human nature is human nature, and that
at certain patterns of bad leadership repeat
erns include the importance of followers to
ns among followers, ranging from those
der to those who are remote and detached;
l leaders and bad followers to get trapped
have spun.

ne level every act of bad leadership is sui
; but on another level every act of bad
y other act of bad leadership. This is
arge issues." This is why the particulars
are described in this book have some-
dership more generally.

careful in drawing parallels; we must be
t history repeats itself. In fact, Geertz cau-
a remote locality as the world in a teacup."
argues, as do I, that this kind of work—the
study of leadership—will not be done unless
nce with some situations to extrapolate to oth-
underestimate the methodological problem pre-
scopic nature of ethnography. But he argues that
ay by the realization that social actions are com-
han themselves: "Where an interpretation comes
etermine where it can be impelled to go."[8]

students of leadership have not looked to anthro-
scipline that is especially well suited to their labors.
ship scholars properly, and justifiably, insist that
is a multidisciplinary enterprise. But the parallels be-
k on culture and work on leadership are striking. Con-
synergy a gift from which those of us with an interest in
p can benefit.

- Leadership is a dynamic, or a system if you prefe[r], though complicated and convoluted, has a certai[n] coherence.

- Patterns repeat themselves, and this means, amon[g] things, that the types of bad leadership are not in[f] number.

- Patterns repeat themselves, and this means, amon[g] things, that bad leadership will be replayed accord[ing] seven scenarios, with which by now we are familia[r].

Ties That Bind

Leaders and followers literally cocreate, coconstitute, le[ad] This finding is not new; as I noted earlier, the presump[t] followers matter is now widely shared. But students of le[adership] still tend to focus on leaders and shortchange followers.

As this book testifies, it's past time for this to change. time for students of leadership to resist the dominant mo[de] leader-centered model—and embrace a more holistic one. should be looked at *only* in tandem with their followers.

Without followers nothing happens, including bad lea[der] Together, leaders and followers can bring out the best in pe[ople] in, say, the civil rights movement; or they can amplify what' in people and leave murder and mayhem in their wake. Ob[viously] this finding has moral implications. Leaders and follower[s] responsibility for leadership, bad as well as good. Finger-poi[nting] "He did it!"—will no longer wash. None of us is off the hoo[k]

Juan Antonio Samaranch would never have been in a posi[tion] let corruption flourish had he not been supported, nearly [c]and nearly at every turn, by members of the International Ol[ympic] Committee. The national Olympic committees and city o[f] worldwide were eager to pay for the privilege of bidding f[or] games and equally eager to profit from Samaranch's inatte[ntion] Nor did those closest to him warn him that he was getting sl[ack] and no one blew the whistle. Finally, the public at large was also complacent, content to watch the Olympic ideal be shunted aside while big money took over.

Mary Meeker's most obvious followers were fund managers and individual investors for whom greed became a stronger motivator than fear. Ignoring the lessons of history, not wanting to miss out on the possibility of making a killing, and unrealistic in their assumptions about money and markets, they encouraged Meeker to stay relentlessly bullish. Her colleagues covered for her when she made a mistake; and, until the party was obviously over, the media continued to fawn over her and what they seemed to presume was her preternatural fiscal acumen. In other words, until the stocks themselves corrected, Meeker did not. Why should she? She was queen of the Net, with subjects who were loyal to the end and prepared to prop her up past her prime.

In good part because of America's history of racism, Marion Barry was able, in spite of his outrageous public performance, to keep his followers in tow. It can be argued that all of Barry's followers were enablers: They enabled him to stay on as mayor when, even for his own sake, they should have sent him a different message. Barry's time in office lasted as long as it did, first, because voters were willing to continue to elect him to public office; second, because close associates were willing to continue to do his real work as well as his dirty work; and third, because family and friends were willing to continue to cover his tracks.

William Aramony could not have stolen from the United Way of America without the help of a couple of cronies who were in on the deal. In fact, it was bad followers such as Stephen Paulachak and Thomas Merlo who made it possible for Aramony to be a bad leader. Aramony also benefited from a remarkably compliant board, which, without taking much time or trouble, approved of virtually everything he did. No hard questions were asked; the board of the United Way of America was content to follow where Aramony led.

The dynamic that characterized Al Dunlap's tenure as CEO of Sunbeam was rather similar. His most immediate advisers, and his board, were as compliant and complicit as were Aramony's. Although the reasons for the two groups' willingness to go along were more dissimilar than similar, the result was the same: Both leaders were left free to operate without checks and balances, and both were therefore encouraged rather than corrected in the error of their ways. Moreover Dunlap's bad leadership was further sustained by employee followers who felt powerless to stave off the chainsaw directed at them, and by a financial community too heavily invested, literally, in Sunbeam's success. Like the other bad leaders, Dunlap could never have done what he did without the support, however defined and expressed, of large cadres of followers.

Bill Clinton's approach to the calamity in Rwanda was avoidance. Moreover, nearly every high-ranking member of his foreign policy team turned a similarly blind eye. They, along with the president whom they were supposed to serve as independent advisers, were responsible for making Rwanda a "sideshow or, worse, a no-show." Similarly, most members of Congress, of both parties, and most of the American people, were content to go along with Clinton, who in this case took a path entirely uncontroversial. On the matter of America's policy in Rwanda—which was to do nearly nothing, in spite of the genocidal outcome—Clinton's constituents went quietly along.

Finally, there was Radovan Karadzic. As far as we know, he did not rape or in any other way torture anyone. Nor, as far as we know, did he murder a single man, woman, or child. So we can leave it at this: Without followers, Karadzic would not have been, could not have been, a leader charged with crimes against humanity.

Jason Epstein offers a perfect conclusion: "History does not repeat itself, but human nature is constant."[9] The particular dramas I have related, these small facts, will not be replayed. But the dynamic that underlies them, the exchange between leaders and followers that *is* leadership, will never be different. As far as bad leadership is concerned, this raises the question, what is to be done?

CHAPTER TWELVE

COMMENTS AND CORRECTIONS

H OW CAN the benefit of hindsight be converted into foresight? How can we get from bad leadership to better leadership? These are haunting and difficult questions, to which there are no easy answers. Still, there are lessons to be learned from these stories of bad leadership, and these lessons have broad implications. In this last chapter I pull together the earlier threads and offer some thoughts on how bad leadership can be stopped, or at least slowed.

Leaders

There is this: It is more likely now than it was in the past that bad leaders—leaders who are ineffective, unethical, or both—will be held to account. Although the evidence for this is only beginning to accumulate, it suggests that things are changing.

- Evil leaders and evil followers are more likely now to face charges in national or international tribunals than they were even a couple of decades ago. Slobodan Milosevic and others charged with crimes against humanity in the Balkans are being tried in The Hague. In December 2003, in Tanzania, an international court convicted three media executives for fanning the flames of genocide in Rwanda in 1994. Two were sentenced to life in prison. In Rotterdam, Sebastien Nzapli is being prosecuted in a groundbreaking trial in a Dutch court on charges of torture and rape in the Congo, in violation of the 1984 United Nations Convention Against Torture. And in Iraq, Saddam Hussein awaits his day in court, his trial being the first ever of a world-class mass murderer. (The number of potential counts against Hussein exceeds a half million.[1])

- Corrupt leaders and their followers are also being held to account, at least in some of the most egregious and well-publicized cases. For example, as we have seen, Andrew Fastow pleaded guilty to two felonies, becoming the highest-ranking officer (as of this writing) at Enron to admit to crimes that contributed to the company's collapse; and four executives from HealthSouth were found guilty of fraud in a $2.7 billion accounting scam.

- Around the world, corporate leaders are being pushed out in record numbers. In 2002, nearly one hundred CEOs of the world's two thousand five hundred largest companies were replaced—almost four times the number in 1995.[2] It's clear that boards are finally judging CEO performance more strictly, and that the rest of the world is moving toward U.S.–style "deliver-or-depart" leadership, especially Europe and Japan.[3]

- The hugely unpopular Democratic governor of California, Gray Davis, was subjected to a recall vote only one year into his second four-year term. And in Nevada, the Republican governor, Kenny Guinn, also faced a nascent recall movement, although he was not forced from office. Recall movements such as these suggest not only a mutation of politics as usual, but also imply a decreasing level of tolerance for poor performance by elected officials.

- Extreme greed is now likely to be considered a punishable offense. Henny de Ruiter, board chairman of the Dutch food retailer Royal Ahold, was obliged to resign shortly after it became known that he had approved an outsized multimillion-dollar pay package for Ahold's new chief executive. And only three weeks after the eruption of blistering criticism of the size of his bonus, Richard Grasso was compelled to quit as chairman and chief executive of the New York Stock Exchange.

Convictions, dismissals, recall movements, and forced resignations such as these seem to signal a growing intolerance of bad leadership, as well as a trend in which bad leaders and followers are increasingly held to account. But let's not kid ourselves: Change is slow. Since the end of World War II, there have been nearly fifty genocides and mass murders, with no punishment to fit the crime.[4] And even though during the 1990s corporate greed was pandemic, only a few have paid for their sins.

Moreover, for no obvious reason Radovan Karadzic remains at large; and Idi Amin, who in the 1970s ordered the death of three hundred thousand of his own citizens (among other crimes), was permitted to die a natural death in Saudi Arabia, in "obscenely easy exile."[5] In addition, although nearly one hundred top CEOs were replaced in 2002, it's hard to imagine that the other two thousand four hundred fully deserved to remain where they were—not to speak of the legions of political leaders whose ineffectiveness or unethical behavior have gone unpunished. Eleven months after ethics issues forced him to drop his bid for reelection to the Senate, Robert Torricelli resurfaced as a significant behind-the-scenes player in New Jersey politics, with influence in major government contracts, the governor's office, and multimillion-dollar business deals.[6]

To repeat: What is to be done? How can we all, leaders and followers alike, begin truly to correct for and prevent bad leadership? My response is preceded by three assumptions.

First, we cannot stop or slow bad leadership by changing human nature. No amount of preaching or sermonizing, no exhortations to virtuous conduct, uplifting thoughts, or wholesome habits, will obviate the fact that even though our behavior may change, our nature is constant.

Second, we cannot stop or slow bad leadership without stopping and slowing bad followership. If we have learned nothing else from the tales told here, we have learned that leaders and followers are interdependent. Without oxygen, fire dies out.

Finally, we cannot stop or slow bad leadership by sticking our heads in the sand. Amnesia, wishful thinking, lies we tell as individuals and organizations, and all the other mind games we play to deny or distort reality get us nowhere. Avoidance inures us to the costs and casualties of bad leadership, and that is why it festers, virtually unabated.

In recent years leaders, corporate leaders in particular have been deluged with advice on how to be good leaders and managers. But most of this counsel depends rather heavily on getting leaders to change in some fundamental way. And most of it is focused on leaders, to the nearly complete exclusion of followers.

The problem is not that change in adulthood is impossible or even rare. Rather, it is that leaders are likely to change only when they decide it's in their interest to do so. Bad leaders will not become good leaders unless (1) they calculate the costs of bad leadership as greater than the costs of good leadership, and (2) they calculate the benefits of good leadership as greater than the benefits of bad leadership.

This is where followers come in. *Bad leadership will not, cannot, be stopped or slowed unless followers take responsibility for rewarding the good leaders and penalizing the bad ones.*

Therefore, this book concludes with corrections for both leaders and followers. Each piece of advice is drawn, directly or indirectly, from the chapters highlighting the primary types of bad leadership that constitute part II of this book.

First, though, a cautionary note: The following lists do not protect against pathology. In particular, they do not pertain to evil leaders, nor to followers who are anesthetized or terrorized. But they do pertain to the countless other situations in which bad leadership threatens or has already taken root.

Leaders: Self-Help

The following corrections suggest how leaders can strengthen their personal capacity to be at once effective and ethical.

- *Limit your tenure.* When leaders remain in positions of power for too long, they tend to acquire bad habits. For example, they are increasingly prone to become complacent and grandiose, to overreach, to deny reality, and to lose their moral bearings. Samaranch and Aramony were chief executives for two decades or more. Both should have left earlier—and Barry should have quit the mayor's office after his second term.

- *Share power.* When power is centralized, it is likely to be misused, and that puts a premium on delegation and collaboration. The advice Mary Meeker gave affected the financial decisions of many people; still, she worked alone. Similarly, Al Dunlap was a corporate tyrant who brought Sunbeam down at least in part because of his refusal to work with others in any meaningful way.

- *Don't believe your own hype.* Samaranch ruled the Olympic movement as if it were his own fiefdom. Meeker seemed actually to believe she was queen of the Net. And Dunlap was in thrall to the portraits of himself as "Rambo" and "Chainsaw Al." For leaders to buy their own publicity is the kiss of death.

- *Get real, and stay real.* Virtually every bad leader named in this book lost touch with reality to some degree. Samaranch blocked out the fact that corruption had crept into the Olympic movement. Meeker came to believe that the history of markets was irrelevant to the "New Economy."

Barry dismissed his addiction to coke. Dunlap never understood that his callousness was self-destructive. Aramony did not grasp that he had morphed into a liar and thief. Clinton came to conclude that genocide was a problem the United States could choose to ignore. And Karadzic considered crimes against humanity justified as long as they were committed against Bosnian Muslims.[7]

- *Compensate for your weaknesses.* When he came into office Clinton knew that his strength was domestic policy and his weakness was foreign policy. So when Rwanda became a crisis, he should have made it a point to surround himself with experts on Africa. At a lower level of importance, Meeker should have made it a point to acquire in-depth knowledge about stocks other than the tech issues she had long followed and favored.

- *Stay balanced.* More than a few leaders named in this book were famous workaholics, far more dedicated to their jobs than they were to family and friends. This is a danger. As Bill George, former chairman and CEO of Medtronic, points out, "Balanced leaders develop healthier organizations." They make more thoughtful decisions and lead more effectively.[8]

- *Remember the mission.* Arguably, this matters most when the group or organization is dedicated to public service. Samaranch lost sight of the original Olympic ideal, and Aramony of the fact that the United Way of America was a charitable association.

- *Stay healthy.* Marion Barry is an egregious example of a leader whose physical and mental health was impaired throughout most of his time in public office. He should have sought professional help.

- *Develop a personal support system.* All of us should have aides, associates, friends, or family members who will save us from ourselves. Every leader named in this book would have benefited from tough love.

- *Be creative.* The past should never determine the future nor narrow the available options. If Atal Bihari Vajpayee, the prime minister of India, and General Pervez Musharraf, the president of Pakistan, have the imagination to break from the past and restart peace talks between their two countries, then Clinton could have helped to create a resolution to the crisis in Rwanda.

- *Know and control your appetites.* These include the hunger for power (Karadzic), money (Dunlap), success (Meeker), and sex (Barry).

- *Be reflective.* Virtually every one of the great writers on leadership—Plato, Aristotle, Lao Tzu, Confucius, Buddha—emphasizes the importance of self-knowledge, self-control, and good habits. But we have seen that acquiring and sustaining such virtues is hard. Intent is required, but so is time for quiet contemplation.

Leaders: Working with Others

The following corrections suggest how leaders can work with followers to get the best work done in the best possible way.

- *Establish a culture of openness in which diversity and dissent are encouraged.* The outcome in Washington might have been different if Barry had made clear that calling attention to wrong is a virtue and not a vice. The outcome in Rwanda might have been different if, on a matter so desperate, Clinton had made certain to give the few dissenting voices a full hearing.

- *Install an ombudsman.* In the wake of the fiasco of Howell Raines, his successor as executive editor of the *New York Times*, Bill Keller, appointed the first "editor for standards." The purpose of this new position was to have someone serve as the "main internal sounding board for staff members who have doubts or complaints about the paper's

content, whether already published or in the works."⁹
Imagine if Samaranch had heard a voice of this kind.

- *Bring in advisers who are both strong and independent.*
  Every leader in this book was ill served by close aides who,
  for various reasons, did not tell truth to power.

- *Avoid groupthink.* Groupthink discourages healthy dissent
  and encourages excessive cohesiveness. When members of
  groups are more motivated to get along with each other
  than they are to realistically appraise alternative courses of
  action, the quality of decision making suffers.¹⁰ By failing
  to have full and frank discussions about decisions as important as dismissing thousands from their jobs, Dunlap
  doomed Sunbeam.

- *Get reliable and complete information, and then dissemi-
  nate it.* James W. Johnston did not lack the evidence that
  indicated cigarette smoking was harmful to health. But the
  information was so closely held that for many years neither
  he nor anyone else in the tobacco industry was obliged to
  take it into account.

- *Invite an historian to the table.* Every group or organization should have a senior manager who knows it well and is
  charged with making certain that the traditional mission
  continues to matter. James Bakker and Henry Lyons would
  have benefited from having church elders responsible for
  holding them to account and reminding them regularly
  of their roles and responsibilities as moral models to their
  followers.

- *Establish a system of checks and balances.* Samaranch,
  Dunlap, and Aramony are only some of the leaders named
  in this book who would have benefited from policies and
  procedures designed to short-circuit bad leadership. These
  practices include limiting the tenure of leaders, rotating
  responsibilities, implementing regular performance reviews,
  measuring performance by more than one metric (e.g.,

profits), and holding CEOs and CFOs in particular accountable for organizational performance. Leaders with boards
should enlist their help as well. For example, boards will
become stronger and more independent if they have clear
and open criteria for board selection, go into regular executive sessions, and require evaluations of both themselves
and all senior managers.[11] The 2002 Sarbanes-Oxley Act
mandates some changes along these lines; but the degree to
which reforms are effectively implemented will depend, as it
always does, on those charged with carrying them out.

- *Strive for stakeholder symmetry.* Leaders should scan the
  horizon to make certain that they connect to all their constituents and not just to a chosen few. By the end of his
  tenure Samaranch had effectively isolated himself from the
  Olympic games at the grassroots. Dunlap cut himself off
  from his own employees from the beginning. And as far as
  Karadzic was concerned, Bosnia's Muslims were another
  species entirely.

Followers

Bad followers mirror bad leaders. If leaders are incompetent or
corrupt, so are at least some of their followers. Because followers
range from those who are apathetic to those who are deeply committed, to imagine them a homogeneous lot is to imagine wrongly.

It is clear that followers matter a great deal. It is equally clear
that if bad leadership is to be stopped or even slowed, followers
must play a bigger part.

The first appeal is to the better angels of our nature. In an essay
originally published in the 1930s, when Germany was already
under Nazi rule, Bertolt Brecht wrote eloquently of the writer's
obligation to speak up. Those who would "combat lies and ignorance," he wrote, had to be smart enough to know the truth and
courageous enough to speak the truth, even when it was everywhere

opposed.[12] The stories in this book make the same point: Someone, or several someones, who were intent on stopping or slowing bad leadership could have intervened before the damage was done, or at least before it became extensive. One or more followers could have stepped in, usually at something less than mortal peril, and said, "Stop!"

But by itself, appealing to the better angels of our nature is not sufficient. As was discussed in chapter 2, the problem is not that intervention, even to the point of opposition and resistance, is impossible. The problem is that the price of intervention is generally considered too high. We derive benefits from going along; and there are often real costs and risks to *not* going along. The question then is how followers can stop or slow bad leaders while also providing some cover for themselves.

Before I respond let me point out, again, that evil is a special case. Herbert Kelman and V. Lee Hamilton found that followers who committed "crimes of obedience"—illegal or immoral acts in response to orders from their superiors—can be taught to break the "habit" of obedience.[13] In other words, even evildoers can change.[14] But they don't change often or easily. Moreover, as we have seen, evil leaders depend not only on evil followers but also on others, especially bystanders, who are willing for reasons of their own to go along.

In fact, bystanders present an especially thorny problem. How, exactly, should we judge them? And what is it fair to expect of them—of us? By definition, bystanders do nothing wrong other than doing nothing when, arguably, they should be doing something. The situation is especially murky when intervening seems the right thing to do, but in defense of those other than our own kind. Human suffering far from home rarely mobilizes political leaders into action. In this book we have seen how easy it was for outsiders to be bystanders in both Rwanda and the Balkans, a circumstance that repeats itself over and over again. Between 1998 and 2003, roughly 3.3 million people died of sectarian violence in the Congo, a calamity that prompted *New York Times* columnist Nicholas Kristof to ask, "So, what did you do during the African holocaust?"[15]

On the one hand, bystanders make an easy target. How *could* they stand by and do nothing while evil was being perpetrated? But on the other hand, we understand better than we did before that doing something incurs costs that we ordinary mortals, more often than not, are unwilling to pay.

This returns us to the fundamental point: Leaders are like you and me, and so are followers. We act in our own interest, however it is determined and defined. Thus, it might seem reasonable to expect that when things go bad, people—followers—will intervene, but often they—we—choose not to do so. Often, we choose instead to mind our own business.

This said, there are nevertheless ways of increasing the likelihood of good followership, and of decreasing the likelihood of bad followership.

Followers: Self-Help

The following corrections suggest how followers can strengthen their personal capacity to resist leaders who are ineffective or unethical.

- *Empower yourself.* How strange, on the face of it, that every key player on Clinton's foreign policy team, even Madeleine Albright, who deviated in her opinion on Rwanda slightly from the majority, was willing, like the president himself, to turn a blind eye to genocide. The fact is that people who think of themselves as followers don't usually think of themselves as powerful. But they (we) are or, better put, they (we) can be. Sherron Watkins laid it on the line for her boss, Kenneth Lay. African-Americans took to the streets in protest against their mayor, Rudolph Giuliani, and got his attention. And the real Leona Helmsley was ultimately exposed by "the little people" she had so strongly disdained.

- *Be loyal to the whole and not to any single individual.* One cannot read the story of Marion Barry without being struck by the fact that his followers continued to follow, even as he was an addict running his city into the ground.

- *Be skeptical.* Leaders are not gods. Had Mary Meeker's subjects been less loyal to their queen, they likely would have saved money. Had Marion Barry's constituents been tougher on their mayor, they likely would have had a healthier city. Had Bill Clinton's aides and advisers been less willing to go along with the president on Rwanda, they likely would have cleaner consciences.

- *Take a stand.* With the benefit of hindsight, it is now almost unanimously agreed that the January 2000 merger between America Online and Time Warner was a corporate catastrophe. But if many claimed after the fact to have thought the deal a folly, at the time no one said a thing. CEOs Gerald Levin (Time Warner) and Stephen Case (AOL) were able to execute the miserable transaction only because of "pliant boards, submissive underlings, and craven accountants, bankers and lawyers."[16] Similarly, Samaranch, Meeker, Barry, Dunlap, Aramony, and Clinton got away far too long with bad leadership. And Karadzic is getting away far too long with murder.

- *Pay attention.* More followers contribute to bad leadership by inattention, either deliberate or inadvertent, than by any other single lapse. Samaranch did not mismanage in secret. Meeker did not stay stuck in a closet. Barry did not steer Washington into the abyss while in hiding. Dunlap's callousness was on public display. Aramony's corruption would have been obvious to anyone choosing to take a careful look. Clinton's foreign policy was a matter of public record. And the murder and mayhem under Karadzic were widely reported even as they were taking place.

Followers: Working with Others

The following corrections suggest how followers can work with each other, and with their leaders, to get the best work done in the best possible way.

- *Ensure that the punishment fits the crime.* Bad leaders must be made to pay for their transgressions. As long as someone like Radovan Karadzic is permitted to remain at large, as long as the likes of Samaranch and Dunlap are rewarded for poor performance, bad leadership will thrive.

- *Find allies.* The easiest way for the powerless to become powerful is to find other like-minded people with whom to work. There is strength in numbers. Had there been an effective working coalition against him, Samaranch could have been compelled to resign years before he did. Had more than a few members of Clinton's foreign policy team banded together to protest his policy on Rwanda, they would at least have gotten him to reconsider his course. Had Karadzic met with stiff resistance early on, from within or without, crimes against Bosnian Muslims would likely never have been committed.

- *Develop your own sources of information.* Relying on people in positions of authority for correct and complete information is not smart. This is not to say that people in positions of authority always lie. Rather, it is to remind us that the interests of leaders and followers do not necessarily coincide. Why was Aramony able to lead a double life for so long? Because except for his own closest advisers, no one bothered to check the books.

- *Take collective action.* Collective action can be taken on a modest scale, such as getting a small group together to talk to the boss or getting residents of an apartment building to withhold the rent until heat is restored. Or it can be taken on a much larger scale. In an article titled "Shareholders to the Rescue!" Roger Martin argues that major or controlling shareholders are in a position to "influence the culture of a firm and the behavior of its managers."[17] Since the mid-1980s, people power has made a difference in the Philippines, in the former Soviet Union and in Eastern Europe, and even in China. An example: In 2004 public fury resulted

in the sudden ouster of Eduard Shevardnadze, president of
Georgia. Shevardnadze was forced from office after three
weeks of nonstop street demonstrations against him.

- *Be a watchdog.* More striking than anything else about the
  spate of recent corporate scandals is the degree to which
  boards abdicated their responsibility exercise oversight, to
  mind the store. Scandals at Enron, WorldCom, and the New
  York Stock Exchange, among others, have all been "traced
  to a failure on the part of a board of directors to handle its
  responsibilities."[18] What's most curious about all this is
  that on paper, CEOs are responsible to their boards. In this
  sense, board members are supposed to be leaders. But as we
  have seen repeatedly in this book, board members who
  were supposed to exercise oversight did not and in fact
  went along with whatever the CEO was doing. The cases of
  Samaranch, Dunlap, and Aramony all involve board members who fell down on the job, *who followed rather than
  led.* To preclude this proclivity, every board should consider
  reforms such as: establishing a governance committee;
  naming a lead director with ultimate responsibility for the
  board as a whole; dividing the responsibilities of the chair
  of the board from those of the chief executive officer; and
  opening regular channels of communication to those on the
  outside, for example, shareholders.

- *Hold leaders to account.* Earlier I suggested that leaders
  establish a system of checks and balances. Followers have
  this responsibility as well. Stakeholders of all kinds should
  secure transparency, open discussions, and meaningful
  participation. And they should seek to effect institutional
  changes that will make leaders more responsible and
  accountable. As legal ethicist Deborah Rhode puts it, there
  should be mechanisms in all groups and organizations that
  require "clear standards of accountability, obligations, and
  protections."[19]

This book probes bad leadership. It covers the spectrum, from incompetence to evil, from ineffective to unethical. It considers bad leadership in context, and from the perspective of the followers as well as the leaders. Finally it explores the question of how bad leadership might be stopped, or at least slowed.

I have no illusions: Work of this kind does not provide a quick fix. But, as I said at the start, my claim is that we promote good leadership not by ignoring bad leadership, nor by presuming it immutable. To the contrary, our only hope is to take it on, to decode and decipher it, and then to attack it as we would any disease that damages, debilitates, and sometimes even kills.

The good news is that the balance of power between leaders and followers has shifted in recent years, however slightly. More followers are divesting leaders of some power, authority, and influence. This is all to the good. For as this book testifies, once they're entrenched, bad leaders seldom change or quit of their own volition. This means it's up to us to insist either on change— or on an early exit.

NOTES

INTRODUCTION

1. Robert Sapolsky, *A Primate's Memoir* (New York: Scribner, 2001), 16–17.

2. Robert Caro, *The Years of Lyndon Johnson: Master of the Senate* (New York: Knopf, 2002), xxii–xxiv.

3. James O'Toole, *Leading Change: Overcoming the Ideology of Comfort and the Tyranny of Custom* (San Francisco: Jossey-Bass, 1995), 2.

4. Ibid.

5. Harlan Cleveland, *Nobody in Charge: Essays on the Future of Leadership* (San Francisco: Jossey-Bass, 2003), 123.

CHAPTER 1

1. Lawrence H. Summers, "Installation Address of Lawrence H. Summers," Harvard University, 12 October 2001.

2. Thomas J. Peters and Robert H. Waterman Jr., *In Search of Excellence: Lessons from America's Best-Run Companies* (New York: Warner, 1982).

3. Rosabeth Moss Kanter, *The Change Masters: Innovation & Entrepreneurship in the American Corporation* (New York: Simon and Schuster, 1983).

4. Warren Bennis and Burt Nanus, *Leaders: The Strategies for Taking Charge* (New York: Harper & Row, 1985).

5. John P. Kotter, *A Force for Change: How Leadership Differs from Management* (New York: Free Press, 1990).

6. Noel Tichy with Eli Cohen, *The Leadership Engine: How Winning Companies Build Leaders at Every Level* (New York: Harper Business, 1997).

7. Jay Conger and Beth Benjamin, *Building Leaders: How Successful Companies Develop the Next Generation* (San Francisco: Jossey-Bass, 1999).

8. See, for example, Spencer Johnson and Kenneth Blanchard, *The One Minute Manager* (New York: Morrow, 1982).

9. John Gardner, *Leadership Papers #1: The Nature of Leadership* (Washington, DC: Independent Sector, 1986), 6.

10. Niccolo Machiavelli, *The Prince* (Chicago: University of Chicago Press, 1998), 37, 38.

11. Talcott Parsons, introduction to *The Theory of Social and Economic Organization*, by Max Weber (Free Press, 1947), 36.

12. Mark Lilla, "The New Age of Tyranny," *The New York Review of Books*, 24 October 2002, 29.

13. There are some exceptions to this general rule. See, for example, Christine Clements and John B. Washbush, "The Two Faces of Leadership: Considering the Dark Side of Leader-Follower Dynamics," *Journal of Workplace Learning: Employee Counseling Today* 11, no. 5 (1999); M. F. R. Kets de Vries, *Prisoners of Leadership* (New York: John Wiley & Sons, 1989); *Leaders, Fools and Imposters: Essays on the Psychology of Leadership* (San Francisco: Jossey-Bass, 1993); *The Leadership Mystique: An Owner's Manual* (London: Pearson, 2001), especially chapters 4 and 7; Jean Lipman-Blumen, "Why Do We Tolerate Bad Leaders: Magnificent Uncertitude, Anxiety, and Meaning" in *The Future of Leadership: Today's Top Leadership Thinkers Speak to Tomorrow's Leaders*, eds. Warren Bennis, Gretchen M. Spreitzer, and Thomas G. Cummings (San Francisco: Jossey-Bass, 2001), 125–138; and Craig E. Johnson, *Meeting the Ethical Challenges of Leadership: Casting Light or Shadow* (Thousand Oaks, CA: Sage, 2001).

14. Edward Rothstein, "Defining Evil in the Wake of 9/11," *New York Times*, 5 October 2002, B7.

15. Daniel J. Goleman, "What Is Negative About Positive Illusions? When Benefits for the Individual Harm the Collective," *Journal of Social and Clinical Psychology* 8 (1989): 191.

16. Eviatar Zerubavel, "The Elephant in the Room," in *Culture in Mind*, ed. Karen A. Cerulo (New York: Routledge, 2002), 21.

17. James MacGregor Burns, *Leadership* (New York: Harper & Row, 1978), 18.

18. Warren Bennis, introduction to the revised edition, *On Becoming a Leader* (Cambridge, MA: Perseus, 2003,) xxi, xxii.

19. Kanter, *The Change Masters*, 17, 18.

20. George Washington, Farewell Address, 17 September 1796.

21. Abraham Lincoln, second inaugural address, 4 March 1865, Washington, DC.

22. Dr. Martin Luther King, Jr., "I Have a Dream" speech, 28 August 1963, Washington, DC.

23. Ronald Reagan, the Anderson-Reagan presidential debate, 21 September 1980, Baltimore, MD. John Kennedy used the phrase in a speech delivered to the Massachusetts legislature on 9 January 1961, and Reagan also used it earlier, in a speech he delivered in 1974.

24. Barbara Kellerman, "Hitler's Ghost: A Manifesto" in *Cutting Edge: Leadership 2000*, eds. Barbara Kellerman and Larraine Matusak (College Park, MD: Burns Academy of Leadership, 1999), 65–68.

25. Bernard Bass, *Stogdill's Handbook of Leadership: A Survey of Theory and Research* (New York: Free Press, 1981), 7.

26. Martin Malia, "Foreword: The Uses of Atrocity," in Stephane Courtois et al., *The Black Book of Communism: Crimes, Terror, Repression* (Cambridge, MA: Harvard University Press, 1999), x.

27. Herbert C. Kelman and Lee Hamilton, *Crimes of Obedience: Toward a Social Psychology of Authority and Responsibility* (New Haven, CT: Yale University Press, 1989), 26.

28. Desmond Tutu, "Let South Africa Show the World How to Forgive," *Knowledge of Reality* 19 (2000).

CHAPTER 2

1. Sigmund Freud, *Group Psychology and the Analysis of the Ego* (New York: Norton, 1954), 54.

2. Thomas Hobbes, *Leviathan* (New York: Cambridge University Press, 1996).

3. Maurice Cranston, introduction to ibid., 9–43.

4. Jean-Jacques Rousseau, *The Social Contract* (Middlesex, UK: Penguin, 1968).

5. Niccolo Machiavelli, *The Prince* (Chicago: University of Chicago Press, 1998).

6. John Locke, *The Second Treatise of Government* (Indianapolis: Bobbs-Merrill, 1952).

7. Clinton Rossiter, introduction to *The Federalist Papers* (New York: Mentor, 1961), xiv.

8. William Golding, *Lord of the Flies* (New York: Perigree, 1954), 75, 78.

9. For a fuller discussion of why the trait approach is considered dated, see Stanley Renshon, *The Psychological Assessment of Presidential Candidates* (New York: Routledge, 1998), 179–180. For more on how leadership emerges, see also Ken K. Smith, "An Intergroup Perspective on Individual Behavior," in *Perspectives on Behavior in Organizations*, by J. Richard Hackman, Edward Lawler III, and Lyman W. Porter (New York: McGraw Hill, 1977), 397–408.

10. Bernard M. Bass, *Stogdill's Handbook of Leadership* (New York: Free Press, 1981), 43–72.

11. See, for example, Alexander George, "Power as a Compensatory Value," *Journal of Social Issues* 24, no. 3 (July 1968): 29–49.

12. See, for example, the fourth edition of James David Barber's enormously influential *The Presidential Character* (Englewood Cliffs, NJ: Prentice Hall, 1992).

13. Renshon, *Psychological Assessment of Presidential Candidates*, 184, 288.

14. Betty Glad, "When Tyrants Go Too Far: Malignant Narcissism and Absolute Power," *Political Psychology* 23, no. 1 (March 2002): 20.

15. For more on Abraham Maslow's seminal work on the hierarchy of needs, see *Motivation and Personality* (New York: Harper and Brothers, 1954).

16. Sigmund Freud, *Moses and Monotheism* (New York: Knopf, 1939), 140.

17. For another discussion of why people follow evil leaders, see Neil J. Kressel, *Mass Hate: The Global Rise of Genocide and Terror* (New York: Plenum, 1966), chapter 5.

18. Sonja M. Hunt, "The Role of Leadership in the Construction of Reality," in *Leadership: Multidisciplinary Perspectives*, ed. Barbara Kellerman (Englewood Cliffs, NJ: Prentice Hall, 1984), 175.

19. Herbert Kelman and V. Lee Hamilton, *Crimes of Obedience* (New Haven, CT: Yale University Press, 1989).

20. Stanley Milgram, *Obedience to Authority: An Experimental View* (New York: Harper & Row, 1974).

21. David J. Luban, "Milgram Revisited," *Researching Law* 9, no. 2 (Spring 1998).

22. On this general point, see Jean Lipman-Blumen, "Why Do We Tolerate Bad Leaders—Magnificent Uncertitude, Anxiety, and Meaning," in *The Future of Leadership*, eds. Warren Bennis et al. (San Francisco: Jossey-Bass, 2001), 129. Lipman-Bluman also discusses why bad leaders are not toppled more often.

23. Jerome Barkow, quoted in Fred H. Wilhoite Jr., "Primates and Political Authority," *American Political Science Review* 70 (December 1976): 1110–1126.

24. David M. Rosen, "Leadership Systems in World Cultures," in *Leadership: Multidisciplinary Perspectives*, 43.

25. Quoted in Jared Diamond, "The Religious Success Story," *New York Review of Books*, 7 November 2002. Review of David Wilson, *Darwin's*

Cathedral: Evolution, Religion, and the Nature of Society (Chicago: University of Chicago Press, 2002).

26. Robert Michels, *Political Parties* (New York: Free Press, 1962), 66.

27. Richard Rhodes, *Masters of Death: The SS-Einsatzgruppen and the Invention of the Holocaust* (New York: Knopf, 2002).

28. Ian Kershaw, *Hitler: 1889–1936: Hubris* (New York: Norton, 1998), 183.

29. Ibid., 283, 284.

CHAPTER 3

1. Letter dated 9 December 2001 to the president of a leading West Coast university.

2. Warren Bennis and Burt Nanus, *Leaders: The Strategies for Taking Charge* (New York: Harper & Row, 1985), 21. Bennis and Nanus were making a distinction between managers "who do things right" and leaders "who do the right thing."

3. Mark Lilla, interviewed by Eric Alterman, "Q & A: Why Are Deep Thinkers Shallow About Tyranny," *New York Times* (10 November 2001), A15.

4. For a full accounting of how the investigative staff of the *Boston Globe* uncovered this story, see Investigative Staff of the *Boston Globe, Betrayal: The Crisis in the Catholic Church* (Boston: Little, Brown, 2002).

5. Robert E. Kelley, *The Power of Followership: How to Create Leaders People Want to Follow and Followers Who Lead Themselves* (New York: Doubleday, 1992), 166.

6. James MacGregor Burns, *Leadership* (New York: Harper & Row, 1978), 18, 20.

7. James MacGregor Burns, foreword to Joanne B. Ciulla, *Ethics: The Heart of Leadership* (Westport, CT: Praeger, 1998), x.

8. Robert K. Greenleaf, *Servant Leadership: A Journey into the Nature of Legitimate Power* (New York: Paulist Press, 1977).

9. Joseph C. Rost, *Leadership for the Twenty-First Century* (Westport, CT: Praeger, 1991), 82.

10. Edwin P. Hollander, "Ethical Challenges in the Leader-Follower Relationship," in Ciulla, *Ethics: The Heart of Leadership*, 49–61.

11. Confucius, *Analects of Confucius* (New York, Norton, 1977), 6, 8.

12. Arthur Isak Applebaum, "Democratic Legitimacy and Official Discretion," *Philosophy and Public Affairs* 21, no. 3 (1992): 240. Also see Dennis F. Thompson, "Moral Responsibility of Public Officials: The Problem of Many Hands," *American Political Science Review* 74 (1980): 905–915.

13. Joanne B. Ciulla, "Carving Leaders from the Warped Wood of Humanity," *Review Canadienne des Sciences de l'Administration* (Montreal) 18, no. 4 (December 2001): 313.

14. Aristotle, *The Ethics* (London: Penguin, 1953), 91.

15. Kelley, *The Power of Followership*, 168.

16. John Rawls, *A Theory of Justice* (Cambridge, MA: Harvard University Press, 1971), 364.

17. Martin Luther King, Jr., "Letter from a Birmingham Jail," in *Blessed Are the Peacemakers*, by S. Jonathan Bass (Baton Rouge: Louisiana State University Press, 2001). The letter is dated 16 April 1963.

18. Max Weber, *The Theory of Social and Economic Organizations* (New York: Free Press, 1947), 329.

19. "Presidential Rankings," 2000 poll from C-Span survey of historians, CNN, 21 February 2000.

20. Deborah Solomon, "Is the Go-Go Guggenheim Going, Going . . ." *New York Times Magazine*, 20 June 2002.

21. For an excellent description of Healy's tenure at the Red Cross, see Deborah Sontag, "Who Brought Bernadine Healy Down?" *New York Times Magazine*, 23 December 2001, 32.

22. Daniel Goleman, *Working with Emotional Intelligence* (New York: Bantam, 1999), 317. For an interesting exchange about leadership and practical intelligence, see Robert Sternberg and Victor Vroom, "The Person Versus the Situation in Leadership," *The Leadership Quarterly* 13, no. 3 (June 2002): 301–321.

23. For example, the failure by South Carolina governor Jim Hodges to communicate during Hurricane Floyd resulted in a monumental traffic jam. "Traffic Backs Up for Miles as Coastal Dwellers Flee Island," *St. Louis Post-Dispatch*, 16 September 1999, A9. See also Leigh Strope, "Hodges Said He Should Control Emergency Response," Associated Press State and Local Wire, 1 October 1999; and David Firestone, "Hurricane Floyd: The Overview," *New York Times*, 16 September 1999, A1.

24. "S. African Leader Claims AIDS Drug Is Unsafe," *St. Louis Post-Dispatch*, 3 November 1999, A5; Barton Gelman, "S. African President Escalates AIDS Feud: Mbeki Challenges Western Remedies," *Washington Post*, 19 April 2000, A1; Samson Mulugeta, "S. Africa: A Country in Denial—AIDS Victims Suffer in Silence, President Dismisses Problem," *Newsday*, 21 August 2001, A16; Rachel Swarns, "In a Policy Shift, South Africa Will Make AIDS Drugs Available to Pregnant Women," *New York Times*, 20 April 2002, A8. In 2002 Mbeki's position on antiretroviral drugs softened slightly, at least in part because of the intervention of Canadian Prime Minister Jean

Chretien. For a fuller description of Mbeki's rigid intransigence, see Samantha Power, "The AIDS Rebel," *New Yorker*, 19 May 2003.

25. Barbara Tuchman, *The March of Folly: Troy to Vietnam* (New York: Ballentine, 1984), 7.

26. Fred Hiatt, "Ex-Aides Raise Questions about Yeltsin's Drinking," *Washington Post*, 8 October 1994, A21.

27. Ronald A. Heifetz and Marty Linsky, *Leadership on the Line: Staying Alive Through the Dangers of Leading* (Boston: Harvard Business School Press, 2002), 164.

28. "Image and Reality for Martha Stewart," *Greenwich Time*, 10 June 2003. See also Jerry Oppenheimer, *Just Desserts: The Unauthorized Biography of Martha Stewart* (New York: William Morrow, 1997), especially 236 ff. and 308 ff; and Christopher M. Byron, *Martha, Inc.: The Incredible Story of Martha Stewart Living Omnimedia* (New York: John Wiley & Sons, 2003).

29. Peter Watson, "Under the Hammer," *The Guardian*, 7 December 2001, 2; Carol Vogel and Ralph Blumenthal, "Ex-Chairman of Sotheby's Gets Jail Time," *New York Times*, 23 April 2002, B1.

30. Nicholas D. Kristof, "Hearing Liberia's Pleas," *New York Times*, 29 July 2003, A23.

31. Chester Crocker, "A War Americans Can Afford to Stop," *New York Times*, 1 August 2003, A21.

32. James Traub, "The Worst Place on Earth," *New York Review of Books*, 29 June 2000, 61–65. The quotation is from Somini Sengupta, "African Held for War Crimes Dies in Custody of Tribunal," *New York Times*, 31 July 2003, A6.

33. Psychiatrist Michael Weiner has this view of evil, as cited by Sharon Begley, "The Roots of Evil," *Newsweek*, 21 May 2002, 32.

34. Sidney Goldberg, "Learning Lexicons: Dictionaries Call Castro a 'Leader' and Stalin a 'Statesman,' " 5 July 2002, *Wall Street Journal Online*, <www.opinionjournal.com/taste/?id=110001946> (accessed 5 July 2002).

35. Alan Ehrenhalt, "The Paradox of Corrupt Yet Effective Leadership," *New York Times*, 30 September 2002, A25.

36. For example, in a 2002 presentation titled "Crisis in Corporate Governance," Bill George estimated that corrupt leaders at Global Crossing, Enron, Qwest, Tyco and WORLDCOM cost shareholders $460 billion.

CHAPTER 4

1. Marcus Mietzner, "Abdurrahman's Indonesia: Political Conflict and Institutional Crisis" in *Indonesia Today: Challenges of History*, eds. Grayson

Lloyd and Shannon Smith (Singapore: Institute of Southeast Asian Studies, 2001), 29–44.

2. Paridah Abd. Samad, *Gus Dur: A Peculiar Leader in Indonesia's Political Agony* (Kuala Lumpur: Penerbitan Salafi, 2001).

3. "Wavering Wahid: Indonesia's President Has a Deft Political Touch," *Economist*, 20 May 2000.

4. Terry McCarthy, "Time for Leadership," *Time Asia*, 3 July 2000.

5. "Nightmare: Toy Industry," *Economist*, 16 December 1995.

6. Kathleen Morris, "The Rise of Jill Barad," *Business Week*, 25 May 1998.

7. Ibid.

8. Abigail Goldman, "Beleaguered Mattel CEO Resigns as Profit Sinks," *Los Angeles Times*, 4 February 2000, A1.

9. Geraldine Laybourne, quoted in Morris, "The Rise of Jill Barad."

10. Morris, "The Rise of Jill Barad"; Lisa Bannon, "Makeover Artist: She Reinvented Barbie, Now, Can Jill Barad Do the Same for Mattel?" *Wall Street Journal*, 5 March 1997, A1; Debra J. Hotaling, "A Girlfriend to the End," *Los Angeles Times Magazine*, 27 June 1999, 10; and Lisa Bannon and Andy Pastor, "Mattel Names Sony Official to No. 3 Post," *Wall Street Journal*, 8 August 1999, A3.

11. Robert K. Barney, Stephen R. Wenn, and Scott G. Martyn, *Selling the Five Rings: The International Olympic Committee and the Rise of Olympic Commercialism* (Salt Lake City: University of Utah Press, 2002), xi.

12. Kim Clark et al., "The Olympic Movement," *U.S. News and World Report*, 28 January–4 February 2002, 42.

13. Ibid.

14. Barney et al., *Selling the Five Rings*, x.

15. International Olympic Organization, <www.olympic.org/uk/organization> (accessed 5 September 2002).

16. Barney et al., *Selling the Five Rings*, 100.

17. Ibid., 147.

18. Ibid., 151.

19. David Miller, "Juan Antonio Samaranch," in *International Olympic Committee: The Centennial President*, ed. Ferrán Brunet, (Lausanne: International Olympic Committee, 1997), 123.

20. International Olympic Organization, <www.olympic.org/uk/organization> (accessed 5 September 2002).

21. Roger Cohen and Jere Longman, "Master of the Games," *New York Times*, 7 February 1999, A1.

22. Andrew Jennings, *The New Lord of the Rings: Olympic Corruption and How to Buy Gold Medals* (London: Simon and Schuster, 1996), 31.

23. Cohen and Longman, "Master of the Games."

24. Ibid.

25. Ibid.

26. Jennings, *The New Lord of the Rings*, 43.

27. Cohen and Longman, "Master of the Games."

28. Miller, "Juan Antonio Samaranch," 125, 126; and Jason Zengerle, "Unspecial Olympics," *The New Republic*, 15 February 1999, 6.

29. Cohen and Longman, "Master of the Games."

30. Barney et al., *Selling the Five Rings*, xi, 151.

31. Ibid., 276.

32. Cohen and Longman, "Master of the Games"; John Meyer, "Passing of the Torch," *Denver Post*, 15 July 2001, C1; and Kirk Johnson, "Tarnished Gold," *New York Times*, 11 March 1999, A1.

33. Cohen and Longman, "Master of the Games."

34. Ibid.

35. Ibid.

36. For a full description of the Salt Lake City scandal, see Johnson, "Tarnished Gold."

37. William Drozdiak, "IOC Chief Parries Criticism," *Washington Post*, 26 January 1999, A1.

38. Zengerle, "Unspecial Olympics," *The New Republic*.

39. Cohen and Longman, "Master of the Games."

40. Drozdiak, "IOC Chief Parries Criticism."

41. Meyer, "Passing of the Torch."

42. Johnson, "Tarnished Gold." See also Alan Abrahamson and Mike Penner, "Olympic Panel Purges Leaders Amid Scandal," *Los Angeles Times*, 9 January 1999, A1.

43. Jack Todd, "Pound in Olympic Dogfight," *Ottawa Citizen*, 10 July 2001, C7. For more on the ultimate acquittal of Welch and Johnson, see Lex Hemphill, "Acquittals End Big Scandal that Dogged Winter Games," *New York Times*, 6 December 2003, D1.

44. Quoted in Meyer, "Passing the Torch."

45. Jennings, *The New Lord of the Rings*, 18.

46. Paul Witteman, *Time*, Special Olympic Supplement, Summer 1992, quoted in Jennings, *The New Lord of the Rings*, 174.

47. Alan Abrahamson and David Wharton, "Behind the Rings: Inside the Olympic Movement," *Los Angeles Times*, 28 August 2000, A1.

48. Richard Sandomir, "3 Quitting Panel on Olympic Ethics," *New York Times*, 18 January 2003, A1.

CHAPTER 5

1. Stratford Sherman, "Levi's: As Ye Sew, So Shall Ye Reap," *Fortune*, 12 May 1997, 104–116.

2 Nina Munk, "How Levi's Trashed a Great American Brand," *Fortune*, 12 April 1999, 82–90.

3. Michael Wolff, "Sumner Squall," *New York*, 18 February 2002, 38.

4. Thomas Friedman, "A Russian Dinosaur," *New York Times*, 5 September 2002, A27.

5. Quoted in John Cassidy, *Dot.con: The Greatest Story Ever Sold* (New York: HarperCollins, 2002), 63. This section draws heavily from Cassidy's book.

6. Ibid., 111.

7. Ibid., 118.

8. Ibid., 120.

9. Ibid., 125.

10. Ibid., 158.

11. Ibid., 169.

12. Ibid., 192.

13. Ibid., 295.

14. Quoted in ibid., 309.

15. John Cassidy, "The Woman in the Bubble," *New Yorker*, 26 April 1999.

16. Ibid.

17. Ibid.

18. "Fortune Picks the Brains of Four Scary-Smart Investors," *Fortune*, 29 December 1997.

19. Andrew Bary, "Net Queen: How Mary Meeker Came to Rule the Internet," *Barron's*, 21 December 1998, 23.

20. Ibid.

21. Cassidy, *Dot.con*, 164.

22. Andrew Bary, "The Queen Told You So," *Barron's*, 4 January 1999.

23. Cassidy, "The Woman in the Bubble."

24. Steven Mufson, "Conventional Firms Are Back in Favor," *Washington Post*, 20 April 1999, E1.

25. Cassidy, *Dot.con*, 208. See chapter 15 for more on Meeker's conflict of interest.

26. Ibid., 209.

27. *New York Times*, 16 August 2002, A1.

28. Emily Lambert, "Queen of the Internet Dethroned," *New York Post*, 23 October 2000, 50.

29. Steve Hamm, "Tech's Cheerleader Won't Say Die," *BusinessWeek*, 30 April 2001, 90.

30. Peter Elkind, "Where Mary Meeker Went Wrong," *Fortune*, 14 April 2001, 68–82. All the quotations in this section are taken from Elkind's article.

31. Steve Hamm, "Tech's Cheerleader Won't Say Die."

32. Elkind, "Where Mary Meeker Went Wrong."

33. David Brooks, "Why the U.S. Will Always Be Rich," *New York Times Magazine*, 9 June 2002, 90.

34. Ibid., 91.

35. Ibid., 124.

36. Cassidy, "The Woman in the Bubble."

37. Cassidy, *Dot.con*, 168.

38. Adam Lashinsky, "Telling Congress About the Rigged Research Game," TheStreet.com, <www.thestreet.com/markets/adamlashinsky/1506924.html>.

39. Steven Pearlstein, "U.S. Economic Forces Seem to be Realigning," *Washington Post*, 21 March 2001, A1.

40. Gretchen Morgenson, *New York Times*, 31 December 2000, C1, and 27 May 2001, C1, respectively.

41. Amy Baldwin, *Montreal Gazette*, 19 February 2002, C10.

42. Michael Lewis, "Jonathan Lebed's Extracurricular Activities," *New York Times*, 25 February 2001, Section 6, 26.

43. Cassidy, *Dot.con*, 309.

44. Tamara Loomis, "Analyst Accountability: Suits Over Stock Recommendations Pose New Wrinkle," *New York Law Journal*, 16 August 2001, 5.

45. Stephen Labaton, "Wall Street Settlement," *New York Times*, 29 April 2003, A1.

46. Riva Atlas, "Citigroup Picks a Former Star of Research for a New Unit," *New York Times*, 31 October 2002, C6.

47. J. R. P. French Jr., and B. Raven, "The Bases of Social Power" in *Studies in Social Power*, ed. Dorwin Cartwright (Ann Arbor: University of Michigan, 1959), 150–167.

CHAPTER 6

1. Quoted in Rick Perlstein, "Gary Hart's Dare," *Columbia Journalism Review* (Nov/Dec 2001), 102. My discussion of Hart is based on this article and on Matt Bai, "The Outsider: Gary Hart," *New York Times Magazine*, 2 February 2003, 31–33.

2. Lynette Clemetson et al., "A Confession from Jesse," *Newsweek*, 29 January 2001, 38.

3. Quoted in Angie Cannon, "The Jackson Reaction," *U.S. News & World Report*, 29 January 2001, 18.

4. Quoted in ibid.

5. "The Fight for Might," *Time*, 28 May 2001, 47.

6. Andrew Sullivan, "Endgame," *New Republic*, 19 February 2001, 6.

7. "TV Evangelist Bakker Resigns in Sex Scandal," *World News Digest*, 27 March 1987.

8. Frances Fitzgerald, "Jim and Tammy," *New Yorker*, 23 April 1990, 76.

9. Ibid., 45, 76.

10. Peter Applebome, "Scandals Aside, Preachers Thrive," *New York Times*, 8 October 1989, 24.

11. Edward Gilbreath, "Redeeming Fire," *Christianity Today*, 6 December 1999, 38.

12. Ibid. Also see *Christian Century*, 12 October 1994, 921.

13. "National Report," *Jet*, 28 July 1997.

14. Earl R. Riggins Jr., "Cheap Grace," *Christian Century*, 5 November 1997, 996.

15. "Rev. Lyons Ordered to Pay $5.2m for Bank Fraud and Tax Evasion; Sentenced to Four Years," *Jet*, 5 July 1999, 14.

16. Alexandra Starr, "Bully Pulpit. Lucrative Too," *Business Week*, 5 March 2001, 62–66.

17. Joshua Green, "The Bookie of Virtue," *Washington Monthly*, June 2003, <www.washingtonmonthly.com/features/2003/0306.green.html>.

18. William J. Bennett, ed., *The Book of Virtues* (New York: Simon and Schuster, 1993), 48, 53, 88.

19. Jonathan Alter and Joshua Green, "Bennett: Virtue Is as Virtue Does?" *Newsweek*, 12 May 2003, 6.

20. Frank Rich, "Tupac's Revenge on Bennett," *New York Times*, 18 May 2003, B1.

21. Quoted in ibid.

22. *National Review*, 2 June 2003, 12.

23. Michael Elliot and Martha Brant, "America's Worst-Run City," *Newsweek*, 13 March 1995, 26.

24. Harry S. Jaffe and Tom Sherwood, *Dream City: Race, Power, and the Decline of Washington, D.C.* (New York: Simon and Schuster, 1994), 22.

25. Ibid., 28.

26. Ibid., 30.

27. Ibid., 45.

28. Ibid.

29. Ibid., 35. Many of the details on Barry's life are taken from this book.

30. Quoted in ibid., 40.

31. Ibid., 47.

32. Ibid., 87.

33. Ibid., 124.

34. Ibid., 140.

35. Ibid., 183.

36. Ibid., 224.

37. T. Morgenthau and M. Miller, "Busting the Mayor," *Newsweek*, 29 January 1990, 24. This article provides a vivid and complete description of the episode.

38. Jonetta Rose Barras, *The Last of the Black Emperors: The Hollow Comeback of Marion Barry in the New Age of Black Leaders* (Baltimore: Bancroft, 1998), 4.

39. Jaffe and Sherwood, *Dream City*, 120.

40. Michael Schaffer, "End Run," *New Republic*, 22 April 2002, 21.

41. "Back from the Dead," *Economist*, 17 September 1994, 32.

42. "The Lady Who Shamed Marion Barry," *Economist*, 9 August 1997, 21.

43. Jaffe and Sherwood, *Dream City*, 274.

44. Quoted by Maureen Dowd, "Resurrection," *New York Times Magazine*, 11 September 1994, 48.

45. Jaffe and Sherwood, *Dream City*, 275.

46. Rev. A. Knighton Stanley, quoted in Barras, *The Last of the Black Emperors*, 51.

47. Barras, *The Last of the Black Emperors*, 30.

48. Jaffe and Sherwood, *Dream City*, 197.

49. Ronald A. Heifetz and Marty Linsky, *Leadership on the Line: Staying Alive Through the Dangers of Leading* (Cambridge, MA: Harvard Business School Press, 2002), chapter 8.

50. Barras, *The Last of the Black Emperors*, 6.

CHAPTER 7

1. Joseph C. Rost, *Leadership for the Twenty-First Century* (New York: Praeger, 1991), 102.

2. Dan Barry, "The Diallo Shooting: The Mayor," *New York Times*, 28 March 1999, A1.

3. Dan Barry, "A Reopened Divide," *New York Times*, 11 February 1999, A1.

4. Dan Barry, "Giuliani Softens His Tone but Still Defends the Police," *New York Times*, 24 March 1999, A1.

5. Dan Barry, "Political Memo: At Very Least, the Mayor Is Listening," *New York Times*, 14 July 1999, B1.

6. Robert D. McFadden with Kit R. Roane, "U.S. Examining Killing of a Man in Police Volley," *New York Times*, 6 February 1999, A1.

7. Elisabeth Bumiller with Ginger Thompson, "Giuliani Cancels Political Trip Amid Protest Over Shooting," *New York Times*, 10 February 1999, A1.

8. Jodi Wilgoren, "The Diallo Shooting: The Dialogue," *New York Times*, 28 March 1999, A47.

9. Barry, "A Reopened Divide."

10. Barry, "The Diallo Shooting."

11. John Lewis, "Symbolism in Action," *New York Times*, 30 March 1999, A23.

12. Adam Nagourney with Marjorie Connelly, "Giuliani's Ratings Drop Over Actions in Dorismond Case," *New York Times*, 7 April 2000, A1.

13. Richard Hammer, *The Helmsleys: The Rise and Fall of Harry and Leona* (London: Penguin, 1990), 142.

14. Ibid., 166.

15. Ibid., 181.

16. Albert Scardino, "New Yorkers & Co: The Helmsley Palace's Embattled Queen," *New York Times*, 18 April 1988, D1.

17. Hammer, *The Helmsleys*, 182–185.

18. John J. O'Connor, "TV Weekend: Self-Proclaimed Royalty on the Rise," *New York Times*, 21 September 1990, C30.

19. Ken Auletta, "The Howell Doctrine," *The New Yorker*, 10 June 2002.

20. David Margolick, "The *Times's* Restoration Drama," *Vanity Fair*, August 2003, 142.

21. Ibid.

22. Ibid., 197.

23. This and other quotations in this paragraph are from ibid., 197, 198.

24. Warren Bennis, "Caesar's Problem," *CIO Insight*, October 2003.

25. Rakesh Khurana, "Al Dunlap at Sunbeam," Case 9-899-218 (Boston: Harvard Business School, revised December 30, 1999), 1.

26. Ibid., 3.

27. Ibid., 10.

28. John A. Byrne, *Chainsaw: The Notorious Career of Al Dunlap in the Era of Profit-at-Any-Price* (New York: HarperBusiness, 1999), 80. Much of the information in this chapter is based on Byrne's book.

29. Ibid., 81.

30. Ibid., 88.

31. Khurana, "Al Dunlap at Sunbeam," 2.

32. Byrne, *Chainsaw*, 92.

33. Khurana, "Al Dunlap at Sunbeam," 2.

34. John Byrne with Joseph Weber, "The Shredder," *BusinessWeek*, 15 January 1996, 56.

35. Byrne, *Chainsaw*, 26.

36. Ibid., 98.

37. Ibid., 106.

38. Ibid., 22.

39. Ibid., 23.

40. Albert J. Dunlap, *Mean Business: How I Save Bad Companies and Make Good Companies Great* (New York: Fireside, 1996), xii.

41. Sam Perkins with David Wylie, "Albert Dunlap and Corporate Transformation (A)," Case BAB032, Babson College (Boston: Harvard Business School Publishing, 1999, rev. 2000), 4.

42. Ibid., 9.

43. Ibid.

44. Ibid.

45. Byrne, *Chainsaw*, 47.

46. Ibid., 153, 154.

47. Matthew Schifrin, "The Dunlap Effect," *Forbes*, 24 March 1997, 42.

48. Patricia Sellers, quoted in Khurana, "Al Dunlap at Sunbeam," 8.

49. Matthew Schifrin, "The Unkindest Cuts," *Forbes*, 4 May 1998, 44.

50. Ibid.

51. Quoted in Byrne, *Chainsaw*, 284.

52. Ibid., 324.

53. John Byrne, "How Al Dunlap Self-Destructed," *BusinessWeek*, 6 July 1998, 58.

54. "Want to Be a Better Investor?" *Pittsburgh Post-Gazette*, 25 November 2002, A13.

55. John Byrne, "Book Excerpt: *Chainsaw*," *BusinessWeek*, 18 October 1999, 128.

56. Byrne, *Chainsaw*, 143.

57. Ibid., 125.

58. Ibid., 185.

59. Ibid., 43.

60. Ibid., 301.

61. Ibid., 157.

62. Ibid., 228.

63. Ibid., 337.

64. Ibid., 3.

65. H. David Sherman, S. David Young, and Harris Collingwood, *Profits You Can Trust: Spotting and Surviving Accounting Landmines* (Upper Saddle River, NJ: FT Prentice Hall, 2003), 31.

66. Byrne, *Chainsaw*, cover photo (unsmiling) and also in the text (smiling).

67. Sydney Finkelstein, *Why Smart Executives Fail—And What You Can Learn from Their Mistakes* (New York: Portfolio, 2003), 238.

CHAPTER 8

1. Jonathan Glater, "Survey Finds Fraud's Reach in Big Business," *New York Times*, 8 July 2003, C3. The survey was conducted by the accounting firm of PricewaterhouseCoopers and the law firm of Wilmer, Cutler and Pickering.

2. Philip Gourevitch, "Can You Forgive Me?" *New Yorker*, 2 September 2002, 108. For the most complete account of Cianci's life and times, see Mike Stanton, *The Prince of Providence: The Life and Times of Buddy Cianci, America's Most Notorious Mayor, Some Wiseguys, and the Feds* (New York: Random House, 2003).

3. Gourevitch, "Can You Forgive Me?" 109.

4. Ibid., 118.

5. Ibid., 110.

6. Dan Barry, "Buddy for Life," *New York Times Magazine*, 31 December 2000, 24.

7. Lawrence Ingrassia, "Amazing Comeback—Buddy Cianci Is Toast of Providence," *Wall Street Journal*, 21 June 1990, A1.

8. Gourevitch, "Can You Forgive Me?" 111.

9. Tim Weiner, "U.S. Drug Indictment Chronicles King of Cancun's Fall," *New York Times*, 11 June 2001, A4.

10. Bill Berkeley, "A Glimpse into a Recess of International Finance," *New York Times*, 12 November 2002, C1.

11. Jose de Cordoba and David Luhnow, "U.S. Targets Account in Mexican Drug Case," *Wall Street Journal*, 14 June 2001, A13.

12. Barnard Thompson, "Ex-Governor Mario Villanueva—Is Extradition to Be or Not to Be?" *Hispanicvista*, 12 May 2003.

13. Ibid.

14. "Corporate Scandals: A User's Guide," *New York Times*, 11 May 2003, D2.

15. Joel Dresang, "Enron Worker to Tell Story of Retirement Loss During Milwaukee Visit," *Knight Ridder Tribune Business News*, 1 April 2002.

16. Mimi Swartz with Sherron Watkins, *Power Failure: The Inside Story of the Collapse of ENRON* (Doubleday, 2003), 35.

17. Ibid., 30.

18. Ibid., 35.

19. Ibid., 167, and Robert Bryce, *Pipe Dreams: Greed, Ego, and the Death of Enron* (New York: Public Affairs, 2002), 204.

20. *World News Digest*, 3 October 2002.

21. Bill Murphy, "The Fall of Enron: Michael Kopper," *Houston Chronicle*, 22 August 2002, Business, 1.

22. David Barboza, "Corporate Conduct: Close Links," *New York Times*, 31 July 2002, C1.

23. Evan Thomas, "Every Man for Himself," *Newsweek*, 18 February 2002, 22.

24. Wendy Zellner, "The Man Behind the Deal Machine," Special Report, *BusinessWeek*, 4 February 2002, 40.

25. Bethany Mclean, "Why Enron Went Bust," *Fortune*, 24 December 2001, 58.

26. John S. Glaser, *The United Way Scandal: An Insider's Account of What Went Wrong and Why* (John Wiley & Sons, 1994), 179.

27. Matthew Sinclair, "William Aramony Is Back on the Streets," *Non-Profit Times*, 1 March 2002.

28. Glaser, *The United Way Scandal*, xxvii.

29. "United Way of American Profile," *Hoover's Online*, 7 April 2003; and Wendy Melillo, "Community-Wide Giving Launched 105 Years Ago," *Washington Post*, 16 February 1992, A39.

30. Glaser, *The United Way Scandal*, 44.

31. Alan S. Cooper, senior vice president at UWA, who had worked in the system for thirty-eight years, quoted in Melillo, "Community-Wide Giving Launched 105 Years Ago."

32. Glaser, *The United Way Scandal*, 44.

33. Ibid.

34. Ibid., 45.

35. Ibid., 70.

36. Ibid., 67, 54–65.

37. Katherine Farquhar, "The Myth of the Forever Leader: Organizational Recovery from Broken Leadership," *Business Horizons*, September–October 1994, 42.

38. Kim I. Eisler, "The Investigator," *Washingtonian*, June 1992.

39. Charles E. Shepard, "Perks, Privileges and Power in a Nonprofit World," *Washington Post*, 16 February 1992, A1.

40. This is the term used in Glaser, *The United Way Scandal*, 9.

41. Ibid., 12.

42. *World News Digest*, 5 March 1992. See also Richard P. Scala, "Aramony Quits United Way," *Fund Raising Management*, April 1992.

43. For details of Aramony's leadership style, see Glaser, *The United Way Scandal*, 69–97.

44. *World News Digest*, 27 April 1995.

45. Cynthia Sanz and Stephanie Slewka, "A Little Help for His Friends," *People*, 17 April 1995, 89.

46. Sinclair, "William Aramony Is Back on the Streets."

47. Shepard, "Perks, Privileges and Power in a Nonprofit World."

48. "Indictments Issued Against Former United Way Execs," *Journal Record* (Oklahoma), 14 September 1994.

49. Tim Weiner, "3 Former United Way Execs Indicted in Theft," *Denver Post*, 14 September 1994, A1.

50. Glaser, *The United Way Scandal*, 123.

51. David Shenk, "Board Stiffs: How William Gates and Paul Tagliabue Helped William Aramony Bilk America," *Washington Monthly*, May 1992, 9.

52. Ibid.

53. Ibid., 10.

54. Pablo Eisenberg, quoted in ibid.

55. Marion Fremont-Smith and Andras Kosaras, "Wrongdoing by Officers and Directors of Charities: A Survey of Press Reports 1995–2003," *The Exempt Organization Tax Review*, October 2003, 34.

CHAPTER 9

1. Quoted in Allen R. Myerson, "Big Oil: The Overview," *New York Times*, 2 December 1998, A1.

2. Quoted in Thaddeus Herrick, "CEO's Controversial Views Lead to Tough Summer for Exxon Mobil," *Wall Street Journal*, 29 August 2001, B1.

3. Daniel Fisher, "Dangerous Liaisons," *Forbes*, 28 April 2003, 84.

4. "Exxon Mobil Shareholders Side with Management on Issues," *Journal Record*, 31 May 2001, 1.

5. Scott S. Smith, "The Man Who Will Lead Exxon Mobil," *Chief Executive*, October 2002, 30.

6. Herrick, "CEO's Controversial Views."

7. *Economist*, 15 March 2003, 64.

8. Janet Raloff, "The Great Nicotine Debate," *Science News*, 14 May 1994, 314.

9. The quotations in this paragraph are in Raloff, ibid.

10. Alix M. Freedman, "The Deposition," *Wall Street Journal*, 26 January 1996, A1.

11. Richard Tomkins, "Johnston to Leave RJR Nabisco," *Financial Times*, 3 June 1996.

12. Myron Levin, "All 7 Tobacco Executives in Perjury Probe Have Quit the Industry," *Los Angeles Times*, 1 June 1996.

13. Philip Gourevitch, *We Wish to Inform You That Tomorrow We Will Be Killed with Our Families* (New York: Farrar, Straus and Giroux, 1998).

14. The history provided in this section is based in part on Alan J. Kuperman, "Rwanda in Retrospect," *Foreign Affairs*, January/February 2000, 95–101. Background to the catastrophe is also provided in Samantha Power, "Bystanders to Genocide," *Atlantic Monthly*, September 2001, 87. For a critically praised, much more complete history and analysis of how the Hutu and Tutsi came to be antagonists, see Jean-Pierre Chretien, *The Great Lakes of Africa: Two Thousand Years of History* (New York: Zone, 2003). Chretien blames the relatively short history of hostility on the colonial powers, the Europeans, who imposed their own racist projection of superiority on the Tutsi "Hamito-Semites," and a corresponding inferiority on Hutu "Bantu Negroes." For a discussion of the book, see John Shattuck, "A Deep Crisis, Shallow Roots," *New York Times*, 30 August 2003, B9.

15. Kuperman, "Rwanda in Retrospect," 96.

16. Power, "Bystanders to Genocide," 87.

17. Kuperman, "Rwanda in Retrospect," 96.

18. Ibid., 98.

19. Gourevitch, *We Wish to Inform You*, 133.

20. Karen Breslau, "Clinton Goes Corporate," *Newsweek*, 17 February 1997, 38.

21. The term *adhocracy* is Roger Porter's, as quoted in Richard Haass, "Bill Clinton's Adhocracy," *New York Times Magazine*, 29 May 1994, 40.

22. Francis Wilkinson, "Is This Any Way to Run a White House?" *Rolling Stone*, 11 August 1994, 40.

23. Philip Zelikow, "Beyond Boris Yeltsin," *Foreign Affairs*, January/February 1994, 45.

24. Power, "Bystanders to Genocide," 90.

25. Ibid.

26. Stanley Renshon, *High Hopes: The Clinton Presidency and the Politics of Ambition* (New York: New York University Press, 1996), 52.

27. Elizabeth Drew, *On the Edge: The Clinton Presidency* (New York: Simon and Schuster, 1994), 144.

28. Kagan quoted in David Halberstam, *War in a Time of Peace: Bush, Clinton, and the Generals* (New York: Scribner, 2001), 273.

29. Halberstam, *War in a Time of Peace*, 273.

30. Samantha Power, *"A Problem from Hell": America and the Age of Genocide* (New York: Basic, 2002).

31. Power, "Bystanders to Genocide," 94.

32. This paragraph is based on Power, "Bystanders to Genocide," 97.

33. Michael Kelly, "Words of Blasphemy in Rwanda," *National Journal*, 28 March 1998, 676.

34. Power, *A Problem from Hell*, 353.

35. Ibid., 366.

36. Ibid., 374, 375.

37. Ibid., 380.

38. *New York Times*, 26 March 1998, A12.

39. Kelly, "Words of Blasphemy in Rwanda," 676.

40. Philip Gourevitch, "The Genocide Fax," *New Yorker*, 11 May 1998, 42.

41. Power, *A Problem from Hell*, 359.

42. Ibid., 362.

43. Power, "Bystanders to Genocide," 97.

44. Quoted in ibid., 97.

45. Ibid., 101.

46. Ibid., 102.

47. Holly Burkhalter, "A Preventable Horror?" *Africa Report*, November–December 1994, 18.

48. Power, *A Problem from Hell*, 369.

49. Michael Barnett, *Eyewitness to Genocide: An Ethical History of the U.N.'s Indifference to Genocide* (Ithaca, NY: Cornell University Press, 2002), 139.

50. Neil A. Lewis, "Papers Show U.S. Knew of Genocide in Rwanda," *New York Times*, 22 August 2001, A5.

51. Holly Burkhalter, "The Question of Genocide: The Clinton Administration and Rwanda," *World Policy Journal*, Winter 1994, 44.

52. Neil A. Lewis, "Word for Word/Defining Moments," *New York Times*, 26 August 2001, D7.

53. Quoted in Power, "Bystanders to Genocide," 93.

54. Barnett, *Eyewitness to Genocide*, 140. For the view that the trauma in Somalia precluded the United States from intervention not only in Rwanda but also in Bosnia, see Kenneth L. Cain, "The Legacy of Blackhawk Down," *New York Times*, 3 October 2003, A27.

55. Barnett, *Eyewitness to Genocide*, 160. See also "Report of the Independent Inquiry into the Actions of the United Nations During the 1994 Genocide in Rwanda," United Nations Document, 15 December 1999. This document criticizes the secretary-general as well as the secretariat, the Security Council, and various governments and alliances.

56. Nat Hentoff, "The Holocaust without Guilt," *Village Voice*, 16 March 1999, 28.

57. For an excellent overview of the genocide in Rwanda and related cases, see the review article by Benjamin Valentino, "Still Standing By: Why America and the International Community Fail to Prevent Genocide and Mass Killing," *Perspectives on Politics*, September 2003, 565–576. For more on this subject, see also Roger Shattuck, *Freedom on Fire: Human Rights Wars and America's Response* (Cambridge, MA: Harvard University Press, 2004).

CHAPTER 10

1. Ron Rosenbaum, "Degrees of Evil," *Atlantic Monthly*, February 2002, 63. The term "malignant wickedness" is also Rosenbaum's.

2. For an interesting discussion of moral relativism in the wake of 9/11, see Timothy Garton Ash, "Is There a Good Terrorist?" *New York Review of Books*, 29 November 2001, 30–33.

3. Osama bin Laden has been as vilified in the United States as Hussein. But academics distinguish between the latter, who as president of Iraq held a formal position of authority, and the former, who is the informal leader of a network of terrorists. See Barbara Harff, "No Lessons Learned from the Holocaust? Assessing Risks of Genocide and Political Mass Murder Since 1955," *American Political Science Review*, February 2003, 58.

4. Kenneth M. Pollack, *The Threatening Storm: The Case for Invading Iraq* (New York: Random House, 2002).

5. David Remnick, "Making a Case," *New Yorker*, 3 February 2003, 32.

6. This paragraph is based on John F. Burns, "How Many People Has Hussein Killed?" *New York Times*, 26 January 2003, E4. For Burns's lengthy and elaborate description of Saddam's brutality, written after the

war, see "Last, Desperate Days of a Brutal Reign," *New York Times*, 26 April 2003, 1. See also Susan Sachs, "A Grim Graveyard Window on Hussein's Iraq," *New York Times*, 1 June 2003, A1.

7. Stephane Courtois et al., *The Black Book of Communism: Crimes, Terror, Repression* (Cambridge, MA: Harvard University Press, 1999), 577. For more on Pol Pot, see David P. Chandler, *Brother Number One: A Political Biography of Pol Pot* (Boulder, CO: Westview, 1999).

8. Courtois et al., *Black Book of Communism*, 601. See also Seth Mydans, "Death of Pol Pot," *New York Times*, 17 April 1998, A14.

9. Courtois et al., *Black Book of Communism*, 606.

10. Mark Bowden, "It's Not Easy Being Mean," *Atlantic Unbound*, 25 April 2002, 3.

11. Anthony Storr, *Feet of Clay: Saints, Sinners, and Madmen: A Study of Gurus* (New York: Free Press, 1996), 3, 4.

12. This paragraph is drawn from Storr, *Feet of Clay*, 4.

13. Ibid., 9–17.

14. Ibid., 4.

15. Indictment available at <www.un.org/icty/indictment/english/kar-ii951116e.htm>.

16. Timothy Garton Ash, "Cry, the Dismembered Country," *New York Review of Books*, 14 January 1999, 29.

17. Paul Garde, "Testimony to the International War Crimes Tribunal for the Former Yugoslavia," PBS *Frontline* Web site, <www.pbs.org/wgbb/pages/frontline/shows/karadzic/bosnia/eindex.html>, (accessed 25 June 2002).

18. Warren Zimmerman, "The Last Ambassador: A Memoir of the Collapse of Yugoslavia," in *Bosnia: What Went Wrong?* (New York: Council of Foreign Relations, 1998), 3. First appeared in *Foreign Affairs*, March–April 1995.

19. Garde, "Testimony to the International War Crimes Tribunal."

20. Zimmerman, "The Last Ambassador," 16.

21. Ibid., 18.

22. These two paragraphs are based on ibid., 18, 19.

23. Ibid., 20.

24. Dusko Doder and Louise Branson, *Milosevic: Portrait of a Tyrant* (New York: Free Press, 1999), 114.

25. Quoted in Doder and Branson, *Milosevic: Portrait of a Tyrant*, 115. See also Louis Sell, *Slobodan Milosevic and the Destruction of Yugolslavia* (Durham, NC: Duke University Press, 2002), 159.

26. Semezdin Mehmedinovic, "A Small Map of the World," *Village Voice*, 4 June 1996, V29.

27. Ibid., V30.

28. John Lampe, *Yugoslavia as History: Twice There Was a Country* (New York: Cambridge University Press, 2000), 363, 364.

29. Sell, *Slobodan Milosevic and the Destruction of Yugolslavia*, 159.

30. Slavoljub Djukic, *Milosevic and Markovic: A Lust for Power* (Montreal: McGill-Queens University Press, 2001), 69.

31. Doder and Branson, *Milosevic: Portrait of a Tyrant*, 119.

32. Sell, *Slobodan Milosevic and the Destruction of Yugolslavia*, 167. The quotation in the preceding paragraph is also from Sell, 166.

33. Roy Gutman, "Bosnia Rape Horror," *Newsday*, 9 August 1992, 5.

34. Jordana Hart, "In Bosnia, Legacy of Rape," *Boston Globe*, 22 February 1993, 2.

35. Leonard Doyle, "Bosnia Rapes 'Horrifying' Says Amnesty," *Independent* (London), 22 January 1993, 10.

36. Stephen J. Hedges et al., "Will Justice Be Done?" *U.S. News and World Report*, 25 December 1995–1 January 1996, 44–47, 49–51.

37. This paragraph is based on Mark Danner, "Bosnia: The Turning Point," *New York Review of Books*, 5 February 1998

38. Lampe, *Yugoslavia as History*, 379. Lampe's figure of six thousand dead has been updated to seven thousand.

39. Rob Siebelink interviewed Karadzic in April 1997. Siebelink's story was published in a Dutch newspaper on May 18 and is now available at <http://users.bart.nl/-papafinn/kara3-gb.html>.

40. Kevin Sim, writer and director, Pippa Scott, producer, *Frontline*, "The World's Most Wanted Man," PBS, 26 May 1998.

41. Hedges et al., "Will Justice Be Done?" 49–51. See also Gary J. Bass, "Milestone in the Hague," *Foreign Affairs*, May–June 2003, 82–96.

42. Sim and Scott, "Frontline."

43. Interview with Marco Vesovic, PBS *Frontline* Web site, "The World's Most Wanted Man," <http://www.pbs.org/wgbh/pages/frontline/shows/karadzic/interviews/vesovic.html>, 1998 (accessed 25 June 2002).

44. Interview with Dr. Ismet Ceric, PBS *Frontline* Web site, "The World's Most Wanted Man," <http://www.pbs.org/wgbh/pages/frontline/shows/karadzic/interviews/ceric.html>, 1998 (accessed 25 June 2002).

45. Robert Jay Lifton, *Medical Killing and the Psychology of Genocide* (New York: Basic, 1986). Lifton's argument is far more sophisticated than the brief reference indicates. See especially 418. The quote is from Danner, "Bosnia: The Turning Point," 35.

46. Interview with Marco Vesovic, PBS *Frontline* Web site. See also Jerrold M. Post, *Leaders and Their Followers in a Dangerous World: The Psychology*

of Political Behavior (Ithaca, NY: Cornell University Press, 2004). Even Post, a psychiatrist, has trouble explaining Karadzic's sudden transformation, although he makes the interesting point that the themes of Karadzic's poetry presaged those of his leadership (178).

47. Interview with Jacques Klein, PBS *Frontline* Web site, "The World's Most Wanted Man," <http://www.pbs.org/wgbh/pages/frontline/shows/karadzic/interviews/klein.html>, 1998 (accessed 25 June 2002).

48. Ed Vulliamy, "The Guardian," in Sim and Scott, *Frontline.*

49. Djukic, *Milosevic and Markovic,* 71.

50. "Croat Is First to Be Convicted by Balkan War Crimes Panel," *New York Times,* 1 June 1996, A4. By 2003 others were convicted as well, including two officers in the Bosnian Serb army who pleaded guilty before the war crimes tribunal at The Hague to crimes against humanity. They admitted that they helped plan the massacre at Srebrenica and agreed to testify against other officers similarly indicted. See Emir Suljagic, "Truth at The Hague," *New York Times,* 1 June 2003, 4, 13. Also see Marlise Simons, "Officers Say Bosnian Massacre Was Deliberate," *New York Times,* 12 October 2003, A12.

51. Siebelink, Karadzic interview.

52. Djukic, *Milosevic and Markovic,* 116.

53. Daniel Jonah Goldhagen, *Hitler's Willing Executioners: Ordinary Germans and the Holocaust* (New York: Knopf, 1996).

54. Mark Lilla, review of Susan Nieman, *Evil in Modern Thought: An Alternative History of Philosophy* (Princeton, NJ: Princeton University Press, 2003), *New York Review,* 12 June 2003, 47.

55. Vesovic interview, PBS *Frontline* Web site.

56. Carla Del Ponte, "Hiding in Plain Sight," *New York Times,* 28 June 2003, A15. See also Elaine Sciolino, "At Balkan Tribunal, Envy Over the Capture of Hussein," *New York Times,* 23 December 2003, A16.

CHAPTER 11

1. For a fuller discussion of the difference between ethical and effective leadership, see Joanne B. Ciulla, "Carving Leaders from the Warped Wood of Humanity," *Revue Canadienne des Sciences de l'Administration* (Montreal) 18, no. 4 (December 2001): 313–319.

2. Sidney Finkelstein, *Why Smart Executives Fail and What You Can Learn from their Mistakes* (New York: Portfolio/Penguin, 2003), ix. See also Donald N. Sull, *Revival of the Fittest: Why Good Companies Go Bad and How Great Managers Remake Them* (Cambridge, MA: Harvard Business School Press, 2003).

3. See, for example, Barbara Kellerman, "Hitler's Ghost: A Manifesto" in *Cutting Edge: Leadership 2000*, eds. Barbara Kellerman and Larraine Matusak (College Park: University of Maryland, 2000), 65–68.

4. Tina Rosenberg, "The Taint of the Greased Palm," *New York Times Magazine*, 10 August 2003, 30.

5. Clifford Geertz, *The Interpretation of Cultures* (New York: Harper-Collins, 1993), 4. The section that follows is based on the first chapter of this book, which was first published in 1973.

6. Ibid., 10.

7. Ibid., 20.

8. Ibid., 23.

9. Jason Epstein, "Leviathan," *New York Review of Books*, 1 May 2003, 13.

CHAPTER 12

1. George Packer, "Trials," *New Yorker*, 5 January 2004, 25.

2. Patrick McGeehan, "Study Finds Number of Chiefs Forced to Leave Jobs Is Up," *New York Times*, 12 May 2003, C2.

3. Chuck Lucier, Rob Schuyt, and Eric Spiegel, "CEO Succession 2002: Deliver or Depart," *Business*Strategy*, Summer, 2003.

4. Barbara Harff, "No Lessons Learned from the Holocaust? Assessing Risks of Genocide and Political Mass Murder Since 1955," *American Political Science Review*, February 2003, 57.

5. Ethan Bronner, "The Obscenely Easy Exile of Idi Amin," *New York Times*, 19 August 2003, A22.

6. David Kocieniewski, "Hardly in Disgrace, Torricelli Gathers Power in New Jersey," *New York Times*, 26 August 2003, A1.

7. For more on leaders' cognitive biases, see Michael Watkins and Max Bazerman, "Predictable Surprises: The Disasters You Should Have Seen Coming," *Harvard Business Review*, March 2003, 74.

8. Bill George, *Authentic Leadership: Rediscovering the Secrets to Creating Lasting Value* (San Francisco: Jossey-Bass, 2003), 46.

9. Jacques Steinberg, "Times Names First Editor for Standards," *New York Times*, 10 September 2003, A20.

10. Irving L. Janis, *Groupthink: Psychological Studies of Policy Decisions and Fiascoes* (New York: Houghton Mifflin, 1982), 9.

11. For more on boards, see Lucian A. Bebchuk, "Making Directors Accountable," *Harvard Magazine*, November–December 2003, 29–31.

12. Bertolt Brecht, "Writing the Truth, Five Difficulties." The essay first appeared in the German publication *Unsere Zeit*, April 1935, 23–34.

13. Herbert C. Kelman and V. Lee Hamilton, *Crimes of Obedience: Toward a Social Psychology of Authority and Responsibility* (New Haven, CT: Yale University Press, 1989), 307.

14. Ibid., 334–336.

15. Nicholas D. Kristof, "What Did You Do During the African Holocaust?" *New York Times*, 27 May 2003, A25.

16. Adam Liptak, "You've Got Travail," *New York Times Book Review*, 18 January 2004, 12.

17. Roger Martin, "Shareholders to the Rescue!" *Compass: A Journal of Leadership*, October 2003, 45.

18. Kurt Eichenwald, "In String of Corporate Troubles, Critics Focus on Boards' Failings," *New York Times*, 21 September 2003, A1.

19. Deborah Rhode, "If Integrity Is the Answer, What Is the Question?" unpublished.

INDEX

fighting bad leadership, 223–224
Finkelstein, Sidney, 221
First World War, 58
followers
  Aramony's, 162–165, 227
  bad, 21–25
  bad behavior of, reasons for,
    25–27, 137–138
  Barry's, 110–114, 227
  changes in attitudes of, 128
  Clinton's, 184–187, 228
  corrupt, 166–167
  dependence of evil leaders on,
    213
  Dunlap's, 137–142, 227–228
  ethical versus unethical, 36
  evil, 211
  Hitler's, 26–27, 216
  incompetent, 54
  ineffective/effective, 33
  Karadzic's, 209–212, 215, 228
  Meeker's, 87–91, 94, 227
  motivations for following bad
    leaders, 21–25, 26
  obligations of, 36–37, 226–228
  opposition by, 26
  punishments inflicted on, 196
  responsibility of, for bad leader-
    ship, 226–228
  Samaranch's, 67–70, 226–227
  self-help for, 239–240
  skepticism of, 240
  stopping bad followership, 232
  suggestions for, 237–243
  weak, 236
  working with, 235–237
Forbes, 135–136, 171
foreign policy crises, 178–179. *See
  also* Clinton, Bill
Free D.C. movement, 105
freedom, security and, 16–17

free will, 16
Freud, Sigmund, 15

Ganga, Jean-Claude, 71
Gardner, John, 4
Gates, Bill, 23
Geertz, Clifford, 224, 225
genocide. *See* Rwanda
"genocide fax," 184
George, Bill, 234
Giuliani, Rudolph, 48, 120–123,
  142, 143, 239
Glad, Betty, 21
Glaser, John, 158–159
Goebbels, Joseph, 26–27
Golden, Tom, 127–128
Golding, William, 17–18, 24
Goldsmith, Sir James, 135
Goldstone, Richard, 197–198,
  214–215
Goleman, Daniel, 7
Göring, Hermann, 26
Gourevitch, Philip, 150
Grasso, Richard, 231
great leaders, American, 10
greed, 19–20, 144, 231
Green, Joshua, 102
Green Party, 202
Greenspan, Alan, 78, 80
groupthink, avoiding, 236
Grubman, Jack, 85–86
Guinn, Kenny, 230–231

Haas, Robert, 76, 220
Habyarimana, Juvenal, 176
Hahn, Jessica, 98–99
Hamilton, Alexander, 6, 8, 17
Hamilton, V. Lee, 238
Hart, Gary, 96–98

ABOUT THE AUTHOR

Barbara Kellerman is Research Director of the Center for Public Leadership at Harvard University's John F. Kennedy School of Government. A pioneer in the field of leadership studies, she has held professorships at Fordham, Tufts, Fairleigh Dickinson, and George Washington Universities. She also served as Dean of Graduate Studies and Research at Fairleigh Dickinson and as Director of the Center for the Advanced Study of Leadership at the University of Maryland, as Executive Director of the Center for Public Leadership, and was cofounder of the International Leadership Association. Winner of a Danforth Fellowship and three Fulbright Fellowships, Kellerman also held the Fulbright Chair in American Studies at Uppsala University. She received her undergraduate degree from Sarah Lawrence College and her M.A. in Russian and East European Studies, as well as her M.Phil. and Ph.D. degrees in Political Science, from Yale University.

Kellerman has served on several editorial boards, including those of the *Presidential Studies Quarterly* and the *Leadership Quarterly*, and was editor of the recently published *Encyclopedia of Leadership*. She has written and edited many books on leadership, including: *Leadership: Multidisciplinary Perspectives* (editor); *Political Leadership: A Source Book* (editor); *Women Leaders in American Politics* (coeditor with James David Barber); *Leadership and Negotiation in the Middle East* (coeditor with Jeffrey Rubin); *The Political Presidency: Practice of Leadership*; *The President as World Leader* (coauthor with Ryan Barilleaux); and, most recently, *Reinventing Leadership: Making the Connection Between Politics and Business.* She has also contributed articles, essays, and reviews to, among other publications, the *New York Times, Washington Post, Los Angeles Times, Boston Globe, Christian Science Monitor*, and *Harvard Business Review.* Kellerman is considered an expert on leadership as broadly defined; as such, she has served as political commentator on such media outlets as CBS, NBC, PBS, and CNN.